Reading Assessment in Practice

Book of Readings

The International Reading Association attempts, through its publications, to provide a forum for a wide spectrum of opinions on reading. This policy permits divergent viewpoints without assuming the endorsement of the Association.

Project Coordinators Kathryn A. Ransom, Springfield, Illinois
Doris D. Roettger, Heartland Area Education Agency, Johnston, Iowa
Phyllis M. Staplin, West Des Moines Community School District, West Des Moines, Iowa

Director of Publications Joan M. Irwin

Produced and Developed by Warger, Eavy and Associates, Reston, VA

Articles in this Book of Readings have been published previously by the International Reading Association in either *The Reading Teacher* or *Journal of Reading* as noted in the credit line accompanying each article.

International Reading Association
800 Barksdale Road, PO Box 8139
Newark, Delaware 19714-8139, USA

ISBN 0-87207-134-0 Video Package
ISBN 0-87207-140-5 Book of Readings Only

Contents

Peter Afflerbach, Editor (1993) ... 5
STAIR: A System for Recording and Using
What We Observe and Know About Our Students

Peter Afflerbach & Barbara Kapinus (1993) ... 11
The Balancing Act

Kathryn H. Au, Judith A. Scheu, & Alice J. Kawakami (1990) ... 15
Assessment of Students' Ownership of Literacy

Wendy Brand (1992/1993) ... 18
Magic Blanket Journals: A Home Writing Activity

Robert C. Calfee & Pam Perfumo (1993) ... 19
Student Portfolios:
Opportunities for a Revolution in Assessment

Beth Davey (1989) ... 26
Assessing Comprehension:
Selected Interactions of Task and Reader

Roger Farr (1992) ... 31
Putting It All Together:
Solving the Reading Assessment Puzzle

Anthony D. Fredericks & Timothy V. Rasinski (1990) ... 43
Involving Parents in the Assessment Process

Claude Goldenberg (1992/1993) ... 48
Instructional Conversations: Promoting Comprehension
Through Discussion

John T. Guthrie, Peggy Van Meter, Ann Mitchell, & Catherine T. Reed (1994) ... 59
Performance Assessments in Reading and Language Arts

Jane Hansen (1992) ... 67
Literacy Portfolios Emerge

Beth Ann Herrmann (1992) ... 71
Teaching and Assessing Strategic Reasoning:
Dealing with the Dilemmas

Peter H. Johnston (1992) ... 77
Nontechnical Assessment

Continued

Barbara Kapinus, Editor (1994) ... 81
Looking at the Ideal and the Real in Large Scale Reading Assessment: The View from Two Sides of the River

Walter H. MacGinitie (1993) ... 86
Some Limits of Assessment

Sheila McAuliffe (1993) ... 91
A Study of the Differences Between Instructional Practice and Test Preparation

Harry Noden & Barbara Moss (1994) ... 99
A Guide to Books on Portfolios: Rafting the Rivers of Assessment

Elizabeth A. Nolan & Martha Berry (1993) ... 105
Learning to Listen

Edward E. Paradis, Barbara Chatton, Ann Boswell, Marilyn Smith, & Sharon Yovich (1991) ... 110
Accountability: Assessing Comprehension During Literature Discussion

Scott G. Paris, Robert C. Calfee, Nikola Filby, Elfrieda H. Hiebert, P. David Pearson, Sheila W. Valencia, & Kenneth P. Wolf (1992) ... 121
A Framework for Authentic Literacy Assessment

Linda J. Pils (1991) ... 133
Soon Anofe You Tout Me: Evaluation in a First-Grade Whole Language Classroom

Lynn K. Rhodes & Sally Nathenson-Mejia (1992) ... 138
Anecdotal Records: A Powerful Tool for Ongoing Literacy Assessment

Elizabeth Sulzby (1991) ... 146
Assessment of Emergent Literacy: Storybook Reading

Sheila W. Valencia & Nancy Place (1994) ... 151
Portfolios: A Process for Enhancing Teaching and Learning

Suzanne E. Wade (1990) ... 156
Using Think Alouds to Assess Comprehension

Peter Winograd (1994) ... 167
Developing Alternative Assessments: Six Problems Worth Solving

Peter Winograd, Scott Paris, & Connie Bridge (1991) ... 172
Improving the Assessment of Literacy

Kenneth P. Wolf (1993) ... 182
From Informal to Informed Assessment: Recognizing the Role of the Classroom Teacher

STAIR: A System for Recording and Using What We Observe and Know About Our Students

Reprinted from *The Reading Teacher* (1993), *47*, 260-263

Peter Afflerbach, Editor

As teachers, our proximity to the action of literacy allows us to observe students' growth and development in reading. Information gathered from this privileged perspective can inform instruction and help gauge student growth and teaching effectiveness. Although observations can produce much that is valuable, this information may not be put to its best use if it is not carefully recorded, easily accessed, or readily communicated.

This month I would like to introduce a system for recording and using classroom observations that was developed for elementary and middle school students who have difficulties reading. Often, students are puzzles whose reluctance to read, inconsistency in reading, or seeming inability to read present a challenge that can be met, in part, through careful and methodical observation. These students often are from the low groups in traditional classroom groupings and are considered for inclusion in remedial programs such as Chapter 1.

Teachers of these students examine questions related to becoming experts in teaching and assessing reading. The questions include:

How can I record the information I gather from observation during reading instruction?

How can my instruction reflect what I know about individual students?

How do I know I'm doing a good job of teaching and assessing my students?

How can I develop my assessment voice so that it is heard and valued by different audiences for different purposes?

Recording and using information from teacher observations is central to answering these questions, and STAIR (System for Teaching and Assessing Interactively and Reflectively) is an approach to assessment that was developed for this purpose. STAIR consists of cycles of teacher entries based on classroom observations, related hypotheses about student strengths and needs, and regular checking and revision of the hypotheses. It provides a source of information for planning reading instruction and allows for teacher reflection on the success of instruction. In addition, STAIR may be used to focus on individual concerns that teachers have for students as well as the benchmarks for student reading performance that may be set at the school or district level. The system also provides structure and permanence to teachers' observations, anecdotes, and mental notes so that they can be presented to and used by students, their parents, and other interested people.

Figure 1

STAIR (System for Teaching and Assessing Interactively and Reflectively)

Student Name: *John Bagley* Date: *4/19*

Hypothesis #: *1*

John often lacks motivation for reading and this prevents him from becoming engaged .in reading class.

Sources of information supporting hypothesis:

Classroom observation of John trying to read Hatchet
Classroom observation of John reading chapter in social studies textbook (Chap. 7: The Plains States)
Discussion w/ John about his reading

Instruction to address hypothesis:

My general plan is to find books that are of great interest to John. Basketball is a love of his, as is motorcycle racing. Choice of reading in these two areas will be helpful, I think.

The development of STAIR was informed by several strands of the assessment and reading research literature. The system revolves around the teacher as evaluation expert (Johnston, 1987). It is anchored strongly to the beliefs that excellence in teaching is due in part to the ability to reflect on instruction, planning, knowledge, and challenges (Schon, 1983) and that information from classroom observations can be helpful in a variety of situations (Calfee & Hiebert, 1991: Stiggins & Conklin, 1992; Wolf, 1993).

Recording Knowledge of Students' Reading

The STAIR includes information about the text or texts a student reads, the contexts in which reading and reading-related activities take place, and the tasks that students engage in related to reading. To illustrate the different procedures and uses of the STAIR we follow Stan, a fourth-grade teacher and his work with one of his students, John. Early in the school year Stan observes John during independent reading. John gives the outward appearance of being a reader, but Stan notes that he does not turn the pages of his book and is rarely able to discuss what he is reading. In contrast, John sometimes shows that he is a competent and enthusiastic reader. John's unpredictable reading is a puzzle that Stan decides to focus on. Stan hypothesizes that a lack of motivation prevents John from becoming engaged in the daily reading experiences. Stan's related initial working hypothesis about John's need is illustrated in Figure 1.

Figure 2

Planning Instruction and Checking Hypothesis

Student Name: *John Bagley* Date: *4/21*

Context: *Individual reading/independent reading*

Text: *Legends of the NBA*

Task: *Share book or story with friends*

Hypothesis ______ Refined __X__ Upheld ______ Abandoned

Sources of information:

I observed John throughout independent reading and he was highly motivated. Knowing that he could finish with a meeting of his friends to describe the book seemed to be extremely motivating. Also, John asked to take the book home, and talked with me at length about the book at the end of the school day.

Instruction to address hypothesis:

Continue to provide motivating texts for John to read. Allowing John to choose from several books on basketball should provide further motivation.

Planning Instruction

In his planning for the next reading session, Stan refers to his STAIR hypothesis. He decides that a variety of books on basketball (a favorite topic for John) will serve as a motivation. Stan plans to ask John to choose a book to read and to tell his classmates about it after reading. As the reading block begins, Stan watches John select *Legends of the NBA.* John is enthralled with the book. He perseveres and rereads frequently, intent on understanding the chapter. Despite the challenge that the book represents, John completes the first chapter. John's comprehension is apparent as he retells what he has read to his interested friends–his basketball buddies. John's enthusiasm remains unquenched as he asks to take the book home and continues discussing the book with Stan at the end of the school day. Stan reviews his lesson and decides his original STAIR hypothesis is accurate (see Figure 2).

Reflecting on Instruction and Updating Hypothesis

Stan plans the next week's reading lessons. He believes that continued attention to John's interest in basketball will help him move from an often reluctant reader to an enthusiastic reader. Yet, the next week brings disappointment. John is not eager to read, even with six different books on basketball from which to choose. During the class share time Stan asks students to review the books they are reading, but John only mumbles briefly about his book, *Hoopster Hijinx!* Stan notes that giving John choices for reading on a topic of high

Figure 3

Reflecting on Instruction and Updating Hypothesis

Student Name: *John Bagley* Date: *4/22*

Context: *John chooses one book to read independently*

Text: *Hoopster Hijinx!*

Task: *Oral report to whole class*

Hypothesis *X* Refined ______ Upheld ______ Abandoned

Sources of information:

Observation of independent reading and subsequent report to the whole class.
It appears book is not only factor. Check the social context of reading and demands it places on John.

Instruction to address hypothesis:

Be clear with John about purpose of reading. What are different aspects of motivation to address with John and his reading?
Maybe whole class oral report is a disincentive for John, so try next reading in context of his "basketball buddies".

interest is not the only ingredient for turning John's reading around. Stan uses this information to update the STAIR. He continues to view motivation as the key to John's success in reading, but notes that book choice alone did not work to this end. Stan notes this in his next entry in the STAIR and revises his hypothesis, as shown in Figure 3.

Revising Instruction

Stan revises his instructional plan while noting that part of his hypothesis seems accurate. John did show an initial interest in the book *Magic!* and he did seem aware of the need to lead a discussion of the book upon completion. But was this incentive enough for John? Through observation, Stan learns that John perseveres in reading unfamiliar text when he knows he will have the opportunity to share what he has read with a small group of classmates who understand the lingo of the basketball court. Stan uses this information to refine his initial hypothesis. Again, the information gathered through observation and John's work is collected and analyzed. A model of Stan's revised hypothesis and the information he used to revise it are presented in Figure 4.

From these brief sketches we see that Stan builds an understanding of John and his reading by using information from his observations. STAIR allows Stan to revisit his hypothesis, to reflect on its accuracy, to change it if necessary, and to use his growing knowledge of John to plan appropriate instruction.

Figure 4

Reflecting on Instruction and Updating Hypothesis

Student Name: *John Bagley* Date: *4/23*

Context: *Independent reading*

Text: *Magic!*

Task: *Share story with friends*

Hypothesis ______ Refined __X__ Upheld ______ Abandoned

Sources of information:

Questions for John about his favorite reading and his favorite reading tasks. Observation of John's independent reading and group retelling.

Instruction to address hypothesis:

Continue to think of John's motivation for reading as a combination of interesting topic and the social context(s) in which John uses the information he gains from reading. Remember to question John about his reading and motivation — he appreciates being asked and gives thoughtful answers.

Through a cycle of observation, planning, teaching, observing, and reflecting, Stan has learned that John is consistently motivated to read books about basketball when he knows part of the outcome will be giving an elaborate retelling to a certain group of classmates. Stan has also reinforced his belief that understanding students is closely tied to observing them. Finally, Stan has again noted the need to consider his knowledge of each student as an unfinished portrait. He originally considered John's motivation to read as inconsistent. Through careful observation and reflection on his own instruction he learned that John's reading was actually quite consistent, as viewed from an increasingly informed perspective on his uses for reading in the social context of the classroom.

Communicating to Different Audiences

STAIR gives permanence and structure to the rich but often fleeting assessment information that Stan can gather each day in the classroom. It provides a running record of his observations, hypothesis generation and testing, and reflections that can be shared with the different people who care about John's reading and Stan's teaching. Stan shares his STAIR with John and describes how he has observed good reading across the last 3 weeks. John is encouraged when Stan mentions the importance of working with friends and the impressive retellings he has heard John share with his classmates. John is happy to hear about some of his strengths in reading

from his teacher, and he is impressed with how well Stan knows him as reader.

At the next parent-teacher conference Stan presents his work to John's parents using STAIR. The use of STAIR provides frequent and detailed documentation of observations of John's growth in reading, demonstrates Stan's careful thinking and planning, and helps John's parents better understand their son's reading strengths and needs. This helps Stan's classroom assessment take center stage—it no longer plays a minor supporting role.

Stan knows that it is not enough to be a competent assessor of his students' growth in reading. People have to trust his information, understand its uses, and find it useful. John's parents are presented with concrete evidence of John's growth in reading. Stan suggests that John's parents continue to take him to the library and provide contexts in which John can share what he has read in discussing, drawing, and acting out scenes from books. Here, the STAIR helps communicate two important messages. First, it describes how John is doing in reading. Second, it demonstrates that Stan's observation is a valid and valuable source of information about John's development as a reader.

Stan's success in using the STAIR revolves around his observations in the classroom and his commitment to reflecting on and updating his knowledge about John. The STAIR requires expertise (or the commitment to developing expertise) in observing students in literate activity and a depth of knowledge of individual students. The system is demanding of time. It requires regular attention, reflection, and updating. Attempting to use the STAIR for every observed behavior of each student will leave little or no time for instruction, or weekends.

STAIR can be a valuable and versatile tool in the assessment process. It can capture the informed observation and hypothesis generation and confirmation that the best teachers do on a regular basis. Teachers' hypotheses about students' needs establish a running record of attention to these needs and students' accomplishments. STAIR provides a means for teachers to reflect on their knowledge of students and to continue their updating of understandings and instructional methods and procedures. Further, STAIR can help communicate increased understandings of students and students' accomplishments in literacy.

Author's Note: I would like to thank the teachers in the University of Maryland Summer Reading Program who provided helpful comments and suggestions related to STAIR.

References

Calfee, R., & Hiebert, E. (1991). Classroom assessment of reading. In R. Barr, M. Kamil, P. Mosenthal, & P.D. Pearson (Eds.), *Handbook of reading research, Volume II* (pp. 281-309). New York: Longman.

Johnston, P. (1987). Teachers as evaluation experts. *The Reading Teacher, 40,* 744-748.

Schon, D. (1983). *The reflective practitioner: How professionals think in action.* New York: Basic Books.

Stiggins, R., & Conklin, N. (1992). *In teachers' hands: Investigating the practices of classroom assessment.* Albany: State University of New York Press.

Wolf, K. (1993). From informal to informed assessment: Recognizing the role of the classroom teacher. *Journal of Reading, 36,* 518-523.

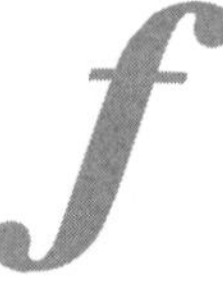

The Balancing Act

Reprinted from *The Reading Teacher* (1993), *47*, 62-64

Peter Afflerbach
Barbara Kapinus

The meaningful assessment of reading results from an often underappreciated but always skillful balancing act. In elementary schools we work with a wide variety of students, using a similarly wide variety of instructional procedures and materials. Both students' progress in reading and our effectiveness in teaching reading are measured using different types of assessment, and the results are sent to different audiences who use the assessment information for different purposes. Achieving a balance in this context is challenging, but it may ensure a reading assessment program that is timely, focused, and useful.

In this column we will take a brief look at reading assessment in the third-grade classroom of Susan Kane at Ferncrest Elementary School and describe some of the balances that she has achieved and the challenges that remain.

As a first step, let's consider the range of reading assessment familiar to Susan and her students. Jackie is reading Elizabeth Fitzgerald Howard's *Aunt Flossie's Hats (and Crab Cakes Later)* aloud while Susan notes Jackie's growth in word recognition, fluency, and self-esteem as a reader. Once shy, Jackie now relishes the opportunity to read aloud with her classmates. Susan observes Jeff choosing a book, reading, pausing to think, and then rereading. Jeff's growing ability to monitor his progress is encouraging. He is eager to discuss books and anxious to listen to others' viewpoints after giving his own. Both Jeff and Jackie are growing in their ability to describe to their teacher, parents, and friends how they are becoming better readers. Using portfolios, both can outline growth in their reading of different books and authors, using different texts to learn about science and social studies, and the areas in which they feel they do their best work.

Throughout the day, Susan notes her students' strengths and needs across a wide range of reading tasks, in a variety of contexts. Susan records her observations using a system developed with her fellow teachers at Ferncrest Elementary School. The recording system accommodates detailed accounts of students' progress, such as Jackie's growing ability to make inferences about characters' motives and her gradually increasing fluency. This information supports the development of Susan's lessons and helps chart students' reading accomplishments, some of which will be included in the narrative section of the Femcrest report card. The class breaks into collaborative groups to continue its work on integrated units, and Susan is heartened by her students' ability, enthusiasm, and willingness to participate, to give each other feedback, and to state their feelings about what they read. She feels increasingly confident in her ability to observe and record students' growth.

The school year also includes reading assessments that are initiated and developed outside Susan's classroom. Jeff, Jackie, and their classmates regularly take unit tests that measure students' mastery of skills and strategies taught with the basal reader. Next month, Susan's students will

take the district criterion-referenced test. The test is geared to the basal reader series used across the district and includes short answer items on vocabulary, main idea, and critical thinking. Susan's students also take a statewide performance assessment in which they read and write to solve problems. The assessment, tied to performance standards in reading and language arts, asks students to respond to what they read in terms of their own experiences and to discuss and critically analyze the texts that they read. This year, the students worked by themselves and in groups, reading to investigate the native animals of their state and writing to develop a plan for protecting the animals.

Susan's Attempts to Achieve Balance

Susan and her students take part in a series of reading assessment procedures that demand careful balance to be effective. In this section we will briefly sketch the balances, some apparent and some not so apparent, that Susan has achieved and the balances that she is working towards. With Susan, we believe they are necessary for reliable and useful reading assessment.

1. There needs to be a balanced representation of experts in the development and use of reading assessment. Ferncrest Elementary School encourages many people to contribute to the assessment program, for there is a strongly held belief that expertise resides in different places. For example, as frequent readers of report cards, parents and students are asked to help create them. Susan and her colleagues use their expertise to develop the classroom observation system that captures the detail and intricacy of students' learning and that informs instruction. Jeff and Jackie know themselves as readers and are adept at explaining their interests in and motivations for reading, the strategies they use while reading, and the uses they have for reading. The state education personnel contributed their expertise in developing a performance assessment that can be reliably scored and that clearly reflects the educational outcomes for reading endorsed at the district and the state levels. In addition, the basal reader developers have designed assessments that provide regular and systematic information about students' growing ability to summarize stories and to monitor their progress while doing so.

This diverse pool of experts contributes to an assessment system that is sensitive to the different aspects of students' development as readers. The experts also provide information that helps address the different purposes and audiences of reading assessment, be it a parent seeking information about how to support a child's reading growth at home or a legislator seeking information on the success of a particular instructional program.

2. Reading assessment must be balanced with the effective communication of the nature, purpose, and results of the assessment. Effective communication can be the universal clamp that holds together different aspects of a successful reading assessment program. For example, the innovative performance assessment used in Susan's state is accompanied by a brochure that explains the nature, purpose, and appropriate uses of assessment information. This helps teachers, parents, and administrators know what questions the assessment can answer. Without this communication the benefits of an exemplary assessment program might be lost on the people who must interpret and use reading assessment information.

Communication contributes to and is a consequence of involvement. Many parents participated in the development of the report card used at Femcrest, and one result is that more parents understand the uses and limitations of the report card. Similarly, the teachers and administrators at Femcrest worked together to develop the schoolwide reading assessment program. Through a series of meetings and discussions, teachers and administrators came to better understand the needs of each group and the nature of reading assessments that best meet those needs.

3. *There needs to be a balance of formative and summative reading assessment.* Susan believes the ideal combination of formative and summative assessment helps the student understand "how you can do it" and helps others understand "what the student can do." Using scaffolded instruction, Susan regularly gives students formative feedback on a variety of reading tasks, including setting purposes for reading, figuring out unfamiliar words, building an understanding of text, and responding to literature individually and in discussion groups. With explicit models and explanations, Susan's students know the details of formative assessment and how it contributes to better reading. This has helped the students become adept at self-assessment.

Susan's students are quite familiar with the summative assessments that are used to demonstrate accountability, to check on student competency, to examine the effectiveness of the reading program, and to make placement decisions. While Susan is aware that different audiences require different types of assessment information, she is concerned about a current lack of balance and the emphasis on summative assessment. The assessments receiving the most attention in the community are the performance assessment and the criterion-referenced test. These assessments will not yield results for several months, and they provide scant information for informing instruction. Teachers and students are simply told that they did or didn't "make the grade."

4. There needs to be a balance of reading assessment for the student and from the student. Susan has seen great growth in her students' ability to self-assess. Jeff knows himself as a reader, and he carefully monitors his reading. He regularly unpacks his portfolio to review his accomplishments, to take account of present challenges, and to plan future work. Susan has also seen a change in students' dependence on her to tell them how they are doing in reading. Of course, Jackie still smiles widely when complimented on her reading, but she is developing the ability and inclination to assess her own growth. Susan's students are learning to "do assessment" for themselves. They are motivated to read and to keep track of their reading.

While acknowledging the importance of her own assessments and those developed by experts outside the classroom, Susan is concerned about the considerable amount of reading assessment that is done for the student: running records, performance assessment, criterion-referenced tests, and the basal unit tests. Without a balance of assessment *for* and *from* the student, she feels that too many students will develop the expectation that reading assessment is not their concern or prerogative, perhaps preventing the development of truly independent readers. Susan believes strongly that effective assessment is reliable and useful, encouraging the reader to examine and assess herself or himself.

5. Reading assessment should include a balance of texts, tasks, and contexts. Across the school day and throughout the school year, Susan observes students reading different texts to perform an array of tasks. Susan's proximity to the action of being literate helps her assess students' reading in varied contexts: responding to literature, reading informational texts, discussing their understandings, and using what they read to solve problems.

Susan notes her own development in assessment. She remembers constructing tests that focused solely on the cognitive aspect of reading. She compares this with the efforts of a local consortium of teachers, parents, administrators, and district and state education personnel. The consortium is investigating ways to assess a range of students' literacy development, including motivation, self-esteem, enthusiasm, visits to the library, and perseverance. By seeking a balance in the texts, contexts, and tasks, Susan and fellow members of the consortium feel confident that they might develop reading assessments that capture the multifaceted nature of student growth in reading.

6. *We must balance the apparent effectiveness of the assessment with the effects of the assessment.* Once a year, statewide scores on the performance assessment are released to the news media. The news is highlighted across the state, and the assessment is touted with considerable testimony to its reliability and validity. It is considered by many an effective test: The assessment outlines areas of strength and need at district level and has been used to help identify districts with exemplary reading programs, as well as districts that need to improve.

But balanced against this "effectiveness" is the *effect* of the assessment. Not included in the television reports or newspaper articles are questions about the sensitivity of the assessment to measuring students' motivation and self-esteem. Susan feels these traits are prerequisites for students' developing habits of lifelong reading, but the assessment is not sensitive to them. Susan is also concerned that the front page news presents the mean achievement of students and by implication, the mean achievement of teachers. She wonders how this can be positive for her colleagues who share commitments to teaching.

7. *Confidence in our current reading assessments must be balanced with a flexibility that anticipates change in both the way we view reading and literacy and the way we view effective reading assessment.* Susan regularly asks students, "How do you want to grow as a reader?" and "What do you think will be important for you as a reader next year?" She believes we should ask related questions of our assessments. Susan knows that things change and that a balanced system of reading assessment is flexible. She remembers a considerable stretch of time when many influential reading assessments seemed immune to what was known about the nature of reading. She is convinced that we must be metacognitive about our assessment processes and products and provide for ongoing discussion among the developers, takers, and users of reading assessment. This should support valid assessment practice, challenge questionable practice, and inform innovative assessments.

An Invitation

We believe that the purpose of reading assessment is to help provide optimal reading instruction and learning for all students. To this end, we have planned columns that allow us to examine the widely varied practices, beliefs, and values related to reading assessment; to share the successes of and challenges to our colleagues; to discuss both new and promising and tried and true reading assessment for elementary classrooms; and to consider the social, political, and interpersonal complexities of reading assessment in elementary schools.

We believe that the best reading assessments are constructed collaboratively, and we would like this column to serve as a forum for collaboration and dialog. Our readers are invited to write to us with concerns, to respond to column content or to make suggestions for future columns. We plan to dedicate a portion of each column to this dialog, and we look forward to hearing from you.

Assessment of Students' Ownership of Literacy

Reprinted from *The Reading Teacher* (1990), *44,* 154-156

Kathryn H. Au
Judith A. Scheu
Alice J. Kawakami

Moana Leong, a second-grade teacher, is proud of James, one of the students in her class. James wrote a book in which he described how he liked to read to his younger sister and how he enjoyed the books his parents bought for him. None of his classmates shows a greater ownership of literacy, although many can read and write much more fluently.

Students like James, who are members of classroom communities of readers and writers, are leading us to new understandings about children's literacy development. In an article in the April 1990 issue of *The Reading Teacher* (Au, Scheu, Kawakami, & Herman, 1990), we proposed that ownership of literacy be the overarching goal in a whole literacy curriculum. In this column, we discuss the concept of ownership of literacy and how ownership can be assessed.

Defining Ownership

Ownership involves looking at the affective as well as the cognitive dimensions of students' literacy development. The need to be concerned about the affective dimensions of literacy is highlighted in research suggesting that many of our students develop the skill but not the will to use literacy. In other words, the problem in many cases is that students can read and write but do not choose to do so on their own. A straightforward solution to this problem is to make students' ownership of literacy a curriculum goal, in the same way that comprehension and word identification are curriculum goals.

We conceptualize ownership as students' attitudes toward literacy and their habits in using literacy. Both seem equally important. Students with a positive attitude about literacy value literacy and understand how it can be useful and enjoyable in their daily lives. Students with the habit of using literacy make reading and writing a part of their everyday routines in school and at home. For example, they read a few pages of a good book before going to sleep, or they make a list of the things they need to remember to take to school.

Assessing Ownership

Ownership of literacy may be assessed by using an observational checklist. Items on the checklist should reflect the literacy curriculum in place in the district, school, or classroom, and the types of activities and opportunities available to students.

The figure shows the checklist we currently use to assess elementary students' ownership of reading (we have parallel items for writing, which are not discussed here). On the left are items we expect to see, even with kindergarten children. On the right are items we generally expect to see with students in the second and third grades and

above. Teachers make a check, jot down the date, or write comments when they see a student showing any of these behaviors.

Here are incidents reflecting students' ownership of literacy taken from classrooms we have visited. Brad showed that he *enjoys reading* by choosing to read a book as he waited for Jeffrey to finish a drawing to complete a project they were working on together. Noel showed her enjoyment during sustained silent reading as she chuckled while reading from *Where the Sidewalk Ends*.

Matthew's *confidence and pride* were evident when he volunteered to read aloud from *Charlotte's Web* in order to clarify for his reading group how he thought Wilbur was feeling. After Nalei discovered *When Bluebell Sang,* she made a poster for the school library to *share book with others*. It was clear that first grader Maile was *developing preferences* when she announced, "I've read all the books Dr. Seuss ever wrote." Third grader Brian's preferences showed in his reading log. His last six entries were mystery stories.

Students who can *recommend books* to others have developed an understanding of specific books and of how books can be matched to the tastes and interests of other readers. Christy had listened to Kelly's report on *Helen Keller* and Kelly's comments that she liked to read books about real women. The next day, Christy brought a copy of *Sally Ride: America's First Woman in Space* from home to share with Kelly. This ability to recommend books grows out of a general willingness to share reading with others but requires a deeper understanding of the workings of a community of readers.

Students have different ways of showing they can *read for their own purposes.* John said he chooses to read "for fun." Suzie wanted a book about guinea pigs, so she would know what to feed her new pet.

Students' involvement with literacy needs to extend beyond the limits of the school day. A kindergarten teacher had just finished reading *The Little Red Hen* and was talking with the children about fairy tales. Pua showed that she *reads outside of school* when she said, "I know *The Gingerbread Boy* is a fairy tale, too, because it's in my fairy tale book at home." Second graders Jessie and Kalei showed that they *obtain books from nonclassroom sources* as they burst into the classroom one Monday morning to announce, "We saw each other at the library Saturday. We checked out the same books." Actions like these show that students are developing and supporting their own habits of literacy.

A group of kindergartners showed they could *learn from reading* as they looked at a book about dogs. As they examined a picture of a collie covered with burrs, their discussion centered upon whether the collie had "fleas" or "those sticky things" on him.

In general, the teachers we work with rely on observations to assess students' ownership of literacy. However, teachers sometimes find it helpful to ask a student one or two of the probe questions matched to each item on the checklist. For instance, suppose that observations have not turned up evidence that a child is *developing preferences* in reading. In this case, the teacher might decide to ask the child one of the following questions: What is your favorite book? Who is your favorite author? What kinds of books do you like to read? Is there any book you've read more than once?

Changes in Assessment Over Time

We have already been through one cycle of change in assessing ownership of literacy. When we first began working with a whole literacy curriculum and portfolio assessment, we did not use an observational checklist to assess ownership. Instead, we interviewed children individually or had them respond in writing to questions such as those listed above. But as teachers became more and more confident

Figure 1

Checklist for Ownership of Reading

Teacher: ____________ **Grade:** ____________

Names	Date	Enjoys reading	Shows confidence, pride	Shares books with others	Is developing preferences	Reads outside school	Reads for own purposes	Recommends books	Learns from reading	Obtains books (nonclassroom)	
Comments											
Comments											
Comments											

about using a whole literacy approach, the classrooms changed, evolving into communities of readers and writers. We found that we no longer had to ask students about their ownership of literacy—it was readily apparent in their actions. At this point, we switched to using an observational checklist. Probe questions were still available, but they were seldom needed. This experience taught us that as classrooms change, assessment will change, too.

In conclusion, ownership and the affective dimensions of literacy have an important place in the curriculum of today's elementary schools. If we want our students to be committed to literacy as a lifelong pursuit, we must give high priority to encouraging and assessing their ownership of literacy.

Reference

Au, K.H.. Scheu, J.A., Kawami. A., & Herman, P.A. (1990). Assessment and accountability in a whole literacy curriculum. *The Reading Teacher, 43*, 574-578.

Magic Blanket Journals: A Home Writing Activity

Reprinted from *The Reading Teacher* (1992/1993), *46*, 348

Wendy Brand

Children need more time than is generally provided during a typical school day to practice emergent writing skills. Parents also need the opportunity to see their children work through the process of writing. The Magic Blanket Journal was introduced as one method of giving the children in my first-grade class additional practice writing at home.

The idea began when I read the book *Snuggle Piggy and the Magic Blanket* by Michele Steptoe (E.P. Dutton, 1987) to the children during story time. The hero of the tale is a little pig whose aunt makes him a beautiful blanket. When he sleeps under it, all the animals and people pictured on it come to life and dance with him. Because the story captured the imagination of the children, we decided to make a Magic Blanket. Parents donated old solid-colored sheets, which I cut into squares. The children then made pictures with fabric crayons and ironed them onto the pieces of sheeting. Under the watchful eye of parent volunteers, the children sewed the squares together, using a flannel sheet as a backing for the completed cover.

When the blanket was done, the children composed a story together patterned after the original *Snuggle Piggy* book. We put their story, the blanket, a blank journal, and an introductory letter to parents into a sturdy canvas bag. The parent letter explained the purpose of the journal, provided suggestions for motivating children to write, the philosophy behind the use of invented spelling, directions for washing the blanket should it become necessary, and encouragement to have fun.

Now children take the bag home on a rotating basis to write about the dreams they have while they sleep under the Magic Blanket. If they can't remember any dreams, they can make up a story. Most children keep the blanket one night, but some choose to keep it for a few days so that they can work on their stories longer. When a journal entry is completed and the bag returned, the story is read to the class and a new dreamer is chosen. When a Magic Journal is filled, it is typed and bound for the class to read, and a new journal is started.

Some of the stories are edited for publication for the class literary magazine, the Young Authors bulletin board, or the Short Story Corner Showcase. Children may choose to revise and expand their original works into full-length books that they bind themselves and place in the school library.

The Magic Blanket Journal is very popular with both children and parents. The activity continues for the entire year, each child taking the journal home an average of six times. The journal is only one technique in a range of home writing activities I employ to spark excitement and build young writers, including creating comic strips based on recommended television specials, writing letters to teachers and other adults in the school, keeping nutrition logs of foods eaten at home, and writing directions for daily routines performed at home. This one, however, is guaranteed to work like a dream.

Student Portfolios: Opportunities for a Revolution in Assessment

Reprinted from *The Journal of Reading* (1993), *36*, 532-537

Robert C. Calfee
Pam Perfumo

Alternative assessment of student achievement has come on the scene during the past decade as a paradigm shift, a fundamental change from earlier reliance on standardized testing techniques (Wolf, Bixby, Glenn, & Gardner, 1991). Several features distinguish the new approaches (Calfee, 1992):

- Production rather than recognition: students must demonstrate competence rather than selecting an answer.
- Projects rather than items: a choice of depth over breadth; validity supersedes reliability as conventionally defined.
- Informed judgment rather than mechanical scoring: the teacher replaces the Scantron in the assessment process.

Theory seems far in advance of practice. Teachers are reportedly "doing portfolios," reviewing student projects, encouraging exhibitions (Harp, 1991; Murphy & Smith, 1991; Smith, 1991; Tierney, Carter, & Desai, 1991). Psychometricians seem uneasy about these developments, uncertain about how to standardize performance, concerned about reliability and validity (Hambleton & Murphy, 1991). Articles in *Education Week* and *Educational Leadership* suggest that regular classroom teachers are taking leadership in this movement. A few states in the U.S. (e.g., Vermont, Connecticut) and quite a few school districts have discussed replacing test programs (in part or whole) with portfolios (e.g., Pelavin, 1991). But for the most part the movement has the flavor of a grassroots revolution: teachers regaining control of assessment policy, tasks that require students to demonstrate what they have learned, "bottom up" rather than "top down" decisions.

This article reviews the concept of portfolio assessment in a specific situation: teacher assessment of student achievement in the literate use of language in the elementary grades. This domain is interesting as a test case. On the one hand, elementary reading achievement has been the centerpiece of the psychometric enterprise during the past half century; standardized tests are more common in elementary reading and language than any other area of school achievement. Writing achievement in the elementary grades has been less commonplace during this time; standardized writing tests typically appear around eighth grade, if at all. On the other hand, portfolios and writing journals have found a welcome reception in the elementary grades during recent years, building on the tradition of informal assessment (Pikulski & Shanahan, 1982).

As a practical enterprise, the classroom-based literacy portfolio comprises a folder containing "situated" samples of student reading and writing performance (Calfee & Hiebert, 1991; Valencia & Calfee, 1991). The student assembles a collection of materials during the school year: lists of books read, reading notes, rough drafts, conference memos, final drafts, and pub-

lished versions. Some tasks are assigned, others are free-form. Some are substantial projects, others a page or less. Each student assembles his or her own folder, although the contents may include collaborative projects. Within a given classroom, portfolio practice is typically rather consistent, but teachers vary considerably in how they choose to frame portfolio design within the dimensions listed above. Unless constrained by district mandates, teachers within a particular school generally describe their portfolio program by the phrase "We each 'do our own thing!'"

The guiding idea is that portfolios provide an opportunity for richer, more authentic, and more valid assessment of student achievement; educators will learn what students can do when given adequate time and resources (Rogers & Stevenson, 1988). While the concept has immediate appeal, questions arise equally quickly, both for researcher and practitioner: What should be included in the folder? What processes should be used to evaluate the student's work? What standards should bear on the adequacy of student work? What are the assessments useful for? Some educators have proposed that portfolios replace standardized tests altogether, but what if every teacher approaches the task with different processes and standards? How can parents, administrators, school board members, and policy makers operate in the midst of anarchy?

In this article, we present preliminary findings from a survey of portfolio practice in selected elementary programs throughout the United States. The survey, designed to inform the preceding questions, suggests that the portfolio movement is broad but thin at the level of teacher practice (the survey did not cover portfolio practices in large-scale testing programs). Hence our suggestion in the title that this movement offers substantial opportunities for enhanced assessment, but much remains to be done to realize the promise of the movement.

The Student Portfolio: Present Practice

Under auspices of the Center for the Study of Writing at the University of California, Berkeley, we conducted a nationwide survey of portfolio practice. The goal of the CSW survey was to move beyond headlines (and newsletter reports) toward a deeper portrayal of what educators mean when they say that they are "doing portfolios." The survey focused on writing assessment, but the products were often equally linked to reading instruction. Further details on the sample, methods, and findings are available in Calfee and Perfumo (1992).

The survey covered 150 nominated contacts, including states, districts, schools, school teams, and individual teachers. The survey was not random but can be viewed as an effort to assess best practice. It employed a qualitative method, webbing, familiar to many elementary and middle-grade teachers. The respondents were instructed to work from a largely blank sheet of paper, which they used to brainstorm and categorize reflections about student portfolios.

To help the respondents (and to provide some degree of structure to the responses), we divided the survey into distinctive chunks: background and history (how did you get into portfolios?); portfolios in the classroom (what does the concept mean in practice?); portfolio process (how do you do it?); portfolio impact (what do you see as the effect of portfolios for your students and for you?). A separate response sheet was provided for each category, along with several starter questions. This methodology proved quite successful, from our perspective. Respondents provided exceptionally rich and informative data, often filling several pages with notes and reflections.

We employed a complementary strategy for obtaining indepth information from a

selected group of 24 respondents. We convened a 2-day conference, where working groups of participants documented and analyzed their collective experience with the portfolio concept, including their own situations but also reports from other projects about which they were knowledgeable. The group sessions were videotaped, and we analyzed the content of these sessions as well as graphic reports prepared by each group. In addition, each individual prepared a postconference reflective essay, the final entry in the portfolio that each individual completed for the conference.

The data set from the survey comprises 70 packets of information. Two state-level projects were represented (both represent their effort as springing directly from practitioner input rather than top-down mandates), along with several districts (about 10% of the sample, including a few that appear to be top-down), and a substantial number of total-school efforts (about 30%). The remaining packets are singletons, individual teachers who adopted the portfolio process on their own initiative with little support, often developing procedures from scratch. Packets from states and districts were generally quite polished; responses from schools and individuals were more homespun but often seemed to capture more of the spirit of authenticity and flexibility that is the hallmark of portfolio assessment.

Analysis of this complex array of information turned up three themes that we think capture the essence of this admittedly nonrandom sample of contemporary practice (see Calfee & Perfumo, 1992, for details): (a) teachers enlisted in the portfolio movement convey an intense commitment and personal renewal; (b) the technical foundations for portfolio assessment appear infirm and inconsistent at all levels; and (c) portfolio practice at the school and teacher level shies away from standards and grades, toward narrative and descriptive reporting. Let us elaborate on each of these themes.

Commitment and Renewal

Across wide variations in approaches and definition, the portfolio approach has energized the professional status and development of educators, especially classroom teachers. This response is partly affective; people who have viewed themselves a subclass report spending enormous amounts of time and energy rethinking the meaning of their work and they feel good about this renewed commitment. A common theme is ownership. Teachers talk about "being in charge" of their instructional programs. They describe the benefit to students of taking responsibility to select and critique their writing.

The following excerpts reflect this theme:

- "By allowing—no, requiring!—teachers to develop their own systems, teachers gained a renewed belief in students and in themselves. Our teachers will fight to keep portfolios in their classrooms."
- "Teachers began to 'toy' with portfolios. We wanted a richer portrait of children's overall growth during the school year. Our district used pre-post tests. We found this was not enough information nor the right kind of information. Our own teachers have served as mentors to each other as some people are farther along in understanding portfolios."
- "I am certain that the power of portfolios lies in helping teachers and students focus on the teaching/learning process."
- "Students have begun to claim 'ownership' of portfolios and strive to 'perform' and do their best. ...[The process] fosters positive feelings. Everything doesn't have to be perfect the first time. Ideas come first."
- "In 19XX the money dried up and the project directors left. ...As a strong proponent, I decided to take over without monetary compensation."

Lack of Technical Foundations

The surveys, interviews, and associated documents all disclose a lack of analytic and technical substance. For instance, respondents claim that an important purpose of portfolios is valid assessment of student progress and growth, yet nowhere in the packets have we found a clear account of how achievement is to be measured. None of the portfolio guide books we listed in this article provides help in analysis, scoring, or grading, although each includes extensive discussions of self-evaluation. None of the books develops the concepts of growth and learning in any detail. District and state activities generally attempt to incorporate judgments and standards, usually through holistic ratings by external groups; school and classroom projects seldom describe how to convert a folder of work into a gauge of achievement. Again, the procedures are normative rather than developmental.

Also missing is discussion of conventional (or unconventional) approaches for establishing validity and reliability. Validity is assumed to inhere in the authenticity of the portfolio process; reliability is simply not discussed. One state-level project employed panel correlation for reliability; each portfolio is scored by a panel of two or more teacher judges to establish consistency. This practice is rare in the districts in our sample and was not mentioned by any school or teacher respondents.

A concern for staff development was expressed by many participants; perhaps the lack of analytic work is due to inadequate preparation. The technical issues listed in the previous paragraph are not high on any of the workshop lists, however. The emphasis instead is on learning about portfolio concepts and techniques, and in establishing and refining a workable model for local implementation. Beyond the pragmatics of implementation, the next concern is how to support students in completing portfolios.

The following excerpts demonstrate intense concern with getting underway, with "doing it:"

- "We embarked on a yearlong research project involving all K-6 teachers [with a consultant]. ... Involving students in selection of portfolio pieces and their own assessment is the heart of our process. [The portfolios] represent student work over time and are interdisciplinary. We have all levels—working files, teacher portfolios, showcases, cumulative records, and competency portfolios. They show the growth of the student, and demonstrate what the student really can do, does, and knows. Students assess their own growth. Standards are developed within each classroom. ...Teachers at each grade level work together to score competencies."
- "Last year we went to training sessions and struggled over purposes. By the end of the year, five teachers really 'tried to do something' with portfolios. ...We are learners, explorers, teachers!"
- "The Literacy Portfolio has three components. The Core kept by all District elementary teachers includes Reading Development Checklist, writing samples, and list of books read. The Core follows each child through the elementary grades. The Optional Component varies according to the teacher; I like first drafts, audiotapes of story readings, etc. This portion is used to confer with parents, to direct instruction, and for report cards. The Personal Folder, used by teachers for parent communication, includes attitude surveys, work samples (and comments), goals for the next term, etc. These go home with report cards."
- "Students receive critiques formally and informally at all stages of work. They confer with teachers and peers and share work with the whole class, with the expectation that every child will eventually produce his/her best quality work. All final drafts are celebrated and displayed for the school or community. They are not graded; they should all be 'A' quality work for that child."

- "While the portfolio model yielded exciting results, over time it did not transfer as well as I had hoped. The records seemed mechanical and routinized. I think this was largely due to the selection criteria into which students had no input. Now I negotiate with students for the portfolio, for time management as well as of obtaining passing grade."

Evaluation Standards

As foreshadowed in the preceding section, respondents exhibit a definite distaste for evaluation. They did not want to set standards or assign grades for students or programs. This reaction is captured by the remark "I wish grades would just go away!" Teachers were willing to judge individual compositions and other student work samples but were uncomfortable about assessing an entire portfolio.

The Evaluation section of the surveys received the fewest and briefest entries, but the substance is captured by these excerpts:

- "Many teachers use criteria written on the report card for giving grades. Others felt grades influenced choices and so did not grade the papers, but noted students' strengths and weaknesses and set appropriate goals."
- "Each student sets goals for self at the beginning, which they review and explain to me. Students decide, based on their projects and goals, what grade they should receive. If I had my say, we'd go through the same process but there'd be no grade. A grade is something the school insists on."

What the Findings Mean

Our survey suggests that complex reactions are materializing in response to the portfolio concept. To be sure, these findings hold for selected situations brought to our attention because of their reputation for "being unique." We have conducted several informal site visits in the immediate vicinity and are impressed by the range of implementations, from intensive commitments where portfolios are a dominant feature of the instructional day to situations where portfolios are little more than manila folders holding assorted papers.

Complementing the three themes from the findings, we venture three interpretive comments about the portfolio movement.

First, the popularity of the portfolio concept often appears as a local reaction to external control. While most elementary and middle school teachers accept standardized tests as the standard, the rebels who "do portfolios" discover in this concept a way to express their professionalism. It is unfortunate that the movement finds so little undergirding conceptual and technical support. Teachers cannot call upon "Cronbach alphas" or "latent trait theory" when asked to reassure policy makers that they know what they are doing.

This leads to the second theme. The portfolio concept amounts to virtual anarchy in many quarters. Most practical articles and newsletters, as well as popular books on alternative and authentic assessment, encourage an "anything goes" approach. Education is subject to pendulum swings, and portfolios may fall into this category. To be sure, the times call for substantial changes in educational practice and policy, but without a more solid conceptual foundation, (e.g., Paris et al., 1992) the portfolio movement is imperiled.

Finally we wonder about the prospects that the portfolio movement will sustain its present fervor. Three possibilities come to mind.

(a) It may disappear for lack of an audience. Portfolio assessment, if taken seriously, entails an enormous amount of work for teachers (and students). "Who's interested?" will eventually become a compelling consideration.

(b) It may become standardized. We have seen examples in our survey artifacts; preprinted folders with sections for often mundane entries.

(c) It may become a genuine revolution. We consider this outcome likely only if accompanied by other systemic changes in the educational process.

The third prospect is compelling, but it remains to be seen whether changes in assessment will become a policy lever for school reform (Newmann, 1991). We think that such leverage is likely to require a more systematic role for student portfolios in the teacher's professional roles inside and outside the classroom.

In our survey, we asked informants for information about who used the portfolios, and what became of them. The main purpose reported was to support teacher-student dialogues, a genuine strength of the method (Richert, 1990). The next most common remark centered around teacher-parent conferences and contacts, again a strength of the approach. At the end of the year, a sample of portfolio materials was occasionally passed on to the student's next teacher, but in most instances either the student took the folder home or it simply "disappeared."

Fewer than 10% of the respondents indicated that this information was of importance in informing either the school or district administration about student achievement. Several respondents remarked that "They use standardized test scores."

This pattern of responses may appear discouraging at first glance, but there is more here than meets the eye. Alternative assessment and student portfolios tend to appear in combination with other elements: whole language rather than basal readers, cooperative instruction rather than didactic teacher talk, school-based decision making rather than top-down direction, the teacher as professional rather than as civil servant. Many of the survey responses described how externally-initiated projects *not* related to portfolios evolved into alternative assessment.

Our sense is that this "package" offers the opportunity for fundamental reform in U.S. schooling. The various components are seldom connected in a coherent manner, and so teachers are easily overwhelmed by the multiplicity of demands. The enthusiasm and commitment of portfolio teachers is impressive, but the costs and benefits are disquieting. The portfolio movement seems likely to falter and fail unless it is connected to the other supporting components in a manner that meets internal classroom needs (e.g., providing valid data for instructional decisions) while satisfying external policy demands (e.g., providing reliable information for accountability purposes) (Fullan, 1991).

Without such support, our guess is that the portfolio movement will eventually fall of its own weight. Selected teachers will rely on their professional judgment for deciding what to teach and how to teach it, and for rendering assessments to interested audiences. External authorities may entertain the idea of portfolios, performances, and exhibitions, but cost effectiveness will eventually carry the day. This shift has happened in the past; witness the early years of NAEP (Tyler, 1969). And another chance to improve the quality of schooling in the United States will have slipped through our fingers.

References

Calfee, R. C. (1992), Authentic assessment of reading and writing in the elementary classroom. In M.J. Dreher & W. H. Slater (Eds), *Research for improving reading/language arts education in the 1990s* (pp. 211-266). Norwood, MA: Christopher-Gordon.

Calfee, R.C., & Hiebert, E.H. (1991). Teacher assessment of student achievement. In R. Stake (Ed.). *Advances in program evaluation.* Vol. 1, Greenwich, CT: JAI Press.

Calfee, R.C., & Perfumo, P.A. (1992). *A survey of portfolio practices.* Berkeley, CA: Center for the Study of Writing, University of California, Berkeley.

Fullan, M. G. (1991). *The new meaning of educational change.* New York: Teachers College Press.

Hambleton, R.K., & Murphy, E. (1991). A psychometric perspective on authentic measurement. *Applied Measurement in Education*, 4, 347-362.

Harp, B.(1991) *Assessment and evaluation in whole language programs.* Norwood, MA: Christopher-Gordon.

Murphy, S. & Smith, M.A. (1991). *Writing Portfolios: A bridge from teaching to assessment.* Markham, Ontario: Pippin Publishing.

Newmann, F.M. (1991) Linking restructuring to authentic student achievement. *Phi Delta Kappan*, 72, 458-463.

Paris, S.G., Calfee. R.C., Filby, N., Hiebert, E.H., Pearson, P.D., Valencia, S.W., & Wolf, K.P. (1992). A framework for authentic literacy assessment. *The Reading Teacher*, 46, 88-89.

Pelavin, S. (1991). *Performance assessments in the states.* Washington, DC: Pelavin Associates.

Pikulski, J.J., & Shanahan, T. (Eds.) (1982). *Approaches to the informal evaluation of reading.* Newark, DE: International Reading Association.

Richert, A.E. (1990). Teaching teachers to reflect: A consideration of program structure. *Journal of Curriculum Studies*, 22, 509-527.

Rogers, V.R., & Stevenson, C. (1988). How do we know what kids are learning in school? *Educational Leadership.* 45(5), 68-75.

Smith, C.B. (Ed.). (1991). *Alternative assessment of performance in the language arts.* Bloomington, IN: ERIC Clearinghouse on Reading and Communication Skills.

Tierney, R.J., Carter, M.A., & Desai, L.E. (1991). *Portfolio assessment in the reading-writing classroom.* Norwood, MA: Christopher-Gordon.

Tyler, R.W. (1969). National assessment—some valuable byproducts for schools. *The National Elementary Principal.* 48(5), 42-48.

Valencia, S.W., & Calfee, R.C. (1991). The development and use of literacy portfolios for students, classes, and teachers. *Applied Measurement in Education*, 4, 333-345.

Wolf, D., Bixby, J., Glenn, J. III, & Gardner, H. (1991). To use their minds well: Investigating new forms of student assessment. In G. Grant (Ed.). *Review of research in education*, Vol.17, Washington, DC: American Educational Research Association.

Assessing Comprehension: Selected Interactions of Task and Reader

Reprinted from *The Reading Teacher* (1989), *42,* 694-697

Beth Davey

Over the years, the assessment of reading comprehension has been particularly problematic due to complex interactions among readers, texts, and tasks during comprehension processing (Johnston, 1983). A recent collection of papers (Squire, 1987) pointed to the need for more theory based measures of reading comprehension, with greater sensitivity to the impact of such interactions on assessment outcomes.

Reading processes, of course, are not directly observable and must be inferred from samples of behaviors assumed to reflect "real reading" (Farr and Carey, 1986). Students' answers to questions provide one such sample, and since the 1930s, questions have remained the predominant tool for assessing reading comprehension (Durkin, 1978-1979; Readence and Martin, 1988).

Educational decisions concerning placements and programs are heavily influenced by students' performance on both formal and informal question measures, and the assumption is often made that all students' performance scores represent the same valid manifestation of the underlying construct, comprehension. However, it has long been recognized that students' responses to questions are influenced not only by text variables and content understandings, but also by ancillary task features of the test itself, and that these features may interact with certain individual differences among readers (e.g., Benson and Crocker, 1979; Carroll, 1972; Drum, Calfee, and Cook, 1981; Johnston and Pearson, 1982; Kendall, Mason, and Hunter, 1980; Traub and Fisher, 1977; Ward, 1982; Ward, Dupree and Carlson, 1987).

What features of questions most affect reading comprehension assessment outcomes, and how do these features interact with differences among readers? We have conducted a series of studies over the past five years to address these questions. This article summarizes key findings from these studies and draws implications for assessment design and instructional practice.

Five Studies

Each study is reported in its entirety elsewhere. For the most part, they assessed features of *question format* (multiple choice or free response), *testing condition* (with or without text lookbacks), and *question type* (text explicit or implicit). Our materials consisted of multiple 250-300 word expository passages, accompanied by a series of experimenter generated questions.

Typically, subjects were somewhere in grades 5-12. They would be assigned certain passages with multiple choice questions, certain passages with free response questions (both types of item had identical stems) and would respond to some of these questions with the passage available for reinspection (lookback) and to others

with the passage unavailable (no lookback). In addition, for some studies, the type of question varied. Some assessed directly stated information (text explicit) and some assessed more reader based inferences (text implicit).

Of particular interest in our studies was the effect of these question task features on performance outcomes for readers who differed in overall reading skill and in language competence (e.g., deaf readers). The majority of our studies focused on comparisons between good and poor readers. Here we used a "matched reading level" design (Stanovich, 1986; Stanovich, Nathan, and Vala-Rossi, 1986), where good and poor readers were matched on overall reading skill but differed substantially in age. With this approach, any observed differences between reader groups could be more reliably attributed to characteristics of the particular readers rather than to differential task or text difficulty.

Effective Factors

General predictors. Some of our work concerning question assessments found that good and poor readers did not differ in terms of surface features, which influence the difficulty of reading comprehension questions. For example, in one study the same two test features–question type (text explicit versus text implicit) and question stem length (number of words in question stems)–proved to be effective joint predictors of question difficulty for both good and poor readers (Davey, 1988a).

Testing time. On the other hand, the same study found a substantial difference between good and poor readers in their test completion times (poor readers were much slower). Like Traub (1983) and others, we concluded that timed testing for reading comprehension adds an additional factor (speed) to the assessment process which might bias outcomes for particular groups of readers (such as less skilled readers).

Several additional studies yielded significant reader task interactions when questions varied in format and in lookback condition.

Question format. Results from several studies indicated that multiple choice question scores were generally higher than free response question scores for all readers. This is not surprising since the multiple choice format (a) provides cues through the response options which can be used for recalling information or inducing additional text processing that might not occur otherwise, (b) heightens the probability of correctly guessing answers, and (c) requires responses that are not dependent on writing skill.

Of particular interest, however, were our findings that, whereas these multiple choice items appeared to be assessing comparable processes and skills for both good and poor readers, this may not have been the case for free response items (Davey, 1987, 1988a; Davey and Macready, 1986).

It appears that questions that require written responses are differentially difficult for readers varying in overall reading skill and English language proficiency. In our studies, poor readers and deaf readers performed comparably to good readers on multiple choice questions, but fared far worse on free response items. Moreover, this finding held for both text explicit and text implicit question types (Davey and LaSasso, 1984).

While these findings concerning the interaction of item formats and reader differences are suggestive of item bias issues, the picture becomes even more complex when one considers the variable of testing condition.

Lookback testing. In our studies, being able to look back to the passage during question answering tended to enhance scores on free response items but not on multiple choice items (Davey, 1987). Moreover, looking back raised these free response scores to a level comparable to that of multiple choice items.

Although this was true for both text explicit and text implicit questions, the im-

pact of looking back was particularly strong when the items assessed information directly stated in the passage (Davey and LaSasso, 1984).

Complicating these rather clear cut findings, however, are the additional observations that readers differed in how effectively they used text lookbacks.

Good readers, compared with poor and deaf readers, appeared to profit most from lookback opportunities (Davey, 1987, 1988b; Davey and LaSasso, 1984). For example, in one study, good and poor readers did not differ when answering questions without passages available, yet good readers' scores substantially exceeded those of poor readers when text lookbacks were permitted. Another study indicated that reading disabled students who used frequent lookbacks did not score better than those who used few or no lookbacks (Keene and Davey, 1987).

Both of these studies concluded that poor readers and deaf readers may not know how to successfully use text lookbacks during assessment.

Student strategies. Most recently, good and poor readers' question answering strategies were studied for free response items with text lookbacks (Davey, 1988b). Our purpose was to compare the strategies used by poor and by good readers. Strategies were inferred from the analysis of response errors on text explicit vs. text implicit questions.

Generally speaking, good readers in this study were quite effective at integrating specific text information with their personal knowledge and reasoning skills when looking back to the passage. They also appeared to be aware of the differential task demands of the two types of questions.

On the other hand, poor readers' strategies were quite different and less successful. When poor readers were not sure of their answers, they did in fact look back to the passage for help, but when they could not find an acceptable answer by "going to the text," they did not "go to the head"; that is, they did not use personal knowledge or reasoning as frequently as did good readers. Instead, the poor readers tended to reproduce inappropriate text segments or to provide no response rather than to guess using their own resources.

Implications from this study were drawn for additional investigations into (a) the etiology of poor readers' ineffective lookback strategies and (b) the value of instruction in shaping more profitable testtaking approaches.

In terms of instruction, training in free response question tasks might show poor readers how the response requirements differ for text explicit and text implicit questions, and how to employ efficient text search strategies, such as skimming. Perhaps most importantly, poor readers need guidance in how to integrate their own knowledge with information from the text so as to generate acceptable and meaningful responses.

One final observation might be made concerning instruction in question responding. The value of such training might be not only to assist poor readers in better test performance, but also to shape the learning consequences of their engagement in these reading comprehension tasks.

Wixson (1983), for example, has demonstrated that the nature of readers' responses to questions can affect what they learn and remember from text. If this be the case, then encouraging poor readers to "go to their heads" during question answering may positively affect both the quantity and quality of what is learned from print.

Need for Caution

Several overall implications can be drawn for assessment practice and further research.

(1) Practitioners and test designers should be aware of how certain question task fea-

tures can affect valid demonstrations of reading comprehension processes for particular groups of respondents. For example, assessments incorporating *speed* or *lookbacks* or requiring *written responses* appear to be differentially difficult for certain types of readers, even when these readers are matched on overall skill level. Continued research is needed to illuminate potential sources of bias due to interactions and to explore the viability of different test administrations for different types of readers.

(2) Awareness of potential test bias resulting from task and reader interactions should result in greater caution when generalizing results from comprehension studies employing certain task features and reader groups to possible outcomes for other reader groups, perhaps assessed using different task features.

(3) More research is needed to clarify the role of educational experiences in the development of question answering strategies. Of particular interest are issues of how and why ineffective testtaking strategies develop, and the degree to which they can be modified through instruction. Systematic observations of classroom teachers' assessment practices could be especially informative: What types of questions do teachers ask? What task directives are provided? What criteria do teachers employ for assessing correctness (e.g., do they overinterpret the meaningfulness of free response answers simply because these contain key text language)? Are classroom question assessments timed? What instruction in question answering strategies do teachers provide?

(4) From a practical perspective, classroom teachers and reading specialists who use free response questions to assess reading comprehension should be aware that allowing students to look back to the passage may advantage some readers and disadvantage others. It seems safe to assume that poor readers in particular could benefit from specific training in the testtaking skills necessary for answering free response questions incorporating text lookbacks.

In sum, much remains to be known concerning factors affecting the optimal measurement of unobservable reading processes. Results from our studies complement those of others in pointing to complex interactions between readers and task features in question assessments. It is anticipated that future investigations will broaden these findings by exploring the impact of other assessment components and reader factors (such as prior knowledge, verbal ability, processing style, interest, and motivation) on valid demonstrations of reading comprehension.

Davey teaches reading courses at the University of Maryland, College Park, Maryland.

References

Benson, Jeri, and Linda Crocker. "The Effects of Item Format and Reading Ability on Objective Test Performance: A Question of Validity." *Educational and Psychological Measurement,* vol. 39, no. 2 (1979), pp. 381-87.

Carroll, John, B. "Defining Language Comprehension: Some Speculations." In *Language Comprehension and the Acquisition of Knowledge.* New York, NY: John Wiley and Sons, 1972.

Davey, Beth. "Postpassage Questions: Task and Reader Effects on Comprehension and Metacomprehension Processes." *Journal of Reading Behavior,* vol. 19, no. 3 (1987), pp. 261-85.

Davey, Beth. "Factors Affecting the Difficulty of Reading Comprehension Items for Successful and Unsuccessful Readers." *Journal of Experimental Education,* vol. 56, no. 2 (1988a), pp. 67-76.

Davey, Beth. "The Nature of Response Errors for Good and Poor Readers When Permitted to Reinspect Text during Question-answering." *American Educational Research Journal,* vol. 25, no. 3 (1988b), pp. 399-414.

Davey, Beth, and Carol J. LaSasso. "The Interaction of Reader and Task Factors in the Assessment of Reading Comprehension." *Journal of Experimental Education,* vol. 52, no. 4 (1984), pp. 199-206.

Davey, Beth, and George B. Macready, "Specification and Validation of Reading Comprehension Components." Paper presented at American Educational Research Association annual meeting, San Francisco, CA, 1986.

Drum, Priscilla A., Robert C. Calfee, and Linda K. Cook. "The Effects of Surface Structure Variables on Performance in Reading Comprehension Tests." *Reading Research Quarterly,* vol. 16, no. 4 (1981), pp. 486-514.

Durkin, Dolores. "What Classroom Observations Reveal about Reading Comprehension Instruction." *Reading Research Quarterly,* vol. 14, no. 4 (1978-1979), pp. 481-533.

Farr, Roger, and Robert F. Carey. *Reading: What Can Be Measured?* Newark, DE: International Reading Association, 1986.

Johnston, Peter H. *Reading Comprehension Assessment: A Cognitive Basis.* Newark, DE: International Reading Association, 1983.

Johnston, Peter H., and P. David Pearson. *Prior Knowledge, Connectivity, and the Assessment of Reading Comprehension.* Technical Report no. 245. Urbana-Champaign, IL: University of Illinois, Center for the Study of Reading, 1982.

Keene, Sylvia, and Beth Davey. "Effects of Computer-presented Text on the Reading Behaviors of Learning Disabled Adolescents." *Learning Disability Quarterly,* vol. 10, no. 4 (1987), pp. 283-90.

Kendall, Janet R., Jana M. Mason, and William Hunter. "Which Comprehension? Artifacts in the Measurement of Reading Comprehension." *Journal of Educational Research,* vol. 73, no. 4 (1980), pp. 233-36.

Readence, John E., and Michael A. Martin. "Comprehension Assessment: Alternatives to Standardized Tests." In *Reexamining Reading Diagnosis,* edited by Susan Glazer, Lyndon Searfoss, and Lance Gentile. Newark, DE: International Reading Association, 1988.

Squire, James R., ed. "The State of Reading Assessment" (Special Issue). *The Reading Teacher,* vol. 40 (April 1987).

Stanovich, Keith E."Matthew Effects in Reading: Some Consequences of Individual Differences in the Acquisition of Literacy." *Reading Research Quarterly,* vol. 21, no. 4 (1986), pp. 360-407.

Stanovich, Keith E., Ruth G. Nathan, and Marilyn Vala-Rossi. "Developmental Changes in the Cognitive Correlates of Reading Ability and the Development Lag Hypothesis." *Reading Research Quarterly,* vol. 21, no. 3 (1986), pp. 267-316.

Traub, Ross. "A Priori Considerations in Choosing an Item Response Model." In *Applications of Item Response Theory,* edited by Ron Hambleton. Vancouver, BC: Educational Research Institute, 1983.

Traub, Ross, and Charles Fisher. "On the Equivalence of Constructed-response and Multiple-choice Tests." *Applied Psychological Measurement,* vol. 1, no. 3 (1977), pp. 355-69.

Ward, William. "A Comparison of Free-response and Multiple-choice Forms of Verbal Aptitude Tests." *Applied Psychological Measurement,* vol. 6, no. 1 (1982), pp. 1-11.

Ward, William, David Dupree, and Sybil Carlson. *A Comparison of Free-response and Multiple-choice Questions in the Assessment of Reading Comprehension* (Research report: April). Princeton, NJ: Educational Testing Service, 1987.

Wixson, Karen K. "Postreading Question-answer Interactions and Children's Learning from Text." *Journal of Educational Pyschology,* vol. 75, no. 3 (1983), pp. 413-23.

Putting It All Together: Solving the Reading Assessment Puzzle

Reprinted from *The Reading Teacher* (1992), *46,* 26-37

Roger Farr

Reading assessment has become a genuine puzzle. Confusion and debate continue about what the goals of school assessment of reading should be and about what types of tests and other assessments are needed to achieve those goals. That debate should focus on the purposes for assessment and whether current tests achieve those purposes. Too often, however, the focus of the debate is on the latest testing panacea. In this article, I first examine the complex components of the assessment puzzle. Next I propose a solution to the puzzle that involves linkages among various assessment audiences and approaches. I conclude with a few remarks about how school districts in the United States might pull together all the pieces and solve the assessment puzzle for themselves.

Examining the Pieces of the Assessment Puzzle

The pieces of the puzzle represent many types of assessments, critical attitudes about them, and attempts to challenge or improve them. One of the truly puzzling aspects of reading assessment to many educators is that the amount of testing appears to increase at the same time that criticism of it intensifies (Farr & Carey, 1986; McClellan, 1988; Salganik, 1985; Valencia & Pearson, 1987).

Criticism of Schools Has Led to More Assessment

Public disappointment with student achievement has led to extensive criticism of U.S. schools. This disapproval intensified in the l950s with a focus on reading. Reading assessment conducted to prove or disprove the criticism has received a great deal of attention ever since. Could Johnny read or not, and how well or how poorly? By the 1960s, and beyond, score declines on tests used to predict how well high schoolers would do in college compounded public concern and criticism (The National Commission on Excellence in Education, 1983.)

The conviction that many students were receiving high school diplomas and yet were almost totally illiterate became firmly established in the public's mind (Purves & Niles, 1984). The Peter Doe case in California exemplified that concern (Saretsky, 1973). The case concerned a high school student who sued the school district for graduating him without teaching him to read. As a result of this kind of dissatisfaction with educational outcomes, the use of standardized, norm-referenced assessment intensified, and state minimum competency testing programs proliferated (Madaus, 1985; Salmon-Cox, 1981).

The data to determine whether scores on reading tests were deteriorating over time is sketchy at best and tends not to substantiate dramatic declines in the reading performance of U.S. students over the years (Farr & Fay, 1982; Farr, Fay, Myers, & Ginsberg, 1987; Stedman & Kaestle, 1987). Nonetheless, the public has remained convinced that performance has dropped rather dramatically. Further, the

prevalence of minimum competency programs has not significantly altered the conviction of the public and press that student achievement, particularly in reading, continues to deteriorate.

This unabated critical concern was at least partly responsible for the establishment of the National Assessment of Educational Progress (NAEP), an ongoing federally mandated study that now provides some reading performance data over time. Any declines it has depicted are small compared to the public's determined assumptions (Mullis, Owen, & Phillips, 1990). And although careful analyses of the ACT and SAT score declines has cited several reasonable causes other than poor schools, that phenomenon did much to sustain and cement public conviction and the demand for accountability testing (Popham, 1987; Resnick, 1982).

The continuing debate about the quality of U.S. schools has now given rise to a new focus on standards and assessment. At the same time that they reaffirm their conviction that children are not learning in school, critics like Chester Finn (1992) echo the call from the White House "for new American achievement tests" that compare student performance to "world class standards" that would be set as criterion references. President Bush (1991) has called for "voluntary national tests for 4th, 8th, and 12th graders in the five core subjects" to "tell parents and educators, politicians and employers, just how well our schools are doing."

The Search for Alternative Assessments Has Also Led To More Assessment

In addition to dissatisfaction with the schools, there has been a quest for assessments that are closely aligned with more holistic views of language development. Some curriculum theorists concerned with the mismatch between curriculum and assessment have determined that if curriculum is to change, the reading tests must change. This has brought about a proliferation of new assessments—both formal and informal (Brown, 1986; Burstall, 1986; Priestley, 1982; Stiggins, Conklin, & Bridgeford, 1986).

Included in this mix have been modifications of conventional tests with new item formats and the addition of the assessment of behaviors not often included on traditional tests, such as background knowledge, student interests and attitudes, and metacognition. Other assessments in reading have taken an entirely different approach to assessment, relying entirely on student work samples collected in portfolios (Jongsma, 1989; Valencia, 1990: Wolf, 1989). Portfolios have themselves taken many different forms from *show portfolios*, which include only a few carefully selected samples, to *working portfolios*, which include a broad sample of work and which are used to guide and organize daily instruction. In addition, numerous professional publications have published articles calling for the use of a broader range of teacher observations and informal assessment techniques (Cambourne & Turbill, 1990; Goodman, 1991).

Different Audiences Need Different Information

Thus, it seems that the increased amount of testing has resulted from greater accountability demands as well as from attempts to find alternatives to traditional assessments. In order to bring some sense to this proliferation of assessment, we need to understand that tests have only one general purpose: Tests should be considered as nothing more than attempts to systematically gather information. The information is used to help children learn about their own literacy development and to give teachers and others concerned with students' literacy the information they need for curriculum planning. *The bottom line in selecting and using any assessment should be whether it helps students.*

A book that I first authored more than 20 years ago regarding the assessment of reading was entitled *Reading: What Can*

Be Measured? (Farr, 1970; Farr & Carey, 1986). I have always felt that the title gave the wrong focus to the review of assessment issues. That book should have been entitled, *Reading: Why Should It Be Measured?* We need to consider who needs information about reading, what kind of information is needed, and when it is needed. Only then can we begin to plan for more sensible assessment.

In order to think more clearly about overall assessment plans, we need to know why we want to test. There are, of course, different groups that need information. Without considering these groups and their information needs, the assessment program in any school system will remain as a set of jumbled puzzle pieces. The general distinctions between audiences are covered in Figure 1.

The public. Members of the general public, who make decisions through their elected officials, including school boards, have a vested interest in the future of children and in their effective and cost-efficient instruction. It is recognized as vital to Americans' and their nation's future that schools produce educated students. Indeed, the most recent federally supported efforts to improve education have been on establishing standards that presumably will result in the development of assessments related to those standards. At the present time, those involved with establishing the standards are moving in the direction of holistic kinds of performance assessment.

Administrators. Ideally school administrators would rely most heavily on performance assessments that are criterion-ref-

Figure 1. Assessment Audiences

Audiences:	The Information Is Needed To:	The Information Is Related To:	Type of Information:	When Information Is Needed:
General Public (and the press)	Judge if schools are accountable and effective	Groups of students	Related to broad goals: norm- & criterion-referenced	Annually
School administrators/ staff	Judge effectiveness of curriculum, materials, teachers	Groups of students & individuals	Related to broad goals: criterion- & norm-referenced	Annually or by term/semester
Parents	Monitor progress of child, effectiveness of school	Individual student	Usually related to broader goals; both criterion- & norm-referenced	Periodically; 5 or 6 times a year
Teachers	Plan instruction, strategies, activities	Individual student; small groups	Related to specific goals; primarily criterion-referenced	Daily, or as often as possible
Students	Identify strengths, areas to emphasize	Individual (self)	Related to specific goals; criterion-referenced	Daily, or as often as possible

erenced. These performance measures should compare student performance against a clearly defined curriculum. But since we live in a complex world where mobility and diversity are the reality, administrators also need norm-referenced comparisons of their students' performance.

Parents. While parents share the public's interests, they have a vested interest in their own individual children. In order to monitor their children's progress and to be active in their education, parents want criterion-referenced reports; additionally parents are also typically interested in how their children perform on normed tests in comparison to children from across the United States.

Teachers. A teacher's primary concern is helping students learn. While teachers are necessarily aware of normed assessment's comparative reports as a kind of bottom-line accountability, they are primarily interested in the kind of information that will support the daily instructional decisions they need to make. This kind of information has been generated by criterion-referenced tests and by other types of assessment that can be utilized more effectively in the classroom as a part of instruction.

Students. Students need to become good self-assessors if they are to improve their literacy skills. They need to select, review, and think about the reading and writing they are doing. They need to be able to revise their own writing and to revise their comprehension as they read. If students understand their own needs, they will improve. Students should, in fact, be the primary assessors of their own literacy development.

The Wall Between Understanding

It is important for each of these audiences to recognize, understand, and respect the needs of the others if we are to pull the assessment puzzle together. Audience needs cluster around those of teachers and students on the one hand and those of other decision-makers on the other.

The assessment needs of these two general groups tend to be dramatically different and even contradictory, and if the users of assessment do not recognize one another's needs, it is because these distinctions create a kind of wall depicted in Figure 2. It is essential that we breach that wall if we are to get our assessment act together!

Some Tests Attempt To Do It All

No single assessment can serve all the audiences in need of educational performance information. Yet developments in standardized tests have attempted to do so. The tests have added criterion-referenced interpretations, special interpretations for teachers, special reports for parents, individual score reports, and instructional support materials of various kinds. These developments have made the tests longer, more expensive, more time-consuming, and more confusing. Consequently, teachers are expected to justify these investments by making more instructional use of the test results.

At the same time, the increased investment in assessment time and money has tended to give these tests even more importance in determining school accountability and in making high-stakes educational decisions. Specifically, four potential problems have arisen.

Teaching to the test. As accountability became more and more of a concern, teachers have felt pressured to place emphasis on what the standardized tests covered, regardless of what the school curriculum called for. Over time, reading curricula have begun to reflect the skill breakdown of many tests, and reading textbooks have tended to emphasize the skills tests cover as well.

Contaminating the evidence. Standardized reading tests used to mean something. They were genuine indications that a stu-

Figure 2. Opposing Views of Assessment

A Teacher's View of Assessment	A Lack of Understanding/Acceptance	Other Decision Makers' Views of Assessment
Assessment is for:		*Assessment is for:*
Nurturing		Gate keeping
Guiding the development of students		Judging the success of students, teachers, and schools
Promoting student self-reflection		Finding relatively singular correct answers
Enabling the teacher to teach flexibly		Exercising control over school behaviors
Comparing student performance to a task to be completed		Comparing student performance to that of other students
Making decisions based on multiple samples including student-selected activities		Making decisions based on single test scores

dent who performed adequately on them could read. This was so because they *sampled* reading behavior. But now that indication is contaminated. If teachers are deliberately stressing the sub-behaviors that they know are on the tests, the assessments are no longer sampling reading behavior—they are, in effect, covering a very limited definition of it. A good score on a standardized reading test no longer indicates that the student can read in general. It means only that the student can do those limited things the test covers.

Crunching objectives. Attempts to make reading assessment tests more encompassing have tended to make them much longer. Even so, tests are forced to cover the numerous subskills they contain with only a few items each. "What does it mean," a teacher may legitimately ask, "if a student misses one of three items that report on comprehending cause-and-effect?"

The potential for a mismatch. Teachers have long noted that nationally normed tests do not reflect particular emphases in their classrooms. How can a standardized reading test, they have correctly argued, tell them much about a particular curriculum they are following? What can it tell the public about how well the teacher has done using the curriculum?

The more a teacher adheres to instruction related directly to the needs, interests, and backgrounds of his or her particular students, the less assured is the match of that instruction to standardized test content—and the less likely the test's scores will serve that instruction.

Good Reading Theory Recommends Authentic Performance Assessment

Most published tests have not adequately responded to emerging reading theory, which explains reading comprehension as a meaning-constructing process. Any subskills factored out of the process are not discrete; if they actually exist as behaviors, they appear to operate in such an intricate fashion that it is difficult if not impossible to isolate them.

Authentic assessment. Relatively wide acceptance of a constructivist, context-specific definition of reading has promoted a careful analysis of current reading and language arts test content and format to see how authentic the testing experience is. This analysis has led to the conclusion that the reading required on most tests is not much like the reading behavior that our new understanding describes. How valid is the content of a reading test in terms of

reader purpose, interests, and background, which we now believe are primary influences on reading behavior?

Performance assessment. Attention to authenticity has accompanied and helped generate the development and use of performance assessment. A student's language behaviors need to be assessed, it is contended, as they are used in real-life situations. Students don't comprehend something read, for example, as a multiple-choice response, and marking those answers has nothing to do with the way reading is actually used, except in taking tests. Reading performance assessment must look at the reading act in process or judge comprehension of a text as it is applied in some realistic way.

Observation. Observation is one way to do this and can lead teachers to meaningful insights about the progress and needs of individual students. Yet teachers need to be trained in regard to what they can look for and what those signs suggest. They need to develop useful ways to make discrete notes about observations and to synthesize what they find. Observation generates many details in relatively random order, and they seldom become clearly useful until they are gathered into patterns that can direct instruction.

Portfolios. Another highly valuable form of performance assessment is the portfolio. For these collections, students and teachers select numerous samples from drafts and final versions of various kinds of a student's writing. The idea is to demonstrate the student's progress and development in the combined process of reading, thinking, and writing. Thus many of the samples in the portfolio are responses to reading. The portfolio is reviewed and discussed regularly by the teacher and student, who may arrange it for others to examine.

Integrated assessment. Assessments in which thinking, reading, and writing are integrated have been developed in recent years. Such assessments have been developed by classroom teachers, school districts, and publishers in an attempt to integrate reading and writing and to assess reading and writing with more realistic activities. These vary widely, but for most of them the student is given a writing task related to a text that is supplied. The task has been deemed to be authentic because it is typical of something the student might do in real life, including the kinds of activities often used for learning in the classroom. It is designed to emphasize the use of information in the reading selection in a realistic and interesting writing task.

For example, one such test asks students to read a nonfiction article that categorically discusses and describes how insect-eating plants lure, capture, and digest their victims. The task is to write a fictional piece telling what a mother bug might say to her children in cautioning them about these plants. Teachers use what the students write to assess students' understanding of the text. They rate other integrated behaviors as well, such as the students' organization and application of the text's content to the task and factors related to writing.

Such reading/writing assessments encourage students to develop a variety of responses based on their interpretation of the reading selection, their background knowledge, and the direction they choose to take in constructing a realistic response. These kinds of performance assessments provide teachers with valuable insights regarding a student's ability to read, write, and construct a meaningful response to an interesting task. Prewriting notes, first drafts, and teacher observation notes all make the assessment a valuable source of information.

In addition, the final drafts can be scored to serve as information that can help determine accountability. The responses can be scored following a "rubric," a list of criteria that describes several levels of performance in each of the categories to be analyzed. Samples of actual student papers ("anchors") that represent each score level described by the rubrics can also be used in scoring. Thus these tests are criterion-

referenced. Yet the guides to scoring are somewhat equivalent to normed scores in the sense that the anchor papers were taken from many gathered in field-testing and were judged to be typical of the range of responses described in the rubric.

A Combined Solution to the Assessment Puzzle

None of the preceding types of assessment should be argued to be the single solution to the testing puzzle. Figure 3 depicts how performance assessments can provide direct linkage among the main users of assessment and how the three major types of assessment are linked. The chart is a plan for pulling the pieces of the assessment puzzle together into a solution that can inform all the decision makers involved in a student's development into an effective reader and language user.

Solving the Puzzle Will Require Cooperation

Pulling the assessment puzzle together will require tolerance and compromise on the part of many critics of particular types of assessment. The process would be facilitated if:

- Critics of the schools would become aware that assessment must serve more than school accountability. Ideally, critics will inform their concerns with a better understanding of what schools are trying to accomplish.
- Decision makers would understand that assessment is more than numbers on a test paper. They would begin to understand and use the kinds of assessments that are based on real classroom activities and that represent the types of activities in which students who are effective readers and writers should become proficient.
- The most idealistic of the critics of assessment would become more realistic and flexible, tempering their insistence on authentic performance assessment. It seems fruitless, in particular, for some critics to insist that all assessment revolve around observation of activities that are apt not to involve all children and that reveal language use in highly varying degrees.
- Producers of assessments would acknowledge that no one assessment is going to suffice as a school's examination of reading. This would mean that they would no longer promote any of their products as such a test. It would also mean that future revisions of standardized reading tests would undo much of the complexity they now contain.

None of this is to suggest that critical analysis of reading assessment should stop, nor should attempts to improve tests in response to criticism cease. Efforts to develop and institute the new accountability assessments in Illinois (Pearson & Valencia, 1987), where the assessment allows for multiple correct responses within each multiple-choice item, and in Michigan (Michigan State Board of Education, 1987), where the assessment relies on longer passages followed by more numerous items, have been interesting, if not conclusive, efforts to contribute to a solution to the assessment puzzle. So have attempts to construct items that will reveal students' awareness of how they are processing texts. Although longer reading test passages, different question formats, etc. will not solve the assessment puzzle, they can certainly shape the parts we pull together for a better fit.

Norm-Referenced Tests Need to Change

To solve the assessment puzzle, it will be necessary for teachers and other educators to admit that norm-referenced test results can be of some value to the public and other decision makers, including parents. But these standardized tests should not be of the form that has evolved in response to criticism.

Test authors and publishers should begin to plan assessment *programs* that address

the multiple audiences. Teachers and schools will need assistance in developing portfolios, planning performance assessments, and integrating assessment information. What is not needed are large single test batteries that promise to meet all of a school's assessment needs from classroom diagnosis to accountability. That attempt, especially linking accountability assessment and instructional assessment, has led to a narrowing of the curriculum.

For the large-scale assessments, this suggests the elimination of the designation of items by subskills and reporting on those subbehaviors as if they truly are separable and distinct. More publisher efforts should go into the development of a variety of creative and useful curriculum assessments in which students have to actually perform the behaviors the school is attempting to teach.

What large-scale assessment can and should do is to report a global comprehension score, with no special subtests on traditional focuses like word recognition and vocabulary. Without the time-consuming battery of accompanying tests, reading tests can be shorter while using longer passages of a variety of types. These passages must evoke different purposes for reading that reflect the real reasons students read in and out of school. Thus, the reading test will be more authentic.

Without the burden of reporting on a host of specific reading and thinking subskills, test makers can write items that truly reflect the balance of a passage, the students' probable purpose for reading such a text, and the aspects of the writing that make the text one of quality and worth the students' time.

It should also be remembered that the long-standing primary purpose of large-scale testing has been to provide a general assessment as to how groups of students are progressing in a school district. Such information, if it does not become the focus of instruction, can be one piece of information used to contribute to a broad base of information for planning, supporting, and evaluating school- and system-wide curricula and instruction.

This approach strongly suggests that *matrix sampling* be used for large-scale assessment, thus eliminating the need to administer to all students the same test items or tasks. Testing time can be considerably shorter if carefully selected samples of students take different parts of a test instead of the whole thing. Good sampling should yield results similar to those obtained when all students take the entire test. Nothing is lost in reporting, since individual scores are of little concern. In addition, matrix sampling provides a general indication of the progress of groups of students, not a blueprint for instruction of individual students.

Performance Assessments Can Provide the Key Linkage

Figure 3 illustrates the linkages across three general audience types that will be essential to solving the assessment puzzle. Norm-referenced information provides a link between parents and decision makers other than teachers. However, the key linkage across all three general audiences is criterion-referenced performance assessments. Various approaches to performance assessment are being developed and tried out in school district assessment programs. Such assessments can be designed by teachers themselves. In fact, this has been done in several local school districts around the United States by teachers cooperating and interacting in order to meet their assessment needs. The same procedures are being tried at the state level in Maryland, Arizona, California, and Utah, and other states are sure to move in this direction.

The teachers who have been most successful in using this approach have had the support of administrators who could see over the assessment wall. Their support generated public interest and support. In some school systems, published or teacher-created integrated language performance assessment has already become

Figure 3. The Solution — Linkage

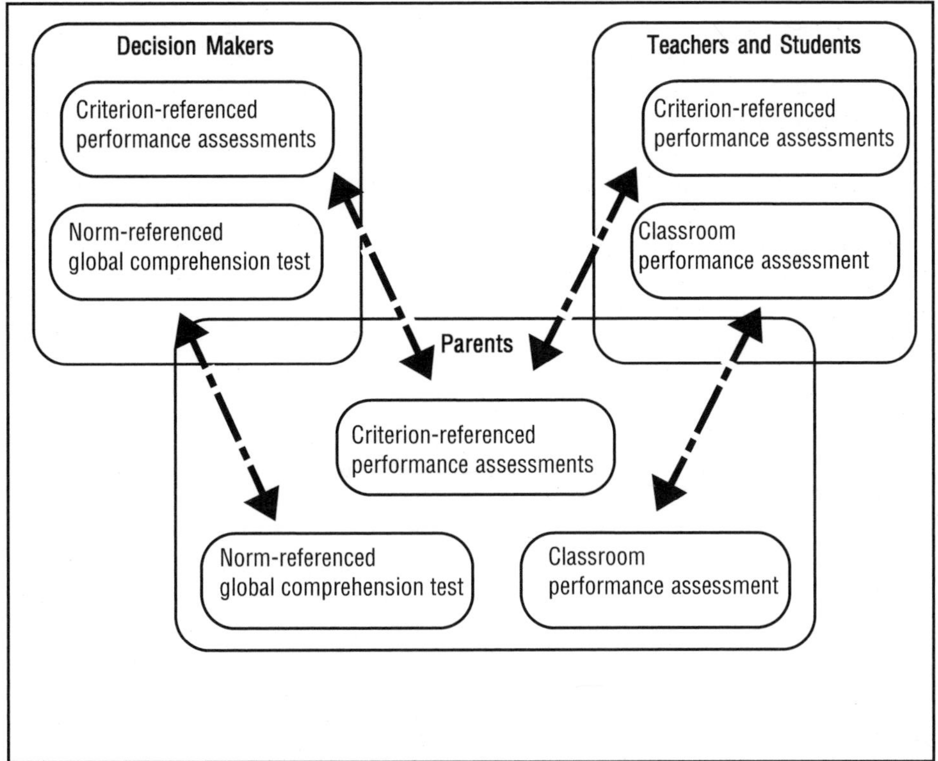

a primary source of information for judging school accountability.

While teachers can create integrated language performance activities on a classroom basis, using them for accountability will require carefully developed or prepared programs that have been made congruent system-wide. This was done in River Forest, Illinois, where teachers developed their own rubrics, anchor papers, and inservice training. This kind of structuring will be necessary if the public, the press, and administrators are to be expected to value these tests as the key indicators of accountability and sources of directions for key decisions, such as curriculum development.

At the same time, of course, these tests can reflect authentic student performance. Not only are they very closely related to instructional activities and thus of high utility to teachers, they are actually instructional activities in and of themselves so the class time they require is doubly well invested.

The Portfolio Is the Flagship of Performance Assessment

Most developers of integrated language assessment programs highly recommend putting the student products into portfolios, a direct acknowledgment that the roots of language performance assessment lie in a portfolio approach to assessment and instruction. So integral is the portfolio performance assessment in good classrooms today that it is vital to note the qualities that make the portfolio approach a successful one.

A successful portfolio approach to assessment must revolve around regular and frequent attention to the portfolio by the student and the teacher. It does minimal good

just to store a student's papers in a big folder and let them gather dust for lengthy periods of time. Papers must be added frequently; others can be weeded out in an ongoing rearrangement and selection process; most importantly, the whole process should involve frequent self-analysis by the student and regular conversations between the teacher and the student.

Too many teachers who contend that they are using portfolios do not do these things. Here are a few requirements if portfolios are to provide good assessment:

- The portfolio *belongs* to the student. It is his or her work and property, not some classroom requirement. Students should have choice about what goes in, and they should be encouraged to decorate and personalize their portfolios in unique ways.
- Portfolios are not primarily display, although students may help arrange them for their parents and administrators to see. They are a shifting, growing repository of developing processes and ideas—a rather personal melting pot that the student uses to reflect on his or her own literacy development and to discuss interesting reading and writing activities with the teacher.
- The teacher's role in portfolio development is that of a consultant who helps convince the student that the work should show a variety of materials reflecting the reading-writing-thinking process as well as examples of responses to common classroom tasks and the student's favorite creations.
- The portfolio should contain numerous and varied pieces written and revised in response to reading. Reading logs reporting ongoing responses to books and articles make valuable contributions to portfolios.
- Portfolios should be reflective collections, revealing genuinely individual and personal responses to classroom activities and to ideas.
- At an absolute minimum, there should be four one-on-one, teacher/student discussions and analyses each semester of a student's developing portfolio. These sessions should not be short and perfunctory. If this requirement is not met, the assessment potential of the portfolio process is forfeited.
- Keeping the portfolio is an ongoing process. Its real value as an assessment tool materializes as the student can analyze his or her progress and development over time.

New Emphases in Assessment Have Common Qualities

Portfolios are part of a group of classroom performance assessments, some of them quite informal, that link the assessment interests of teachers, students, and parents. Portfolios can also be highly revealing to school specialists and administrators who, with the students' permission, take the time to examine them. All of these emerging strategies are both authentic and involve performance assessment. They are:

- Highly individualized, even though they may take place during activities that involve groups of students.
- A part of classroom activities and instruction designed to match an individual student's interests and needs and to use a student's strengths to develop more incisive and creative use of language.
- Activities that integrate several language behaviors.
- Chances to use critical thinking and to express unique and emerging reactions and responses to ideas encountered in text.
- Models that encourage and develop self-assessment by the student, making him or her aware of the language-related strengths that are developing.

How School Districts Can Begin to Solve the Assessment Puzzle

Too often school district testing programs are nothing more than test-and-file procedures. The tests are administered; when the scores are available, they are reported in some way; and teachers are admonished to peruse and use the test results. Yet many educators across the U.S. already embrace the suggestions made here for solving the assessment puzzle. Administrators are aware that testing programs can and do divide educators. Superintendents do not want to abandon their accountability responsibilities, yet they want to support effective ongoing classroom assessment that provides teachers with information that is congruent with current knowledge about reading/writing processes. Teachers want to be more involved in developing an assessment program that serves and matches their instructional needs. They all sense that what is needed is an integrated system that is effective in fostering better teaching and learning.

Many of these school districts need help with developing an assessment program that links audiences instead of dividing them—one that supplies broad-based accountability information yet is customized to the particular system, its teachers, and its students. One way for school districts to begin is to discuss the pieces of the assessment puzzle in their system. Representatives of all the audiences with assessment needs should take part. As this process develops, the discussions need to be recorded in some way and synthesized. Out of all this can come other brainstorming sessions and ultimately inservice workshops to help all teachers understand how a broad-based assessment program can be pulled together. Equally important, many teachers will welcome inservice training on using different types of informal assessments.

These kinds of workshops can be started within school districts right away. For instance, teachers who are exceptionally good observers or use the portfolio approach with great success are almost always easily identified. They could be enlisted and supported by administrators to run workshops that can be conducted while the discussions about broader reading assessment are helping representative groups define the assessment problems and their district's needs.

The assessment puzzle can be solved. The solution, however, is not as simple as identifying a nonexistent test that will do the whole job nor as arbitrary as eliminating most reading assessment. Rather it takes a vision that focuses on what real literacy means and the awareness that various groups have a stake in helping students to develop as literate citizens. Such a vision must not use assessment to isolate. It must respect the complex nature of literacy, it must serve students and help them to become reflective self-assessors, and it must create links that bring instruction and assessment together.

References

Brown, R. (1986). Evaluation and learning. In A.R. Petrosky & D. Bartholomae (Eds.), *The teaching of writing: Eighty-fifth yearbook of the National Society for the Study of Education* (pp. 114-130). Chicago, IL: University of Chicago Press.

Bustall, C. (1986). Innovative forms of assessment: A United Kingdom perspective. *Educational Measurement: Issues and Practice, 5*, 17-22.

Bush, G. (1991). *America 2000: An education strategy.* Washington, DC: U.S. Department of Education.

Cambourne, B., & Turbill, J. (1990). Assessment in whole language classrooms: Theory into practice. *The Elementary School Journal, 90*, 337-349.

Farr, R. (1970). *Reading: What can be measured?* Newark, DE: International Reading Association.

Farr, R., & Carey, R. (1986). *Reading: What can be measured?* (2nd ed.). Newark, DE: International Reading Association.

Farr, R., & Fay. L. (1982). Reading trend data in the United States: A mandate for caveats and caution. In G. Austin & H. Garber (Eds.). *The rise and fall of national test scores* (pp. 83-141). New York: The Academic Press.

Farr, R., Fay. L., Myers. R., & Ginsberg, M. (1987). *Reading achievement in the United States: 1944-45, 1976, and 1986.* Bloomington, IN: Indiana University.

Finn, C.E.. Jr. (1992. January 12). Turn on the lights. *The New York Times.* Sect. 4. p. 19.

Goodman, Y. (1991). Evaluating language growth: Informal methods of evaluation. In J. Flood, J. Jensen, D. Lapp. & J. Squire (Eds.), *Handbook of research on teaching the English language arts* (pp. 502-509). New York: Macmillan.

Jongsma, K. (1989). Portfolio assessment. *The Reading Teacher, 43*, 264-265.

Madaus, G.F. (1985). Public policy and the testing profession: You've never had it so good? *Educational Measurement: Issues and Practice, 4*, 5-11.

McClellan, M.C. (1988). Testing and reform. *Phi Delta Kappan, 69*, 766-771.

Michigan State Board of Education. (1987). *Blueprint for the new MEAP reading test.* Lansing, MI: Author.

Mullis, V.S., Owen, E.H., & Phillips, G.W. (1990). *Accelerating academic achievement: A summary of the findings from 20 years of NAEP.* Princeton, NJ: Educational Testing Service.

National Commission on Excellence in Education. (1983). *A nation at risk.* Washington, DC: U.S. Department of Education.

Pearson, P.D., & Valencia, S. (1987). *The Illinois State Board of Education census assessment in reading: An historical reflection.* Springfield, IL: Illinois State Department of Education.

Popham, W.J. (1987). The merits of measurement-driven instruction. *Phi Delta Kappan, 68,* 679-682.

Priestley. M. (1982). *Performance assessment in education and training: Alternate techniques.* Englewood Cliffs, NJ: Educational Technology Publications.

Purves, A., & Niles, 0. (1984). The challenge to education to produce literate citizens. In A. Purves & 0. Niles, (Eds.). *Becoming readers in a complex society: Eighty-third yearbook of the National Society for the Study of Education* (pp. 1-15). Chicago, IL: University of Chicago Press.

Resnick, D. (1982). History of educational testing. In A.K. Wigdor & W.R. Garner (Eds.), *Ability testing: Uses, consequences, and controversies*, Part 2 (pp. 173-194). Washington, DC: National Academy Press.

Salganik, L.H. (1985). Why testing reforms are so popular and how they are changing education. *Phi Delta Kappan, 66*, 628-634.

Salmon-Cox, L. (1981). Teachers and tests: What's really happening? *Phi Delta Kappan, 62*, 631-634.

Saretsky, G. (1973). The strangely significant case of Peter Doe. *Phi Delta Kappan, 54*, 589-592.

Stedman, L.C., & Kaestle, C.F. (1987). Literacy and reading performance in the United States from 1880 to the present. *Reading Research Quarterly, 22*, 8-46.

Stiggins, R.J., Conklin, N.F., & Bridgeford, N.J. (1986). Classroom assessment: A key to effective education. *Educational Measurement: Issues and Practice, 5*, 17.

Valencia, S. (1990). A portfolio approach to classroom reading assessment: The whys, whats, and hows. *The Reading Teacher, 43*, 338-339.

Valencia, S., & Pearson, P. (1987). Reading assessment: Time for a change. *The Reading Teacher, 40*, 726-732.

Wolf, D.P. (1989). Portfolio assessment: Sampling student work. *Educational Leadership, 46*, 35-39.

Involving Parents in the Assessment Process

Reprinted from *The Reading Teacher* (1990), *44*, 346-349

Anthony D. Fredericks
Timothy V. Rasinski

Involving parents throughout the reading curriculum is one of the most productive, effective ways to enhance children's literacy development. When parents are provided with opportunities to take a sincere, active role in their child's reading growth, reading performance escalates; in addition, pupils' attitudes toward reading improve. Research has convincingly demonstrated that parent involvement can dramatically affect the total reading development of every child.

We believe that parents should be more than passive participants in reading curricula; they should be invited to participate in all aspects of the classroom reading program. Such parent participation assumes a commitment on the part of the classroom teacher to provide parents with opportunities to interact with their children in meaningful, relevant activities.

At the 1990 IRA Convention in Atlanta, Georgia, we saw considerable interest in various literacy assessment procedures. Teachers with a whole language orientation to literacy instruction were eager for ideas and procedures that would make the assessment process purposeful. For example, many educators were looking for assessment procedures that would move assessment beyond norm- or criterion-referenced tools and focus more on an evaluation of processes involved in meaningful, functional reading.

To that end, we believe that parents can and should play a significant role in the assessment process. Any teacher who has attempted to explain standardized test scores to parents at conference time knows the frustration parents feel about their child's performance in reading. Flood and Lapp (1989) note that parents often read more into a single test score than educators do. What often ensues during discussions of test scores is a great deal of misunderstanding between teachers and parents about the actual progress students are making in reading.

Parents' participation in evaluating their children's growth can help to eliminate many misconceptions and misinterpretations that may occur during parent-teacher conferences or at report card time. Moreover, it helps give parents direction in aiding their children's literacy development. We do not mean to imply that parents should take on all or even the major responsibilities of evaluating progress in reading; rather, parents can make a positive contribution to assessment and thus develop a healthy regard for the process and their children's progress.

Inviting parents to take an active role in assessing individual literacy growth is predicated on three interdependent principles:

1. *Involving parents in the assessment process must be an integral part of that program.* By this we mean that the assessment process should be a natural extension of the reading program and not portrayed as an "add-on" to the curriculum.

2. *Parent assessment procedures must be conducted comprehensively.* That is, the information garnered from all assessment measures must be taken from all aspects of the reading curriculum. Purposeful assessment is not a single activity done once or twice during the year, but an activity that is addressed on a regular basis and is pertinent to the direction of that program. Parents need to understand that assessment can and will lead to sound curricular decisions.

3. *Parents' involvement in assessment should be approached systematically.* Parents cannot be expected to assess and monitor their children's reading development without sufficient time or training. Getting them involved and keeping them involved are important to the success of the assessment process.

An effective parental assessment program does not happen overnight; but by the same token it need not be an elaborate or confusing array of tasks that overwhelms parents, either. Nevertheless, when parents take part in observing and assessing their children's literacy development, they will be taking an active role in the reading program; they will have first-hand knowledge about their children's personal progress throughout that program. Regular opportunities to monitor and assess reading growth provide parents with a better understanding of the demands of effective reading instruction. Such opportunities also allow them to develop an appreciation of reading consistent with the goals of the reading program.

Following are six ideas for teachers who want parents to become active partners in the assessment process.

1. Early in the school year, provide a means for parents to state individual expectations for their child. You might ask what kind of progress individual parents like to see. Record parents' responses to these queries and refer to them on a regular basis

2. Ask parents to help design an evaluation instrument that rates home assignments. Develop a brief questionnaire that can be attached to each homework assignment on which parents can indicate such factors as (a) the difficulty level of the assignment, (b) how well their child understood the assignment or the procedures, (c) the appropriateness of the assignment, or (d) suggestions for improvement.

3. Provide parents with a weekly or biweekly summary sheet on which they can record their own observations about their child's reading growth. You may want to prepare some questions ahead of time such as: What were some positive things you noted in your child's reading this past week? What were some negative events? Keep a record of these sheets and refer to them regularly in home telephone calls or face-to-face conferences.

4. Develop a series of simple "question sheets" for parents to complete frequently. Each sheet would be designed to elicit parents' questions about the progress of their child; a space should be included for your responses.

5. Ask parents to compose frequently lists of things their children have learned in reading. Also, direct parents to provide information on lessons or parts of lessons that their children did not understand. Ask that these be submitted at intervals throughout the year and take time to discuss them with parents.

6. Provide opportunities for parents to visit classrooms and observe the reading program in action. Afterward, ask them to evaluate their child's performance in that class and elicit their per-

Figure 1

Attitudinal Scale for Parents

Child's name: ______________________ Date: ______________________

Please indicate your observation of your child's reading growth since the last report. Feel free to comment where appropriate.

A = Strongly Agree B = Agree C = Disagree D = Strongly Disagree

	My child:					Comments
1.	Understands more of what he/she reads	A	B	C	D	
2.	Enjoys being read to by family members	A	B	C	D	
3.	Finds time for quiet reading at home	A	B	C	D	
4.	Sometimes guesses at words, but they usually make sense	A	B	C	D	
5.	Can provide a summary of stories read	A	B	C	D	
6.	Has a good attitude about reading	A	B	C	D	
7.	Enjoys reading to family members	A	B	C	D	
8.	Would like to get more books	A	B	C	D	
9.	Chooses to write about stories read	A	B	C	D	
10.	Is able to complete homework assignments	A	B	C	D	

Strengths I see: ______________________

____

____

Areas that need improvement: ______________________

____

____

Concerns or questions I have: ______________________

____

____

ceptions about their child's strengths or weaknesses. Record these parental observations and keep them in a portfolio for sharing later in the year.

Two of the must useful parental assessment tools are an attitudinal scale and an observation guide (see Figures 1 and 2). These two instruments, if used throughout the year, can provide teachers and parents with a host of relevant information through which joint decisions can be made concerning children's reading progress. More important, however, is "the inside look" these instruments provide parents into salient aspects of literacy growth, giving them an opportunity to take an active role in the assessment procedure. This new role results in a deeper appreciation for the demands of reading instruction and a personal awareness of each stage of their child's growth. Moreover, it establishes im-

Figure 2

Observation Guide for Parents

Child's name: ______________________

Date of last report: ____________ Today's date: ______________

The skills and attitudes you observed in your child on the last report have been recorded in the first column. Please place a check (✓) next to those items in the second column that you have observed in your child since the last report.

			My Child:
_____	_____	1.	Reads from a wide variety of materials such as books, magazines, newspapers, etc.
_____	_____	2.	Takes time during each day to read in a quiet place
_____	_____	3.	Talks with family members about the things he/she is reading
_____	_____	4.	Finds reading to be an exciting way to learn about the world
_____	_____	5.	Brings home books and other reading materials from the school or public library
_____	_____	6.	Seems to understand more of what he/she reads at home
_____	_____	7.	Tries to discover new words and uses them in his/her conversations
_____	_____	8.	Seems to have developed higher-level thinking skills
_____	_____	9.	Uses study skills (e.g., notetaking, organizing time, etc.) regularly
_____	_____	10.	Has shown improvement in his/her reading ability since the last report

My child would be a better reader if:

____

____

My child's greatest strength in reading is: ______________________

____

____

By the next report my child should learn: ______________________

____

____

____
Signature

portant bonds that should exist between home and school.

Parental assessment procedures can become an important component of the reading program. Not only does the assessment process allow parents to take an active role in the reading curriculum, it also gives them valuable data beyond standardized test scores that help them understand the whole reading process.

One school that has begun to actively solicit the involvement of parents in assessing students' literacy growth is the Escondido Elementary School in Stanford,

California. According to principal Julie Ryan, "Procedures which provide parents with active opportunities to take part in the assessment process not only arouse parents' awareness of critical issues in literacy acquisition, but also provide both teachers and parents with valuable information prior to the fall and spring conferences."

Escondido School is located on the Stanford University campus and, as such, has a significant number of students entering and exiting during the school year. Principal Ryan and her staff have designed several assessment forms for children at different grade levels. These forms are sent home prior to the start of school or prior to parent-teacher conferences. As a result. parents take an active role in observing and becoming aware of those behaviors that contribute most to growth in reading and language arts.

The forms Escondido School uses are important for both teachers and parents. Not only do the data provide teachers with important information upon which to make instructional decisions, parents and teachers begin to communicate in positive ways about the literacy activities necessary for individual children. Just as important, the forms will be used to chart progress between parent-teacher conferences to determine the nature and direction of each child's reading development.

The staff at Escondido School feels that these assessment tools are a positive way for parents and educators to share knowledge. As Ryan points out, "Parents are a child's first teacher—and we need to validate that. We hope our assessment forms will allow parents to use information gained at home to work with teachers in designing specific and purposeful reading plans." In short, the staff at Escondido Elementary School believes that informal parental assessment should be a significant part of the entire school program and serves as a foundation for good home-school relationships.

In summary, involving parents in the assessment process does not mean turning them into psychometricians, but rather provides them with opportunities to monitor and supervise the literacy growth of their own children. Such a process requires regular contacts between parents and students and allows parents to understand more fully the entire reading program. Communication bonds are established that lead to a greater understanding between educators and parents—an understanding that can have a significant impact in the lives of all students. Shared assessment processes hold the potential for close and positive relationships—certainly a laudable goal for any effective outreach program.

Note: Readers interested in obtaining copies of the forms used at Escondido School can send a self-addressed, stamped envelope to Julie S. Ryan, Principal, Escondido Elementary School, 890 Escondido Road, Stanford, CA 94305. USA. or call (415) 856-1337

Reference

Flood, J., & Lapp, 0. (1989). Reporting reading progress: A comparison portfolio for parents. *The Reading Teacher, 42*, 508-514.

Instructional Conversations: Promoting Comprehension Through Discussion

Reprinted from *The Reading Teacher* (1992/1993), 46, 316-326

Claude Goldenberg

Since fifth-century Greece, educators and philosophers have argued for a kind of teaching that does more than impart knowledge and teach skills. Knowledge and skills are undoubtedly important. But true education—real teaching—involves helping students think, reason, comprehend, and understand important ideas.

Yet teaching aimed at these important goals is presently most notable for its absence from U.S. classrooms. Goodlad (1984), for example, reports that:

> A great deal of what goes on in the classroom is like painting-by-numbers—filling in the colors called for by numbers on the page....[teachers] ask specific questions calling essentially for students to fill in the blanks: "What is the capital city of Canada?" "What are the principal exports of Japan?" Students rarely turn things around by asking the questions. Nor do teachers often give students a chance to romp with an open-ended question such as "what are your views on the quality of television?" ... (p. 108).

If this portrait is true in mainstream American classrooms, it is even truer in classrooms with low-income, minority children. Because of the perception that these students fundamentally require drill, review, and redundancy in order to progress academically (Brophy & Good, 1986), their learning opportunities are likely to be excessively weighted toward low-level skills and factually oriented instruction (see e.g., Barrera, 1983; Hiebert, 1983; Knapp & Shields, 1990). As important as skills and knowledge are, no less important are more intellectually demanding learning opportunities that promote, as philosopher Mortimer Adler (1982) has written, the "enlarged understanding of ideas and values" (p. 23).

A particular kind of lesson, which we call "instructional conversation" (Tharp & Gallimore, 1988, 1989), might help us redress the imbalance Goodlad and others have noted. Instructional conversations, or ICs, are discussion-based lessons geared toward creating richly textured opportunities for students' conceptual and linguistic development. They suggest a way for educators to reach for the ambitious goals held by thoughtful teachers since the time of Socrates—"to bring [students'] thoughts to birth, to stimulate them to think and to criticise themselves, not [simply] to instruct them" (Rouse, 1956, p. ix).

This article describes and illustrates an instructional conversation model that has been developed in collaboration with elementary grade teachers interested in finding ways to promote these kinds of learning opportunities for their students.

What Is An Instructional Conversation?

In one sense, the idea of instructional conversations is not new. Generations of educators have talked about and encouraged teachers to engage students in interactions to promote analysis, reflection, and critical thinking. The great tutors of classical Greece, of whom Socrates remains the paramount example, employed what Gordon (1990) calls a "conversational form of tutoring... [that] stimulated thinking and sharpened reason in...search of ideal truth" (p. 15).

In this century, although the idea of "ideal truth" has lost currency and the common school has replaced Plato's Academy, educators still put forth conversation—or in larger groups, discussion—as an important educational strategy. In the l920s, Progressive educator Vivian Thayer wrote, "The give and take of class discussion helps. . .test conclusions...and generates ideas that would otherwise remain unborn." Class discussions, Thayer wrote, are invaluable for "opening up new territories for exploration [and] revealing the need of more intensive cultivation of ground already broken" (1928, p. 320).

Contemporary researchers and scholars have also advocated more frequent use of discussion or conversation in the classroom—e.g., Au and Scheu (1989), Bridges (1979), Cazden (1988), Center for the Study of Reading (n.d.), Eeds and Peterson (1991), Perez and Strickland (1987), and Wilen (1990). Thus, the kinds of classroom interactions ICs promote have a long and active history within educational thought and practice.

Although educators have been talking about this type of teaching for millennia, it seems to be talked about more than done. Unfortunately, instructional conversations—or good classroom discussions—are notable not only for their desirable attributes, but also for their rarity. One of the assumptions underlying the work reported here is that the development of an explicit instructional conversation model will help guide teachers in implementing this type of instruction, thereby increasing the likelihood that students will experience these sorts of learning opportunities.

An instructional conversation appears deceptively simple. On the surface, it is simply an excellent discussion by a teacher and a group of students. Most people have a reasonably intuitive sense of what this might be like: It is, first, interesting and engaging. It is about an idea or a concept that has meaning and relevance for students. It has a focus that, while it might shift as the discussion evolves, remains discernible throughout. There is a high level of participation, without undue domination by any one individual, particularly the teacher. Students engage in extended discussions—conversations—with the teacher and among themselves.

Teachers and students are responsive to what others say, so that each statement or contribution builds upon, challenges, or extends a previous one. Topics are picked up, developed, elaborated. Both teacher and students present provocative ideas or experiences, to which others respond. Strategically, the teacher (or discussion leader) questions, prods, challenges, coaxes—or keeps quiet. He or she clarifies and instructs when necessary, but does so efficiently, without wasting time or words. The teacher assures that the discussion proceeds at an appropriate pace—neither too fast to prohibit the development of ideas, nor too slowly to maintain interest and momentum. The teacher knows when to bear down to draw out a student's idea and when to ease up, allowing thought and reflection to take over. Perhaps most important, he or she manages to keep everyone engaged in a substantive and extended conversation, weaving individual participants' comments into a larger tapestry of meaning.

But moving beyond such general descriptions, what characterizes good classroom

instructional conversations? What are their constituent elements? What must teachers know and do in order to implement, successfully and reliably, these types of learning interactions with their students? Working in a low-income, language-minority school district in Southern California, a collaborative team composed of teachers and researchers has attempted to address these questions over the past three years. What has gradually emerged is a more precise model, or description, of instructional conversations.

The Instructional Conversation Model

The Table shows the list of IC elements along with brief descriptions we identified during the course of our work.

The elements, are divided into two groups—instructional (#1-5) and conversational (#6-10)—reflecting the two major dimensions of the IC. As Tharp and Gallimore (1988, 1989) have noted, ICs involve something of a paradox. On the one hand, they are **instructional** in intent, that is, they are designed to promote learning. Teaching through conversation requires a deliberate and self-controlled agenda in the mind of the teacher, which the first five elements reflect. On the other hand, ICs are **conversational** in quality—they appear to be natural and spontaneous interactions, free from the didactic characteristics normally associated with formal teaching. While having specific curricular, cognitive, and conceptual goals, the teacher tries to maintain a high degree of responsiveness and dynamic interaction with students, as the second group of elements suggests.

The metaphor of "weaving" perhaps best captures the spirit of instructional conversations (cf. Tharp & Gallimore, 1988, 1989). The weaving takes place on many levels. First, a skilled teacher weaves together the comments and contributions made by different students with the ideas and concepts she or he wishes to explore with them. Second, a teacher weaves students' prior knowledge and experiences with new knowledge and experiences, thereby broadening the scope of their understanding while building upon understandings they already possess. Finally, during the course of conversation, a skilled teacher weaves together, in appropriate proportions and shadings, the 10 IC elements. While particular elements can be picked out and identified—just as threads of different color can be picked out and identified on a cloth—instruction and conversation are woven into a seamless whole: The conversation is instructional, and the instruction is conversational.

In developing the IC model shown in the Table, we have drawn upon the classroom experiences of practicing teachers. The model evolved as teachers attempted to implement ICs in their classroom, then reviewed and analyzed videotapes of the lessons. We have also drawn upon several currents in educational theory and research—for example, promoting reading comprehension among at-risk minority students (Au, 1979; Tharp & Gallimore, 1988), schema theory (Glaser, 1984; Hacker, 1980), and research on reading comprehension instruction (Dole, Duffy, Roehler, & Pearson, 1991).

Instructional Conversation: An Illustration

To illustrate an instructional conversation, we have chosen an excerpt from a lesson conducted by a fourth-grade teacher, most of whose students were making the transition from Spanish to English reading. (See Author Notes.) These students were in a bilingual education program, but since they were in transition from Spanish to English instruction, all academic work was conducted in English.

The class had just read a story in an English basal reader about two friends, one of whom deviously convinces the other to buy bubble gum with the money his mother had given him for a haircut. The teacher uses the story as an opportunity to engage the children in a discussion about the various facets of friendship—that friends are

Elements of the Instructional Conversation

Instructional Elements

1. *Thematic focus.* The teacher selects a theme or idea to serve as a starting point for focusing the discussion and has a general plan for how the theme will unfold, including how to "chunk" the text to permit optimal exploration of the theme.
2. *Activation and use of background and relevant schemata.* The teacher either "hooks into" or provides students with pertinent background knowledge and relevant schemata necessary for understanding a text. Background knowledge and schemata are then woven into the discussion that follows.
3. *Direct teaching.* When necessary, the teacher provides direct teaching of a skill or concept.
4. *Promotion of more complex language and expression.* The teacher elicits more extended student contributions by using a variety of elicitation techniques—invitations to expand (e.g., "tell me more about that"), questions (e.g., "What do you mean?"), restatements (e.g., "in other words,—"), and pauses.
5. *Elicitation of bases for statements or positions.* The teacher promotes students' use of text, pictures, and reasoning to support an argument or position. Without overwhelming students, the teacher probes for the bases of students' statements—e.g., "How do you know?" "What makes you think that?" "Show us where it says_____."

Conversational Elements

6. *Fewer "known-answer" questions.* Much of the discussion centers on questions and answers for which there might be more than one correct answer.
7. *Responsivity to student contributions.* While having an initial plan and maintaining the focus and coherence of the discussion, the teacher is also responsive to students' statements and the opportunities they provide.
8. *Connected discourse.* The discussion is characterized by multiple, interactive, connected turns; succeeding utterances build upon and extend previous ones.
9. *A challenging, but nonthreatening, atmosphere.* The teacher creates a "zone of proximal development," where a challenging atmosphere is balanced by a positive affective climate. The teacher is more collaborator than evaluator and creates an atmosphere that challenges students and allows them to negotiate and construct the meaning of the text.
10. *General participation, including self-selected turns.* The teacher encourages general participation among students. The teacher does not hold exclusive right to determine who talks, and students are encouraged to volunteer or otherwise influence the selection of speaking turns.

not always perfect, that they can have problems and get mad at each other, and that sometimes they can resolve their difficulties through talking.

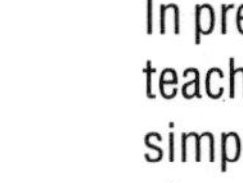

In previous discussions with the class, the teacher realized that students had fairly simplistic and exclusively positive constructions of "friends" and "friendship"—for example, friends always get along, they never fight, and they do things together. Her theme for this lesson, therefore, was the more problematic aspects of friendship—friendship does not always constitute a perfect or idealized relationship between two people. Although she was not trying to impart a particular lesson or moral, the teacher wanted to encourage

her students to consider and weigh various facets of friendship. Her goal was to help students see friendship in a more complex and differentiated light.

In the early part of the discussion, the teacher writes on a chart students' comments and contributions about the characteristics of friends. At one point. a student (Ca) says that friends must demonstrate patience:

Ca:	yep, patience because, he didn't get mad when they cut the hair...
Teacher:	Who didn't get mad when they cut the hair?
Ca:	Rob
S:	Robert.
Teacher:	Rob didn't get mad so you think he fits in here? (points to friendship chart)

This exchange provided the teacher with the opportunity to pursue the theme she wanted to explore with her students—the more problematic aspects of friends and friendship.

The ensuing discussion (illustrated in the following segment) demonstrates various IC features. There is a clear thematic focus (element #1, Table), that of friendship, more specifically, some problematic aspects of friendship. Phrases in **bold** show the theme of the discussion threading its way through the segment.

The teacher clearly uses student background knowledge as she asks students to draw upon their knowledge and experiences about friendship (element #2). She also elicits more speaking, for example, in turns 11 and 36, when she asks students to elaborate ("tell me more") on comments they have made (element #4). The teacher also asks questions for which different answers are acceptable (element #6), for example, if friends don't share "does that keep you from being friends?" (turn 15).

Teacher and students are responsive to what others say (element #7); in fact, the entire segment was in response to Ca's observation that friends must be patient. There are multiple and connected student turns (element #8), all of which are related to the topic at hand. Overall, the tone of the lesson is positive, yet challenging (element #9), as the teacher identifies points of disagreement among the group and challenges students to justify their statements (element #5; e.g., turns 18,29).

Note: In the following segment, these transcribing conventions are used: Single parentheses denote words are unclear, and transcriber has written best guess.Double parentheses denote actions by participants. Pairs of brackets stacked vertically denote speakers speaking simultaneously.

	Turn	Speaker
	Teacher:	why should Rob get **mad**,
00	Ca:	because, because **he cut his hair wrong.** awful, [crooked,and
01	Teacher:	[oh. well, do we sometimes, [get **mad** at our friends?
02	Ca:	[you have to **forgive them,** too, but.
03	Teacher:	do we sometimes **get mad** at our friends?
04	Ss:	yes
05	Ca:	yes, **course**.
06	Teacher:	when do we **get mad** at our friends, (why d'you) say "**course**" (like) **of course**, what happens when you **get mad** at your friends.
07	Ca:	they **get mad** at you,
08	Teacher:	oh, you **get mad** back at each other, ((laughter))
09	Ml:	they do **something** [**that you don't like** or.
10	Ca:	[(they bounce the ball around)
11	Teacher:	okay. tell me a little bit more about that.
12	Ml:	they do **something that you don't like** or. **they'll. not talk to you** or. **not, share** or. **not, be a good friend**
13	Teacher:	okay, so, friendship, I'm gonna add, this time I'm gonna put it in capital letters the new ideas we got. ((writes on chart)) friendship, friends CAN **get mad** at each other. right? what else did you say, they,
14	Ml:	they, they **can not talk to you** or **don't share with you** or nothing.
15	Teacher:	okay,so sometimes they, **DON'T share with you.** does that **keep you from being friends**?
16	S:	[yes
17	S:	[no

18 Teacher: okay. I heard different answers. who said "yes" it keeps, if they don't share it **keeps you from being friends**.
19 Ja: because if you talk to them.
20 MI: **you have problems**.
21 Ce: **you have problems** with them and,
22 Teacher: okay. **friends have problems**?
23 S: ((immediately)) oh yes.
24 Teacher: and I even heard (a word bigger than) problems, **fighting, can friends fight?**
25 Ss: yes.
26 S: no
27 Ss: YES!
28 S: yes. so.
29 Teacher: [okay someone that said yes. tell me (how **friends can fight**)
30 Ca: [my friend my friend one day'. we were out of order and uh.
31 V: like. umm. yesterday. I was playing with my sister, and I told her, let me see that for a second and she said "no you always get it.." and we **started fighting**, and then we went with my mom and then, we said she doesn't wanna give me that, she doesn't wanna give me this, and I started crying, and um, we got in problems because my mom spanked us.
32 Teacher: okay but if that hadn't been your sister, would you still **have been a friend**?
33 V: nope. ((laughter))
34 Teacher: (inaudible) do you agree with Melissa?
35 S: yes
36 Teacher: okay Melissa, you got someone who agrees with you. So (inaudible) tell the rest of they all said, that **true friends (can) fight** you say no. tell me more about it.
37 MI: **If, true friends fight then, that's not true friends**. it just, it just doesn't work out, it's not true friends.
38 Teacher: so, **if you are a true friends you would never fight**. but how **would true friends** solve problems?
39 S: [**talking**.
40 MI: [**by talking, not fighting**.
41 Teacher: **by talking not fighting**.
42 Ce: [aha, Ms. Fuller, so many times, like friends when, when they want to **talk to you**, they **make friends again**, unless they **fight**.
43 Teacher: okay so you're telling me that you can have a FRIEND, that can (keep it COOL) because of the **problem**, maybe even **fight** each other, **real fighting up there**, Melissa said no. you.
44 Co: I said yes.
45 T: changed your mind.
45 Co: I say yes, because, my friend, she always plays with us and. we were playing and. **she gets mad** because she wants to be this or she wants to be that and they don't let her. so **then I told her**, umm. you don't if you don't want to be that you don't have to. And she screamed and then said yes! I wanna be that. but you can change. if you WANT to she said, I can change if I want to and you be something you are gonna have to um. do that! then okay, cause we were both doing the same thing and then, she, she started, winning the others my friends (and I) **fighting with** and, she said that she **wasn't gonna be her friend again** and then she was her **friend again**! **was talking** to her later.
46 T: okay so, **shall I put fighting up here**? ((points to board))
47 S: yeah
48 Ss: yeah

In this segment, beginning with the teacher's follow-up question ("Do we sometimes get mad at our friends?") to Ca's comment that Rob did not get mad, the teacher has prompted her students to consider aspects of friendship that previously had not formed a part of their discussions. The teacher led the students in discussing a more complex and differentiated view of the concept, while framing an important context for the story they have read and will discuss. Notice the progression of ideas in this segment—from the suggestion that friends need to be patient, to the idea that sometimes friends get mad at each other because they do things the other does not like (turn #12 and following), to the idea that friends sometimes have problems or can even fight with each other (turns #22-23 and following). On this last point there was some disagreement, as one of the students (MI) insisted that if friends fight, they are no longer friends (e.g., turns #36, 37, and 43). The rest of the students, however, argued that friends can fight, then talk over or otherwise resolve their difficulties.

We have found that when students participate in discussions such as this, their writing about a complex concept such as friendship demonstrates greater sophistication and depth of understanding without sacrificing literal comprehension of the story they have read (Saunders & Goldenberg, 1992).

Planning and Implementing Instructional Conversations

Conducting ICs is more challenging than at first appears. Many teachers seem to assume that they do ICs naturally, as a matter of course, in their classrooms. Our experience in Southern California (Goldenberg & Gallimore, 1991), in addition to earlier experiences in Hawaii (Tharp & Gallimore, 1988, 1989), suggests otherwise—that instructional conversations are professionally and intellectually demanding teaching/learning events that come neither easily nor naturally.

Perhaps because they require balancing or juggling a number of potentially conflicting elements — e.g., maintaining a clear thematic focus while being responsive to unanticipated opportunities offered by students—successful ICs seem to require considerable time and effort from teachers. Learning to manage such inherent tensions requires repeated attempts to implement ICs, coupled with videotapings, discussion, and analysis of lessons.

In our ongoing work in Los Angeles, we have found it productive to have teachers meet weekly in a small group to discuss, plan, and evaluate IC lessons. At the beginning of the year, teachers read and discuss relevant papers and articles. They also identify aspects of their classroom programs that they feel could benefit from the use of instructional conversations. Teachers see videotaped examples of ICs and are encouraged to try them out on their own. Teachers are also encouraged to focus on no more than one or two IC elements at first before attempting to incorporate all 10 into any one lesson. As teachers become more comfortable, they volunteer to bring in stories or books they plan to use when teaching an IC lesson. The entire group then discusses possible approaches that can be taken. Teachers are videotaped conducting the lessons in their classrooms, and the tapes are viewed and analyzed at the next meeting.

In planning for an instructional conversation around a story or a book, the following steps seem helpful:

1. *Select a story or book that is appropriate for your students.* We have found that suitable texts can be found in many places—anthologies, basal readers, and trade or literature books.
2. *Read the story (or book) several times until you feel you understand it thoroughly.* It is also helpful to have colleagues, friends, or family members read the story and discuss it with you, since there are often dimensions of meaning not immediately apparent to a single reader. Although this can be time consuming, we have found this sort of teacher scholarship to be indispensable; it provides the intellectual foundation for discussing a text with students and for being prepared to respond to their contributions (Fuller & Gallimore, 1992).
3. *Select a theme to focus the discussion, at least initially.* Any good story will have a number of possible themes; choose one that is meaningful and interesting to you. But also consider what will be meaningful and interesting to students. Remember that the theme you select will be a starting point. During the course of the discussion, a better or more compelling theme might emerge.
4. *Identify and provide, as needed, background knowledge students must have in order to make sense of what they will be reading.* Students sometimes need factual information, for example, if they are reading a story that requires an understanding of native peoples' cosmology and religious beliefs. Sometimes students do not need factual information as much as they

need an opportunity to bring into conscious awareness things they might already know but have not consciously considered, such as the attributes of friendship. In either case, teachers need to be sure that relevant background knowledge and schemata are activated and accessible. This can often be accomplished in lessons or activities (e.g., a writing or research assignment) that precede the actual IC.

5. *Decide on a starting point for the discussion to provide an initial focus.* This might be a key word (e.g., "friendship") or a key question, either of which can be written on the board or a chart to help focus students' and the teacher's attention. It is often very effective then to write student contributions on the board or chart as the discussion proceeds. This can be done as a simple list or organized semantically, using one of many semantic mapping techniques (e.g., Alvermann, 1991; Pehrsson, 1985).

6. *Plan and think through the lesson mentally.* Think about possible ways the discussion might proceed, how the initial focus might eventually lead to an exploration of the theme and, ultimately, how the theme will tie into the story students are reading. Consider, for example: How might students respond to the initial focal point you have chosen? What will you do if they do not respond? Do you have a story, illustration, or anecdote you can share that will help the discussion begin? How will you "chunk" the text, that is, what portions will you read, before stopping for discussion? What meanings and interpretations might students bring to this theme or text?

7. *Finally, consider some suitable followup activities, particularly ones that will help you gauge what students have learned from the IC.* We have used writing as one way to determine whether students have actually learned something from the discussion. Depending upon the age and abilities of students, we would expect that student writing will reflect a more sophisticated understanding of the topics discussed (Saunders & Goldenberg, 1992). Other follow-up activities might include projects or reports or simply answering questions designed to probe student comprehension.

Clearly, all of the above is time- and labor-intensive; indeed we have found that time is an absolute requirement, particularly to allow for adequate planning. Teachers have found they cannot conduct satisfactory ICs if they attempt to glance at a story hurriedly and attempt to teach it "cold." One of the major lessons of our first year's work was precisely this—teachers had to prepare themselves intellectually by reading the story several times, analyzing it, and thinking about possible ways to approach it with a group of students. The intellectual, as opposed to procedural, side of lesson planning is rarely mentioned, yet we found it to be critical. One teacher, for example, commented at year's end.

> ... if you read it [the story], and if you think about it, and you think about the kind of ways that you can present it and what you're gonna do with it, it makes all the difference in the world.

This sort of analysis is so important that we have made it a regular feature of our weekly meetings; the entire group discusses possible themes, meanings, and approaches to stories. Invariably, teachers comment that as a result of these discussions (which themselves resemble ICs, see Saunders, Goldenberg, & Hamann, 1992), they make new discoveries about the texts they have brought in.

Selecting an appropriate theme is especially important, since the theme becomes the focal point of successful ICs. In the words of one teacher, a good theme provides the glue that gives an instructional conversation coherence. Selection of a good theme and its successful elaboration in the lesson requires planning and prepa-

ration in order to search out important ideas that might be brought to bear in discussing texts with students. Planning carefully and selecting a good theme also make it more likely that the teacher will take advantage of unanticipated opportunities students provide for extending the discussion. For example, when Ca observed in the earlier example that friends often need patience, the teacher was able to use her comment as the entry-point for a discussion on problematic aspects of friendship.

The Place of Instructional Conversations in the School Curriculum

Instructional conversations stand in contrast to many relatively "traditional" forms of teaching (e.g., lectures, recitation, direct instruction), which are based upon the assumption that the teacher's role is to help students learn what the teacher already knows and can do. ICs represent an approach to teaching that is more in keeping with the contemporary shift toward a "constructivist" curriculum. According to constructivist views, students are expected actively to *construct* their own knowledge and understanding—e.g., making connections, building mental schemata, and developing new concepts from previous understandings—rather than to *receive* knowledge transmitted by their teachers (see, e.g., California State Department of Education, 1987; Resnick, 1987; Resnick & Klopfer, 1989; Shuell, 1986). In this sense, ICs can be seen as consistent with perhaps this most important shift in mainstream educational thinking since the "back to basics" movement of the l970s.

Nevertheless, even when expertly done, instructional conversations do not constitute an all-encompassing instructional method; nor, much less, do they offer educational panaceas. Rather, we suspect that ICs might be particularly suited to certain educational goals, such as helping students comprehend texts, learn complex concepts, and consider various perspectives on issues. Other forms of teaching, such as direct or explicit instruction, are probably more suited to different, but no less important, purposes.

Rosenshine (Rosenshine, 1986; Rosenshine & Stevens, 1986), for example, has argued that explicit teaching is highly effective for "well-structured" skill and knowledge domains. Well-structured domains, as the name suggests, are well-defined knowledge or skill areas—e.g., mathematical computations, explicit reading comprehension strategies, map reading, reading decoding, and conventions of punctuation and grammar. In these areas, the procedures and criteria for successful performance can be made explicit. Explicit, or direct, teaching—which comprises teacher functions such as stating an objective, providing step-by-step instruction, modeling, guiding practice, and giving feedback—has been shown to be highly effective for these goals and objectives (e.g., Gage, 1978; Rosenshine & Stevens, l986; Walberg, 1990).

Instructional conversations, in contrast, will be more suitable for domains of learning that are relatively less clearly or hierarchically organized. In these so-called "ill-structured" domains, concepts are fuzzier and, therefore, explicit steps toward successful performance cannot be followed. Examples of such areas of learning include analysis of literary or historical themes, learning and understanding complex concepts, mathematical reasoning, applying quantitative understandings, and oral or written composition (Rosenshine, 1986; Simon, 1973; Spiro & Myers, 1984). It is in these domains that we expect instructional conversations to be powerful instructional tools.

In the work described here, ICs have been used primarily to guide reading comprehension lessons and activities with small groups of elementary-age students. However, the general model is probably applicable for promoting comprehension of ideas and concepts in a wide range of situ-

ations. Schneider, Hyland, and Gallimore (1985) provide examples of a similar approach in junior high social studies classes. Other educators have explored the utility of discussions for high school social studies and English (Wilen, 1990), and for learning science vocabulary (Stahl & Clark, 1987) and mathematical reasoning (Lampert, 1991, April). In our own work, we are also investigating the use of ICs to guide teacher-student interactions that contribute to children's development as writers.

As educators, we are responsible for student growth and learning in many areas, and it seems unlikely that any one approach or strategy will be sufficient. We would therefore expect professional teachers to have at their disposal a wide range of skills and knowledge suited to particular goals they have for students' learning. Improving our educational system—and more specifically, improving teaching itself—depends upon achieving a successful synthesis of instructional strategies that will enable educators to accomplish important educational goals. To this extent, instructional conversations suggest a way to expand teachers' instructional repertoires while fulfilling the visions of generations of educators.

References

Adler, M. (1982). *The Paideia proposal: An educational manifesto.* New York: Macmillan.

Alvermann, D. (1991). The Discussion Web: A graphic aid for learning across the curriculum. *The Reading Teacher 45*, 92-98.

Au, K. (1979). Using the experience-text-relationship method with minority children. *The Reading Teacher 32*, 677-679.

Au, K., & Scheu, J. (1989). Guiding students to interpret a novel. *The Reading Teacher 43*, 104-110.

Barrera, R.B. (1983). Bilingual reading in the primary grades: Some questions about questionable views and practices. In T.A. Escobedo (Ed.), *Early childhood bilingual education: A Hispanic perspective* (pp. 164-184). New York: Teachers College Press.

Bridges, D. (1979). *Education, democracy & discussion.* Windsor, England: NFER Publishing.

Brophy, J., & Good, T. (1986). Teacher behavior and student achievement. In M. Wittrock (Ed.), *Handbook of research on teaching* (3rd ed.) (pp. 328-375). New York: Macmillan.

California State Department of Education. (1987). *English-language arts model curriculum guide, kindergarten through grade eight.* Sacramento, CA: California State Department of Education.

Cazden, C. (1988). *Classroom discourse: The language of teaching and learning.* Portsmouth, NH: Heinemann.

Center for the Study of Reading (n.d.). *Teaching reading comprehension: Experience and text* (videotape). Champaign, IL: The University of Illinois.

Dole, J., Duffy, G., Roehler, L., & Pearson, P. (1991). Moving from the old to the new: Research on reading comprehension instruction. *Review of Educational Research, 61,* 239-264.

Eeds, M., & Peterson, R. (1991). Teacher as curator: Learning to talk about literature. *The Reading Teacher 45,* 118-126.

Fuller, W., & Gallimore, R. (1992, April). *Let's talk: Conversation, instruction, and the teaching of reading comprehension.* Paper presented at the annual meeting of the American Educational Research Association, San Francisco, CA.

Gage, N.L. (1978). *The scientific basis of the art of teaching.* New York: Teachers College Press, Columbia University.

Glaser, R. (1984). Education and thinking: The role of knowledge. *American Psychologist. 39*, 93-104.

Goldenberg, C., & Gallimore. R. (1991). Changing teaching takes more than a one-shot workshop. *Educational Leadership. 49* (3), 69-72.

Goldenberg, C., & Patthey-Chavez, G. (in press). Discourse processes in instructional conversations: Interactions between teacher and transition students. *Discourse Processes.*

Goodlad, J. (1984). *A place called school.* New York: McGraw-Hill.

Gordon, E. (1990). *Centuries of tutoring: A history of alternative education in America and Western Europe.* Lanham, MD: University Press of America.

Hacker, C. (1980). From schema theory to classroom practice. *Language Arts, 57,* 866-871.

Hiebert, E. (1983). An examination of ability grouping for reading instruction. *Reading Research Quarterly 18,* 231-255.

Knapp. M., & Shields, P. (1990). Reconceiving academic instruction for the children of poverty. *Phi Delta Kappan, 71*(10), 753-758.

Lampert. M. (1991. April). *Representing practice: Learning and teaching about teaching and learning.* Invited address presented at the annual meeting of the American Educational Research Association. Chicago, IL.

Pehrsson, R. (1985). *The semantic organizer approach to reading and writing instruction.* Rockville, MD: Aspen Systems Corp.

Perez, S., & Strickland, E. (1987). Teaching children how to discuss what they read. *Reading Horizons, 27,* 89-94.

Resnick, L. (1987). Constructing knowledge in school. In L. Liben (Ed.). *Development and learning: Conflict or congruence?* (pp. 19-50). Hillsdale, NJ: Erlbaum.

Resnick, L., & Klopfer, L. (Eds.) (1989). *Toward the thinking curriculum: Current cognitive research.* Alexandria. VA: Association for Supervision and Curriculum Development.

Rosenshine, B. (1986). Synthesis of research on explicit teaching. *Educational Leadership, 43*, 60-69.

Rosenshine, B., & Stevens, R. (1986). Teaching functions. In M. Wittrock (Ed.), *Handbook of research on teaching (*3rd ed.*)* (pp. 376-391). New York: Macmillan.

Rouse, W.H.D. (Trans.) (1956). *Great dialogues of Plato.* New York: New American Library.

Saunders, W., & Goldenberg, C. (1992, April). *Effects of instructional conversations on transition students' concepts of 'friendship': An experimental study.* Paper presented at the annual meeting of the American Educational Research Association, San Francisco, CA.

Saunders, W., Goldenberg, C., & Hamann, J. (1992). Instructional conversations beget instructional conversations. *Teaching and Teacher Education, 8*, 199-218.

Schneider, P., Hyland, J.T., & Gallimore, R. (1985). The zone of proximal development in eighth grade social studies. *The Quarterly Newsletter of the Laboratory of Comparative Human Cognition, 7*(4), 113-119.

Schuell, T. (1986). Cognitive conceptions of learning. *Review of Educational Research, 56*, 411-436.

Simon, H. (1973). The structure of ill-structured problems. *Artificial Intelligence, 4*, 181-201.

Spiro, R., & Myers, A. (1984). Individual differences and underlying cognitive processes in reading. In P. Pearson (Ed.), *Handbook of reading research* (pp. 471-501). New York: Longman.

Stahl, S., & Clark, C. (1987). The effects of participatory expectations in classroom discussion on the learning of science vocabulary. *American Educational Research Journal, 24*, 541-555.

Tharp, R., & Gallimore, R. (1988). *Rousing minds to life: Teaching, learning and schooling in social context.* Cambridge, England: Cambridge University Press.

Tharp, R., & Gallimore, R. (1989). Rousing schools to life. *American Educator 13*(2), 20-25.

Thayer, V. (1928). *The passing of the recitation.* Boston. MA: D.C. Heath.

Walberg, H. (1990). Productive teaching and instruction: Assessing the knowledge base. *Phi Delta Kappan, 71*, 470-478.

Wilen, W. (1990). Forms and phases of discussion. In W. Wilen (Ed.), *Teaching and learning through discussion (pp. 3-24).* Springfield, IL: Charles C. Thomas.

Performance Assessments in Reading and Language Arts

Reprinted from *The Reading Teacher* (1994), *48*, 266-271

John T. Guthrie
Peggy Van Meter
Ann Mitchell
Catherine T. Reed

Teachers are inventing a wide variety of exciting new ways to integrate reading and writing instruction into the teaching of literature, history, geography, and science. These integrations reflect the view that reading and writing are inextricably linked to knowledge, strategies, and dispositions for learning. Teachers see students as builders and explorers who use resources including texts, peers, and experience to discover meaning and solve self-defined problems. For these teachers, traditional assessments seem incomplete. When instruction is based on trade books, group thinking activities, and projects that may involve the home and community, traditional assessments often fail to capture students' motivational development and higher-order competencies. In this column, we discuss a performance assessment designed to reflect a wide spectrum of literacy processes that appear in an integrated curriculum (Grant, Guthrie, Bennett, Rice, & McGough, 1993).

What is a Performance Assessment in Reading?

Our performance assessment in reading has three fundamental qualities. First, the assessment is instructional, simulating the teaching environment that we maintain in the classroom. As students participate in the assessment, they interact with texts, draw, write, and use their newfound knowledge to solve problems in ways that parallel the typical instructional unit. Consistent with classroom instruction, we expect students to learn, and we record the new concepts they acquire. The assessment is a small unit of instruction for both the students and teachers.

Second, this performance assessment is realistic. It is a mirror of classroom literacy, reflecting authentic and regularly occurring tasks in reading, writing, and problem solving. In integrated curricula, students may write observations from a field trip into a journal, read journals to each other, discuss trade books on topics observed in the field trip, and develop ways to teach what they have learned to other students. Similar connections across learning activities are part of this performance assessment in reading.

Third, this performance assessment provides a public record of tasks students have accomplished. The task in this assessment includes a text (something to read), a response to the text (a way of writing or expressing understanding), and a quality statement (which describes the student performance). This sequence of tasks

brings literacy learning to light, enabling students, teachers, and others to observe students as they interact with instruction.

What Does Student Performance Look Like?

This performance assessment accompanies an integrated curriculum, Concept-Oriented Reading Instruction (CORI; Grant et al., 1993), for the third and fifth grades in two schools. Topics used for the assessments include owls, phases of the moon, trees, tides, ponds, and simple machines. To chart growth, we use two topics, one that is closely tied to the curriculum and a second that is less related to it. This permits teachers to see content-based gains as well as generalized gains in reading strategies. Our performance assessments are designed to enable students to perform seven distinct but connected tasks: (1) statement of prior knowledge (stating what they know about the topic), (2) searching (finding resources and ideas about the topic), (3) drawing (expressing what they have learned through drawing), (4) writing (communicating their learning through composition), (5) problem solving (addressing a related problem using conceptual knowledge learned during the unit), (6) informational text comprehension (understanding an expository text related to the theme), and (7) narrative text comprehension (understanding and responding to a literary text on the theme of the unit).

These assessments are conducted in classrooms as instructional units lasting 4-6 days. One teacher began the performance assessment on owls and how they adapt to their environment by asking the whole class what they knew about owls. Discussion was brief and did not convey new information to students. The teacher then moved the class into Stage 1 and asked students to write down their prior knowledge by responding to the question: "What are the different parts of an owl and how do these parts help it live?" We will follow two third grade students, Sandra and William, as they perform each of the tasks.

Stage 1: Statement of prior knowledge. Sandra recorded her prior knowledge as follows (we have not edited this excerpt): "A owl can eat a lot of food. The owl lives like people. The eat corn. He can live like people. The owl will live good like people."

The quality of the student's performance on each stage is judged using a rubric, which distinguishes lower levels of quality from higher levels of quality. Rubrics enable us to chart student growth, to profile a student's strengths and weaknesses, and to discuss the effectiveness of instruction. Here we present the general rubric for each stage, although specific rubrics for each topic are also needed for complete coding. We created five levels for most rubrics and assigned points to each level.

The rubric for statement of prior knowledge was:

1. No conception (student writes nothing at all or the answer does not contain information relevant to the question).
2. Preconception (student may list objects or parts and their functions may be vaguely described; the answer is scientifically incorrect but demonstrates an understanding that there are relationships among objects or events relevant to the concept).
3. Partial conception (student answer is scientifically correct and shows a limited understanding of some of the relationships among a few of the relevant objects or events but the statements are vague).
4. Incomplete conception (student answer is scientifically correct, shows an understanding of relationships among many but not all of the relevant objects or events, and the relationships are clear but incomplete).
5. Full conception (student answer is scientifically correct, shows an understanding of relationships among all important objects or events, and the relationships are depicted in clear and complete form).

Table 1

Sandra's Search Log

A Packet Letter	B Why did you pick this packet?	C What did you learn from this packet?
1. D	The owl eat a lot of mouse and can get quiet	I learn the owls can get quiet mouse and eat the mouse to
2.	mouse to Because it is good	and owls do not miss a thing.
3. B	Birds can fly to trees and some Birds can not fly to a trees.	King Birds, the mother a father will have a baby and Be it will Be Birds.
4.	I put this is about Birds mother has the baby	I put this about the father go get the Baby and get and love.
5.		
6. A	Introducing like to end fish and like to eat Sea birds.	it eat a lot to like and eat fish to like.
7.		
8.		

Sandra's statement of prior knowledge was a Preconception, which we assigned a level of 2. An example of an Incomplete conception (4) was given by William, whose statement was that: "the eyes help it see at night to catch its prey and he takes his prey with his clawed feet and he swoops to get it with his giant wings."

William's prior knowledge contained an understanding of several parts of the owl and the survival value of these parts.

Stage 2: Search. Next, we gave students a booklet containing 12 selections of text, which simulated the format of a trade book containing a table of contents, index, glossary, and chapter headings. Each selection was a 1-3 page excerpt from a trade book on the topic of birds. Half of the selections were relevant to the question (What are the different parts of an owl and how do these parts help it live?) and half were not. As the students read through the packets, they maintained a log to record the packet they were reading, why they chose the packet, and what they learned from it. We gave students a form for their logs, divided into sections 1-8, one for each packet they read, as illustrated here. We did not have 12 sections because we did not expect third graders to read all 12 packets.

Sandra's search log looked like Table 1.

To describe the quality of search for information we coded the logs into 5 levels:

1. No search (no evidence of search or selection of materials).
2. Minimum (students chose at least two relevant packets as well as some irrelevant ones, took good notes from one packet, and gave one clear reason for choosing one of the packets).
3. Moderate (students chose at least three relevant packets and very few irrelevant ones with appropriate reasons for their selections and good notes on two packets).
4. Adequate (students chose at least four relevant packets with few or no irrelevant ones, giving clear reasons for all their selections and clear notes).

Table 2

William's Log of Activities

A Packet Letter	B Why did you pick this packet?	C What did you learn from this packet?
1. D	I picked it because it tells alot about owls and how they are.	I learned that owls can see in the dark and I learned that they can twist there head all the way around. I also learned that they can twist it.
2. I	I picked it because it shows you how birds get their food.	I learned that birds need their sharp claws to get their food.
3. G	I pick this packet because it tells how birds feed their babies.	I learned that birds feed their babies by dropping worms, insects, and bread in their mouth.
4. H	I picked it because it tells (no continuation)	I learned that they need their feet to help them swim.

5. Proficient (students selected all of the relevant packets with no irrelevant ones and all of their notes were related to the theme. Their reasons for choosing packets were diverse, and their notes showed that they learned during the course of the reading and note taking activity).

Sandra's log of her activities (rated a 2) contained two packets that were related to the theme. She did not, however, know the difference between a reason for choosing a packet and what she learned from the texts that she chose. Sandra's notes from the first packet clearly stated that owls can "get a quiet mouse and eat the mouse." But her notes from the second packet were not highly elaborated beyond the notion that birds have babies. This was a Minimum search (2).

William used a more well-developed search strategy than Sandra. The log of his activities, which is given in Table 2, was rated Adequate (4).

William chose four packets related to the theme and no irrelevant ones. He showed that he could distinguish the reasons for his choices from what he had learned from the texts. He first learned about how owls see in the dark and turn their heads around. From the next packet he learned that owls use their claws during hunting. From the third text he learned that birds feed babies by dropping food into their mouths, and last he discovered that different birds have different types of feet which are adapted to their environments.

Stage 3: Drawing. After students searched for information, we asked them to make a picture that showed everything they knew about owls. These third graders were asked to make a drawing to teach second graders about owls, without using their notes. We described the quality of student drawings with the same rubric used for describing their statements of prior knowledge: No conception, Preconception, Partial conception, Incomplete conception, and Full conception. Sandra's drawing was a Preconception (2) because she presents some of the parts of the owl, but the functions are not described and the relationships among the parts were vague (see Figure). William's drawing was an Incomplete Conception (4). It is scientifically correct and

Figure 3

Students' Drawings About Owls

Sandra

William

it shows an understanding of relationships among parts of an owl, but his drawing omitted several parts of the owl that were described in the text. Because this part of the assessment focused on students' understanding, we accepted invented spelling and punctuation.

Stage 4: Writing. We next asked students to write a statement that showed their un-

Read
64

derstanding of the topic using their drawing and what they remembered. As in the Concept-Oriented Reading Instruction, we did not encourage copying or rote learning. Students were expected to construct and reorganize their thoughts continually to express them in writing, without using notes from their search activity. Sandra's written statement of how the parts of an owl help it to live was the following: "The owl can see thing and get the thing and it eat them. Owl like mouse and water and owl can get quite thing. Owl eat a lot to be love and live from food and can fly to and fly to a tree and like tree to and eat thing in tree. I thing owl will like it."

Using the same rubric that we used to describe prior knowledge, we classified Sandra's written understanding as a Partial conception (3). Comparing Sandra's written statement to her prior knowledge, we can see that she gained conceptual knowledge during the assessment. As the notes in her search log indicate, she learned that owls have exceptional eyes for hunting mice.

William's written understanding was an Incomplete conception (4) as follows: "The eyes help it see in the dark. A hooked beak to tear meat in half and a long wing span help it fly swiftly. The claws help catch mice and hang on branches."

Although William understood the owl as a predator more fully than Sandra at the time of the writing task, Sandra learned more new concepts during the assessment than William. William's task performance does not give evidence that he gained conceptual knowledge about owls.

Stage 5: Problem solving. Students then used their knowledge to write a solution to a new problem: "Suppose you saw a type of owl that was blind. But these owls are living a very good life. What things would these owls have to be good at to be able to keep living? What would the body parts of these owls be like? Please explain your answer."

Sandra wrote: "The owl can hear thing but this is not so good. I will like to know what can do when owl are blind. I will not like to be blind. I will like to know how it is some owl have friend and friend like to help people. Maybe the friend will help her or him see thing and hear thing and eat thing. I think owl will not go out in the day and will be wild."

During her search activity, Sandra learned that owls could see even in the dark and capture "quiet things." In the new problem when the owl was deprived of sight, Sandra could not employ the concept of adaptation to generate newly developed senses for the owl, although she understood that such information was called for. She solved the owl's problem by giving the owl a friend. Although Sandra was aware that the question called for information about the senses and their adaptations, her solution did not illustrate the concepts of adaptation of body parts to the environment. In contrast, William solved the new problem by writing: "he will have to hear his prey and then catch it, if it was a great horned owl he would have to keep his tufts of feathers up so that he could signal his family, maybe he would have to use his wings to feel around when he is flying, maybe he could smell where his prey is in the woods."

The rubric for problem solving consisted of the following:

1. No solution (no answer given).
2. Presolution (solution is scientifically incorrect or not relevant to the problem; some conceptual knowledge of the topic is evident).
3. Partial solution (some objects are present but the concepts are not applied to solving the problem; solution is scientifically correct, but the answer is vague or incomplete).
4. Incomplete solution (all objects and/or events are present and the concepts are related to solving the problem, but the answer is incomplete or vague).

5. Full solution (all objects and events are present; the concepts are fully applied and the answer is complete).

In solving the new problem, Sandra's notion that the owl could make friends which would help her see things was not realistic (a Presolution 2), although she showed that serious adjustments would have to take place. William's solution contained the generative concept that adaptations of other senses such as hearing and feeling in the wings would increase to help support the owl in hunting. But his statement was an Incomplete solution (4) because there are many other adaptations that might have been included.

Stage 6: Informational text comprehension. During the search stage of the assessment, different students use different text selections and their notes may not reflect their full comprehension of the material. A relatively low level search performance may reflect a low text-selection strategy or low text comprehension ability or both. Because text comprehension is fundamental, we gave students two tasks. One was a short informational text containing related illustrations. The accompanying question required students to integrate information from both the text and the illustration. This informational text explained the development of a bird inside an egg.

The rubric to describe the quality of students' responses to informational text was:

1. No answer (no answer; answer relies on prior knowledge not related to the text; or information is incorrect, nonspecific, or verbatim copy).
2. Accurate (response accurately integrates information from two or more parts of the text).
3. Elaborated (response connects an integrated statement with additional information in the text that elaborates, explains, or contextualizes the statement).

Sandra's response was not related to the text, nor was it very coherent (No answer 1): "I now that egg has a red line on the yolk and the egg will have to get water a food to grow and you can see the hen babyes and the baby can float in the egg."

William's response was based on appropriate segments of text, and he added shape and color (Elaborated 3): "inside of an egg is a baby chick and yolk for the baby to eat. The baby looks like a bird, the yolk is light yellow."

Stage 7: Narrative text comprehension. Students read a 350-word excerpt from "Izzard the Lizard," a story in which a girl brings to the classroom a lizard that entertains and distracts the students. Three questions required the students to: (a) reproduce a brief portion of text from memory, (b) give an explanation for an important event, and (c) provide a personal reaction to a character, event, or theme. We include narrative because our integrated curriculum contains literary as well as informational books.

Quality of narrative comprehension was judged with a rubric based on responses to all of the questions. Student responses to the reproductive, explanatory, and open-extension questions were rated as appropriate (accurate and text-based) or elaborated (embellished with details and characterizations). The scoring scheme was: 1—no appropriate responses; 2—one appropriate response; 3—two appropriate responses; 4—three appropriate responses; 5—three appropriate responses and at least two elaborated responses. Although all of the responses cannot be given here, Sandra received an overall score of 1 and William received a 4.

To the question, "Why couldn't Izzard go to school anymore?" Sandra wrote, "I thing the Izzard will be good but it will be log and the teacher will be happy."

William said, "Because the class wasn't waching the teacher, they where waching Izzard."

What Are the Advantages of a Performance Assessment and Who Does It Help?

Developing an assessment challenged us to examine our teaching aims and objectives. We clarified what we wanted students to learn and what evidence we would accept as indicators that they had learned. This process helped us to understand where we were going in our teaching as well as where our students had been in their learning (Gaskins et al., in press). Many of these instructional benefits are shared with portfolio assessment (Valencia & Place, 1993). This performance assessment can be placed in a student's portfolio, providing a common task that permits teachers to compare students and to chart growth over time.

Students benefit from this assessment because they can use the tasks as a basis for their own self-appraisal. Students can reflect on whether they used their background knowledge in their search and whether they applied their search findings to their writing and problem solving. We believe that administrators and policy makers may benefit from performance assessments, too, because the assessments reflect the shape of the curriculum and teachers' aspirations for authentic learning. By communicating the outcomes of the assessment to administrators as well as to other teachers, we have been able to make public the higher-order accomplishments of our students on a diversity of important and realistic tasks. We believe that a performance assessment that simulates instruction can be a stage where schooling and its appraisal are acted out together.

What Are the Demands On and Responsibilities of Teachers Who Want to Conduct This Performance Assessment?

One teacher can design, administer, and evaluate the results of this performance assessment, but the demands on the teacher's time will be prohibitive. We recommend that a group of teachers with similar curricula and goals at a given grade level, perhaps across several schools, join together to develop a performance assessment. A cluster of teachers within a school or an entire district may design, administer, score, interpret, and report a performance assessment. The assessment presented in this article may be used as a starting point for the development of instructional assessments that are tailored to the curricula, student populations, and cultural contexts of particular schools or districts.

References

Gaskins, I.W., Guthrie, J.T., Satlow, E., Ostertag, J., Six, L., Byrne, J., & Conner, B. (in press). Integrating instruction of science and reading/writing processes: Goals, assessments, and teacher development. *Journal of Research in Science Teaching.*

Grant, R., Guthrie, J., Bennett, L., Rice, M.E., & McGough, K. (1993). Developing engaged readers through concept-oriented reading instruction. *The Reading Teacher*, 47, 338-340.

Valencia, S.W., & Place, N. (1993). Literacy portfolios for teaching, learning and accountability: The Bellevue literacy assessment project. In S.W. Valencia, E.F. Hiebert, & P.A. Afflerbach (Eds.), *Authentic reading assessment* (pp. 134-167). Newark, DE: International Reading Association.

Literacy Portfolios Emerge

Reprinted from *The Reading Teacher* (1992), *45*, 604-607

Jane Hansen

In the fall of 1990, portfolios emerged as a new concept in the Manchester, New Hampshire, public schools. Twelve of us from the University of New Hampshire and Manchester began to explore evaluation in the context of Literacy Portfolios. Portfolios have many definitions, but the Manchester portfolios grew from these beliefs:

Readers and writers know more about their own abilities and progress than outsiders do. Thus, they can be the prime evaluators of themselves and their work.

Choice is a hallmark of a reading-writing classroom. Thus, teachers and students will each decide what to put in their individual Literacy Portfolios.

In reading-writing workshops, teachers and students work together. Both teachers and students will create portfolios.

In this article I will show how these three concepts unfolded in Karen Boettcher's innercity sixth-grade classroom. I served as a co-researcher with Karen twice a week for the 1990-91 schoolyear and continue during 1991-92.

Prior to the Schoolyear

The teacher volunteers. In May of 1990, Jane Kearns, director of writing for the public schools of Manchester, which is New Hampshire's largest city, invited all interested teachers to an informational meeting about the Literacy Portfolios research project proposed for the next fall. Karen, who taught Grade 6 at the Beech Street School for 17 years, attended the meeting and soon volunteered to participate. She would not only explore the notion of Literacy Portfolios during the next two years, but she would expand her students' writing and reading experiences. In this article I will focus on Karen's reading program and how it paved the way for her students' creation of their Literacy Portfolios.

The teacher plans. Before school began, Karen invited me to her home for lunch. She had created a time schedule and a record keeping system for her new reading, writing, student-as-evaluator venture. Karen said, "It looks workable, but if it doesn't work, I'll adjust it." Then she had a question, "Jane, when I put my little chair down beside a student for a reading conference, what do I say?"

In a reader's conference the student must say something about herself or her work in order for the teacher to learn, support, and help. What should Karen say to ensure that each student would talk? She had never held a reading conference with anyone.

I dug my current book, *Storm in the Mountains* by James Moffett, from my book bag and placed it on the table. We looked at each other. Finally, she blurted, "Tell me about your book." She knew what to say!

We conversed for about three minutes, and during this time she was not the only evaluator. I was constantly thinking, "There's so much to tell. What should I say?" Conferences give readers opportunities to evaluate themselves, their reading, and their books, all skills that Karen's students would practice as they took on the major responsibility for evaluation of themselves as readers, writers, and persons when they created their portfolios.

The Schoolyear Begins

The students read. Karen gave her students 45 minutes each day to read. They spent the majority of that time reading from books of their choice and some time reading from a book they were all reading. Karen and I read with the class for the first 10 minutes of this reading time before we started individual reader's conferences.

The conferences. After only a few days, Karen didn't open conferences with her initial request, "Tell me about your book." As soon as she placed her primary-sized chair beside someone, the student started to tell her about his/her book. Often they chose to read to Karen. The two of them had a good time; frequently, nearby students entered into a conference. When Mouv told about *More Scary Stories to Tell in the Dark*, by Alvin Schwartz, he told about the steps he heard in his attic, and Melissa and Keisha, who sat at his cluster of desks, added their scary stories.

The evaluation practice the students received when they chose which book to read and how to tell about the book gave them experiences they'd need when they created their portfolios. To consider possibilities and make choices is a skill central to a portfolio classroom (Seidel, 1989). The conferences placed the students in an evaluator's chair, as did their reading groups.

Groups to discuss books. The groups that met to discuss one title were nonleveled, a critical feature of reading/writing classrooms (Wansart, 1988). Initially, these groups met to answer Karen's questions about a book, but at the end of September she decided to change the talk pattern. Karen opened the discussion of *The Girl with the Silver Eyes*, by Willo Davis Roberts, with "Who would like to start? Who has something to say to get the group moving?"

Ryan said, "It's interesting to find out how she uses her powers."

April said, "It would be neat to have those powers. They say she's different, but she can take care of herself."

Artie said, "I'd use the power to do my homework."

Later, Kristen said, "She should be careful."

Artie said, "If she doesn't do it right. ..."

Karen (teacher), said "Has she hurt someone?"

Kristen answered, "Mr. P. twisted his ankle."

The talk continued among the students, and the teacher asked a few questions for clarification. Karen had not brought a list of comprehension questions to ask the students. Evaluation was no longer a matter of students giving answers to the teacher's queries. The students decided which aspects of their books merited discussion, and in the upcoming weeks they would draw on this experience when they selected items for their portfolios (Polin, 1991).

Within about two weeks, the students initiated discussions with ease, and Kim started a new type of talk in the groups. She began, "I don't know what the problem is in this book. I know there is one, but I don't get it."

Prior to this day I hadn't heard a student admit to general lack of confusion about a book. The ability to ask others for help is a necessary aspect of the kind of classrooms the project teachers were trying to create. These students were going to set their goals for what they intended to do to become better readers and writers, and they'd have to be able to write about these plans in their portfolios. In order to do this, they'd have to, in effect, say "I don't get something. I want to learn more about it. I need help."

Groups to discuss choice books. Karen defined "choice books" as books from the school library, class library, or home that each student chose as one of their books to read every day during reading class. The students met in heterogeneous groups to share these books.

These response groups met without Karen, while she conducted reader's conferences. To meet without supervision was a necessary experience in this classroom where self-evaluation was to become the hallmark. The students must realize that their teacher trusted their judgments.

Karen initiated the choice groups at the end of September. Two groups of five met each week, and they signed up, on a rotating basis, for this opportunity. The first group fumbled, not accustomed to discussions about books of their choice, but by mid-October the students could share and respond to books. Artie shared *Sir Cedric*, by Roy Gerrard, Amanda brought *The Horse That Came to Breakfast*, by Marilyn Anderson, Amy was reading *Dawn and the Impossible Three*, by Ann Martin, April told about *Pen Pals*, by Sharon Wyeth, and Eric shared *Mystery of Chimney Rock*, by Edward Packard.

When April, for example, told about *Pen Pals*, she ended her comments with "she must choose between her boyfriend or her girlfriend."

Eric asked, "So, what's the problem?"

April explained some more, and, as part of her explanation, she read a letter from the book.

Eric asked, "So, the whole book is just letters?"

April responded, "No, it's very good ... she's very rich ... like $100.00 a week for allowance."

One of the students said, "I could live off that!"

The talk continued. For each book, the members of the group asked questions of interest to learn more about the book, and the person who shared explained. They had to decide what to say to open their turn and they knew they'd better understand their book. The choices the students made about what to tell and what to ask established more groundwork for the evaluation skills they'd need when they created their portfolios. They'd need to look at their work and find value in it (Paulson, Paulson, & Mayer, 1991).

Literacy Portfolios

At the research team meetings. Karen attended research team meetings twice a month after school with 12 people, 7 from the Manchester Public Schools and 5 from UNH. Of the Manchester people, 5 taught in innercity schools (Grades I, 6, an elementary resource room, junior high English, and high school writing), and the other 2 were administrators, the directors of writing and reading. The UNH researchers were 3 students in the Reading and Writing Instruction Ph.D. program and 2 professors, one being myself.

The Manchester personnel volunteered the 90 minutes for these meetings as part of their responsibility to the project. We held the meetings on a rotation basis in the 5 teachers' classrooms. To these sessions we each brought a one-page piece of writing for distribution. (A collection of these pieces is available in *The Manchester Literacy Portfolios Project*.) Our task was to write about the evolution of the Literacy Portfolios, but at the early meetings we wrote about other reading/writing experiences because we had not started to create portfolios. We continued to do this throughout the project because the portfolios were a part of the entire classroom fabric, so all concerns and joys about students were relevant.

We also shared our own portfolios with the group. When I prepared my portfolio for the team meeting at the end of October, I included a letter from my mother, a recipe, a photocopy of the cover of my book, a list of books I've read during the past 2 years, and several other artifacts that, all together, I hoped would show the group who I am as a literate person. In my self-reflection (Wolf, 1989), I explained who I am, wrote about why I included each item, and dreamed about who I hope to become in this evolution of literate Jane.

In the classroom. Later Karen said to me, "My students have such shaky self-concepts that they first need a portfolio that shows who they are. Then, later, when

they've gained some confidence in themselves, they can assess who they want to be as students." This concept of a portfolio dovetails with the concept of a scholar held by Shirley Brice Heath (Bishop, 1991) as someone who has no seams in her life. The literate self is a combination of school self and nonschool self.

Karen created her portfolio as teachers elsewhere have done (Graves & Sunstein, in press) and shared it with her class. Some of her contents were a page from the journal she keeps whenever she and her husband travel and two parts of an index card. (She writes constant lists and her son cut this one up as a joke.) She had a piece of writing she'd written with her class and three of her onepagers for the research project. As her goal, she wrote that she will show, as she revises her portfolio more about herself as a reader.

After she'd shared it, she invited her students to think of important items that would show who they are and to put them in the blank portfolio folders Karen had stacked on a back table. In time, they would write reflections and goals and revise those statements, as they grew in their ability to evaluate themselves. The Literacy Portfolios in Grade 6 had begun.

The students reflected on their own literacy, both in and out of school. They selected items to show their individual selves, articulated their reasons for each, and showed their growth. Karen could help them with this process, because she made similar decisions when she created her original portfolio and would continue to do so as she revised it throughout the year.

She and her students each made their own decisions about what to place in their Literacy Portfolios. Each of them, whether teacher or student, gained a clearer notion of who they are as they evaluated themselves and their work.

References

Bishop, R.S. (1991). Profile: Shirley Brice Heath, *Language Arts*, 68, 159-163.

Graves, D., & Sunstein, B. (Eds.). (in press). *Portfolios: Diversity in action.* Portsmouth, NH: Heinemann.

The Manchester Literacy Portfolios Project. (1991). Durham, NH: The University of New Hampshire, The Writing Lab.

Paulson, F.L., Paulson, P.R., & Meyer, C.A. (1991, February). What makes a portfolio a portfolio? *Educational Leadership*, 60-63.

Polin, L. (1991). Portfolio assessment. *The Writing Notebook: Creative Word Processing in the Classroom*, 8 (3), 25-27.

Seidel, S. (1989, November). Even before portfolios: The activities and atmosphere of a portfolio classroom. *Portfolio*, 6-9.

Wansart, W. (1988). The student with learning disabilities in a writing process classroom: A case study. *Reading, Writing, and Learning Disabilities*, 4, 311-319.

Wolf, D.P. (1989, April). Portfolio assessment: Sampling student work. *Educational Leadership*, 35-39.

Teaching and Assessing Strategic Reasoning: Dealing with the Dilemmas

Reprinted from *The Reading Teacher* (1992), *45*, 428-433

Beth Ann Herrmann

Strategic reasoning is associated with effective reading and writing (Baker & Brown, 1984; Harris & Graham, 1985), but teaching and assessing strategic reasoning is difficult. In this article, I describe instructional and assessment dilemmas I frequently experience when teaching and assessing strategic reasoning in various classroom and tutorial situations, and how I deal with these dilemmas.

The Nature of Strategic Reasoning

For the purpose of this article, *strategic reasoning* is defined as the complex thinking processes used before, during, and after reading and writing to construct meaningful interpretations of text and to create meaningful texts. Strategic reasoning varies greatly with each reading and writing situation and purpose. To illustrate this, monitor your thinking as you attempt to construct an interpretation of the following passage about induction icing (Douglas, 1990):

> Induction Icing
>
> Carburetor icing is one of the facets of induction system icing (the effects on fuel-injected engines will be discussed later). It is most commonly caused by refrigeration effects inside the carburetor coupled with appropriate atmospheric conditions. The refrigeration effect comes from a combination of lowered air pressure inside the carburetor throat and the vaporization of fuel, which drops the temperature of both the air flowing through the carburetor and the carburetor, itself. The drop can be as much as 70 degrees Fahrenheit.

To construct an interpretation of this text you consciously used prior knowledge from a variety of sources. For example, you probably thought about the words *induction icing* in the title and then predicted a meaning associated in some way with the formation of ice. However, by the time you read the first line, you encountered other words, such as *carburetor* and *fuel-injected engines*, which may have caused you to expand your initial prediction. If you have extensive prior knowledge about engines, you probably predicted an engine topic at that point, but you may not have been able to construct a meaning for induction icing or figure out what it has to do with the topic. However, if you thought this passage might have been taken from a chapter about airplanes, your choice of predictions for induction icing may have narrowed to airplane engines. On the other hand, if you thought this passage was taken from a book for automobile mechanics, you may have formed hypotheses about automobile engines.

You consciously used all these various knowledge sources simultaneously, monitoring your sense-making as you proceeded. Every time you encountered unfamiliar or unknown terminology, such as "carburetor throat," you probably gener-

ated new hypotheses. If you encountered words you could not pronounce, you consciously applied your knowledge of letter-sound combinations or other linguistic units such as prefixes and suffixes. By testing hypotheses triggered by your knowledge of language and the topic working together, you gradually built a meaning for the passage.

If this were an authentic reading experience, your thinking might differ from the example shown here, depending on your purpose for reading the passage. For example, if you were reading the passage to prepare for a test, you would probably pay closer attention to unknown words than if you were reading the passage for recreational purposes. In sum. the thinking you did to construct an interpretation of the induction icing passage was complex, which is what makes teaching and assessing strategic reasoning so difficult. In the following sections, instructional and assessment dilemmas are explored along with suggestions for dealing with these dilemmas.

Instructional Dilemmas

Teaching strategic reasoning is difficult for three reasons. First, instructional actions associated with effective teaching of strategic reasoning are difficult and demanding. Second, instructional materials designed to help teachers teach strategic reasoning don't always provide enough information about strategic reasoning. Third, it is difficult to teach strategic reasoning without overemphasizing content.

Demanding instructional actions. Effective teaching of strategic reasoning requires teacher verbalization of strategic reasoning. Duffy, Roehler, and Herrmann (1988) refer to this type of verbalization as *mental modeling*. For example, the following seventh-grade lesson excerpt illustrates how I attempted to reveal strategic reasoning associated with using context to infer meaning about an unknown word (Herrmann, 1990):

> (Reading:) He took the medicine ball from Stan, reared back, and sent it can ... can ... blank at me. My arms went up, the mass of the ball smacked into them, and I went over backwards. Hmmm. I can't pronounce that word and I'm confused. There must be some clues here to help me. I know what a medicine ball is. It's heavy and some people use one to exercise....I'll think about that as I reread the sentence. (Reading:)...sent it can...cannon. Hmmm. A cannon ball is heavy and it does lots of damage to things it hits. That's a good clue. (Reading:)... sent it cannon...*add*... ing, cannon....*aid*....ing. I don't know which way to pronounce it, but I think I know what it means. The ball was heavy and it was thrown hard—like a cannonball is shot out of a cannon.

This type of modeling differs from other think-aloud techniques in two ways. First, it reveals thinking processes, whereas other techniques reveal the end result of thinking, but not thinking processes, as illustrated in the following lesson excerpts.

> From the title I predict that this season will tell how fishermen used to catch whales. (from Davey, 1983.)

> My question is: What have the people of Butterfly City, U.S.A., done to protect the butterflies? (from Palincsar & Brown, 1984.)

Second, modeling strategic reasoning is difficult to accurately describe. To illustrate this point, consider again the passage about induction icing. If you had to explain to someone else how you went about constructing an interpretation of the passage, chances are your verbal explanation would reduce your thinking to a step-by-step procedure (e.g., "First I....Then I....") which oversimplifies the complex nature of strategic reasoning.

Here are two ways I deal with the modeling dilemma. First, I select short passages from two or three types of texts presenting unfamiliar content. I tape record myself as I talk out loud to construct meaning from these passages. Afterwards, I listen to the tape recordings several times to pinpoint thinking I have done. Then I revise my initial modeling attempt. I prac-

tice modeling this way before teaching a lesson.

Second, I frequently invite students I am teaching to verbalize their thinking, encouraging them to be as explicit as possible in their verbalizations. This helps students become more familiar with the complex nature of strategic reasoning, and it helps me improve my ability to verbalize reasoning processes.

Instructional materials. I have found some new instructional materials helpful in teaching strategic reasoning, but they don't always provide enough information about strategic reasoning. For example, consider the following inference strategy from a fourth grade teacher's edition from a popular basal reader series (Pearson et al., 1989):

> Look for word clues and think about your own experiences to make an inference. Read to see if your inference was right.

The strategy helps students see what to think about when making inferences, but the specific thinking associated with using the clue words and experiences is not specified. Likewise, what the teacher should say and do to show students how to reason with clue words and their background experiences is not specified, as illustrated in the following excerpt (Pearson et al., 1989, pp. 16-17):

> Read the passage and explain that the sentences do not state what RBI is. Point out the word clues *switch, computer, and strange voice.* Tell students that since you know from experience that these clues can describe robots, you can infer that RBI is a robot.
>
> "Okay, RBI, it's time to switch you on." said Professor Blake. She typed the command in the computer.
>
> "WHAT...ARE...MY...ORDERS...FOR...TODAY?" asked RBI in a strange voice. Just then there was a knock on the door.
>
> "Come in," said Professor Blake. "Mark! Why are you here an hour before class?"
>
> "I want to teach RBI how to open a door for our science project," Mark answered.

To provide the missing information, I include verbal descriptions of strategic reasoning, as illustrated in the following example:

> OK. I've read this part but I am confused because it doesn't tell me who RBI is. Watch what I do to figure it out. I know a lot about some concepts included in this passage—commands, computers and science projects. I'll think about what I know about these things to figure out what they have to do with each other in this passage. Let's see. Mark is obviously doing a science project, so that means the professor must be his teacher. You give commands to a computer and it does things for you. If I put all that together, I think RBI is a computer and Mark is going to give it a command to open the door. Let's see if there are any more clues. Yes. It says RBI is talking in a strange voice. I never saw a talking computer, so that can't be right. What's the closest thing to a talking computer that I know—a robot!

Note that my modification includes direct teacher statements describing *how* to reason strategically about clue words and background experiences.

Balancing strategic reasoning and content. I have found that authentic reading and writing experiences, though useful for teaching strategic reasoning, can cause students to focus too much on content. The following fourth-grade lesson excerpt illustrates this point. Note that my modeling of strategic reasoning relies heavily on content.

> I'm going to show you how to use what you already know to figure out hard words when you're reading. Let's pretend I don't know this word *alarmed.* (Reading) "The turtle was alarmed and quickly pulled his head inside his shell." I know a lot about turtles that will help me here. I saw a turtle on the beach at my house one day, and when I walked over to look at it he got scared and pulled his head inside his shell to hide. We backed away and he took his head out, but only a little bit, to look around. When he saw us he zipped his head right back in his shell. So if I think about that as I read, I can make this sentence make sense, even

> though I don't know this word—I could use *scared* instead.

It is necessary to rely on the content to explain reasoning, but sometimes students become confused as they try to sort out what's important from my instructional actions. Too often students conclude that what is important is the content being discussed rather than the reasoning being modeled. For example, when the students were interviewed after the lesson from which the above excerpt was taken and asked to describe what the lesson was about, they said turtles!

I deal with the process/content dilemma in two ways. First, at the beginning of each lesson, I emphasize that two important aspects of reading will be taught—strategic reasoning *and* content, as illustrated in the following second-grade lesson introduction:

> I'm going to be teaching you two things today. I'm going to teach you something about turtles you might not have known before. I'm also going to teach you how to use what you already know to figure out hard words.

This type of lesson introduction helps students understand that how meaning is constructed is just as important as what is understood or learned from the text. Second, each time we stop to discuss the story, we also discuss the reasoning we have used to construct meaning, as illustrated in the following lesson excerpt:

> OK. Let's stop a moment and talk about what we have read and the kind of thinking we have done to construct meaning from this text.

These kinds of discussions help me maintain a balance between strategic reasoning and content, and the students develop more awareness and control of reasoning processes associated with constructing meaning from text.

Assessment Dilemmas

Assessing strategic reasoning is just as difficult as teaching it, even though a number of classroom reading and writing instruments designed for this purpose are now available. Most of these instruments provide useful information about students' awareness of strategic reasoning, but they don't always yield information about *how* students reason about text. For example, the following basal unit test item is designed to assess students' inference-making abilities about an accompanying passage (Pearson et al., 1989):

> Why did David think this was the worst day of his life?
>
> A. He didn't want to move.
>
> B. He lost his baseball cards.
>
> C. He was hungry.
>
> D. He wanted to meet Mr. Rios.

Note that the item focuses on whether or not an inference is made rather than *how* the inference was made. Similar problems exist with a number of newly developed classroom assessment instruments designed to measure strategic reasoning. For example, Schmitt (1990) developed a multiple-choice questionnaire, the Metacomprehension Strategy Index (MSI), for evaluating middle- and upper-elementary students' knowledge of strategic reading processes. Students are told to think about the kinds of things they can do to help them understand a story better before, during, and after they read it. They are then instructed to read four statements following each question (a total of 25) and decide which one would help them the most. They are also told there are no right answers. Consider the following MSI items. The circled responses indicate strategy awareness.

> Before I begin reading, it's a good idea to:
>
> A. See how many pages are in the story.
>
> B. Look up all of the big words in the dictionary.
>
> (C.) Make some guesses about what I think will happen in the story.
>
> D. Think about what has happened so far in the story.
>
> While I'm reading, it's a good idea to:
>
> A. See if I can recognize the new vocabulary words.
>
> B. Be careful not to skip any parts of the story.

C. Check to see how many of the words I already know.

(D.) Keep thinking of what I already know about the things and ideas in the story to help me decide what is going to happen.

After I've read the story. it's a good idea to:

(A.) Underline the main idea.

B. Retell the main points of the whole story so that I can check to see if I understood it.

C. Read the story again to be sure I said all of the words right.

D. Practice reading the story aloud.

The items provide useful self-report information about students' strategy use, but not much information about *how* students reason.

I deal with the assessment dilemma by collecting additional descriptive information from students about their thinking to supplement information obtained from other assessments. For example, I have experimented with individual and small group conversations about strategic reasoning, as illustrated in the following excerpt:

> OK. Let's talk about the thinking you did for this question. (Reading) "Why did David think this was the worst day of his life?" Don, start us off by telling us how you figured out the answer to that question.

I tape record these conversations and keep written notes describing each student's thinking and the kinds of difficulties they are having developing awareness and control of their thinking.

In addition to student conversations, I use teaching situations to obtain additional information about students' strategic reasoning. On several occasions I sit down and read authentic text (e.g., magazines) with small groups of students. As we take turns reading I pay close attention to what they appear to be doing to make sense of the text, frequently asking them to share *how* they are constructing meaning, the kinds of comprehension difficulties they are experiencing, and how they are attempting to resolve them. When pronunciation errors are self-corrected, I ask them to explain the thinking that led to the self-correction, and when unknown words contribute to comprehension difficulties, I inquire about ways they go about restoring comprehension, as illustrated in the following fifth-grade lesson excerpt:

Student: (Reading) There were several roads nearby, but it did not take her long to find the one paved with yellow brick. Within a short time she was walking...walking...

Teacher: Go ahead and skip that word, we'll come back to it later if you get confused.

Student: (Reading).. she was walking blank toward the Emerald City, her silver shoes..blank on the hard, yellow roadbed."

Teacher: OK. good. Let's stop here for a minute. Can you put what you just read in your own words?

Student: Dorothy was following the yellow brick road to the Emerald City.

Teacher: Excellent. Now, did you need those hard words to make sense out of this?

Student: No.

Teacher: OK. This time you understood what you read without having to worry about those hard words, but let's suppose you did get confused because of those words. (Addressing the group) How could Alicia go about figuring out those hard words?

I pay close attention to the responses students make in these instructional situations to track their developing awareness and control of strategic reasoning.

Student journals also provide useful information about students' strategic reasoning abilities. I frequently ask students to dictate to me or write on their own about experiences they have with comprehension blockages and how they go about remov-

ing them, as illustrated in the following student journal excerpt:

> Yesterday I was reading *The Wizard of Oz* and I had trouble with some of the words they used to describe the people in that strange country. The words were *shepherdesses* and *bodices* and *breeches* and *ermine* robes. I thought about what I had already read about the country and different types of clothing, then I tried to picture what those people must have looked like.

I encourage open discussion of journal entries as another way of exploring unique features of strategic reasoning.

Finally, portfolios can provide rich information about students' progress toward awareness and control of strategic reasoning. Portfolios can take many forms (e.g.. Rief, 1990; Valencia, 1990), but I use portfolios by sharing and discussing their contents with my students and their parents so we can examine and document their progress. For example, a small group of fourth-grade students I worked with needed to develop more awareness and control of text editing. Together, we collected their edited compositions along with their written and verbal explanations of the strategic reasoning used to edit them. We frequently discussed these portfolio collections with their parents to report to them their children's progress.

Summary

In this article I have described dilemmas and solutions associated with teaching and assessing strategic reasoning. My intent has been twofold: (a) to highlight that learning to teach and assess strategic reasoning is a trial-and-error process requiring much reflection on the part of the teacher, and (b) to spark discourse among teachers about dilemmas associated with teaching and assessing strategic reasoning. Conversations of this sort should lead to new ideas for teaching and assessing strategic reasoning.

References

Baker, L., & Brown, A. (1984). Metacognitive skills and reading. In P.D. Pearson (Ed.), *Handbook of reading research* (pp. 353-394). New York: Longman.

Davey, B. (1983). Think aloud—modeling the cognitive processes of reading comprehension. *Journal of Reading, 27,* 44-47.

Douglas, A.B. (1990). Induction icing, *Aviation Safety* 10, 4-6.

Duffy, G., Roehler, L., & Herrmann, B.A. (1988). Modeling mental processes helps poor readers become strategic readers. *The Reading Teacher, 41,* 762-767.

Harris, K.R., & Graham, S. (1985). Improving learning disabled students' composition skills: Self-control strategy training. *Learning Disability Quarterly, 8,* 27-36.

Herrmann, B.A. (1990). Teaching preservice teachers how to model thought processes: Issues, problems and procedures. *Teacher Education and Special Education, 13,* 73-81.

Palincsar, A., & Brown, A. (1984). Reciprocal teaching of comprehension-fostering and comprehension-monitoring activities. *Cognition and Instruction, 1,* 117-175.

Pearson, P.D., Johnson, D.D., Clymer, T., Indrisano, R., Venezky, R.L., Baumann, J.F., Hiebert, E., & Toth, M. (1989). World of Reading *Silver Secrets* teacher's manual. Needham, MA: Silver Burdett & Ginn.

Rief, L. (1990). Finding the value in evaluation: Self-assessment in a middle school classroom. *Educational Leadership, 47*(6), 24-29.

Schmitt, M.C. (1990). A questionnaire to measure children's awareness of strategic reading processes. *The Reading Teacher, 43,* 454-461.

Valencia, S. (1990). A portfolio approach to classroom reading assessment: The whys, whats and hows. *The Reading Teacher, 43,* 338-340.

Nontechnical Assessment

Reprinted from *The Reading Teacher* (1992), *46*, 60-62

Peter H. Johnston

One of my clippings from *Newsweek* boasts a subtitle, "We need to produce students who know how to think. And we need new tests to help us" (Leslie & Winger, 1990). Assessment technology is widely viewed as the tool for educational reform, and there is a lot of talk about new and improved tests—"performance-based" and more "authentic"—that will "drive" instruction to "higher standards." The prevailing belief is that if only we had the right tests, then teachers would teach better. But even if the Holy Testing Grail were found, it is a long way from such an instrument to the interactions between teachers and students. The most powerful assessment for students' learning occurs in the classroom, moment-to-moment among teacher and students. Even developing turbocharged portfolios will accomplish nothing unless teachers understand reading, writing, and learning in more complex ways. Improving educational "standards"—the quality of instruction—is not a technical problem but a people problem. It requires creating conditions in which members of the school community will learn.

It is also a people problem because any assessment instrument must be used in a social context and for a social purpose. In a context of high stakes accountability, the most wonderful portfolio system will have its central, reflective function subverted. Under stress of time and accountability, teachers will scan the most thoughtfully constructed checklist to find what is missing, focusing only on what students cannot do rather than what they can do. As a consequence, the weaker student, whose work needs to be framed most positively, will have his work framed most negatively.

Assessment is a people problem in part because, like reading, it is interpretive. When we read, our understanding is influenced by the knowledge and perspectives we bring, the purposes for which we read, and the contexts in which we read. We read students' literate activity just as we would read a book. For example, in interviews my colleagues and I asked teachers for impromptu descriptions of the literate development of a student they knew well (Johnston, Afflerbach, & Weiss, 1990). Teachers who knew more about children's literature were more likely to frame their descriptions in terms of the books children read and their responses to them. Teachers in situations that focused on testing and normative practices both in and out of the classroom rarely mentioned literature, even when they knew about it, and gave less detailed and less personal descriptions than did teachers in less controlling situations. Some teachers, without recourse to files, gave descriptions that filled several pages of transcript. Other teachers' readings filled no more than three or four lines. These brief descriptions came from the teachers whose instructional lives were highly controlled.

Assessment is always interpretive. We *make* sense of children's literate behavior. Sometime we might use tests, but that does not reduce the interpretive nature of the activity. Tests merely constrain the literate behavior that is available for interpretation. The only time testing is free of interpretation is when a computer is scanning bubble sheets. Even though a test produces a number, stripped of its context and process, it must still be interpreted before it is of any use. Even if it were possible to produce an unbiased test (and it is

not), there is little gain for students if the teacher remains biased.

Assessment is a people problem also because it is social. It is not simply a matter of collecting data. Teachers' assessments of children's literate activity are the basis of instructional interactions in the classroom and of students' assessments of themselves. Consequently, merely focusing on what the individual student has to say about her reading and writing is important, not only because doing so yields useful information but also because it lets the student know that you think her perspective is important. Testing is no different. It has consequences for both teachers (Smith, 1991) and students (Paris, Lawton, Turner, & Roth, 1991), most of them less than desirable.

The social nature of literate activity in the classroom influences children's assessments of their own literate activity. For example, when I asked Tara, "What sort of reader are you?" she told me she was "pretty good." When I asked her, "What makes you say that?" she said, "I'm in the Red group." Sheila, in a different classroom, drew her description from a different framework: "I like funny stories and books about animals, but often I just kind of get stuck on the same author for months at a time." Students who evaluate their reading and writing in the simplistic normative terms ("I'm good at writing") will view reading (or writing) as a talent that one either has or does not have, a view that is neither nor instructive.

The propensity for those outside the schools to ignore all this and pose assessment as a technical matter is problematic enough, but as teachers we have lived with this thinking for so long it has become part of us. It is reflected in our own formulations of assessment problems and in the language we use. For example, we formulate the problem of "accountability" instead of the problem of "responsibility." These words reflect entirely different metaphors. You are *held* accountable whereas you *are* responsible. To arrange for responsibility, you focus on building communities, involvement, trusting relationships, and self-assessment. To arrange for accountability you focus on building external assessment, a power differential, and some means for those in power to mete out consequences based on outcomes.

As a second example, we refer to our own observations as "subjective," "informal," and "anecdotal," whereas we refer to tests as "objective" and "formal." Our own language devalues the close knowledge we have and values distance. It would be more helpful if we referred to our own assessments as "direct documentation" and test-based assessments as "indirect" and "invasive."

These uses of language are far from trivial. They show that we do not value our own assessment knowledge. Our unfortunate cultural concern for control, distance, objectification, and quantification is a legacy from Kant, Bacon, and Descartes (Field, 1991), and it does not favor teachers, whose knowledge is often intuitive, usually nonnumerical, more inclined to the narrative, and gained through personal involvement. Not valuing our own knowledge leaves us continually insecure and easily made defensive, which makes learning difficult.

Objective knowledge, in the technological sense, is not the most constructive form of assessment in education. "Objectivity" is only useful as "dynamic objectivity," which Keller (1985) describes as:

> not unlike empathy, a form of knowledge of other persons that draws explicitly on the commonality of feelings and experience in order to enrich one's understanding of another in his or her own right. (p. 117)

Detailed knowledge comes from proximity and involvement, not distance. The problem is to know ourselves, our practice, and our students more deeply--developing awareness of ourselves while maintaining involvement. Current assessment practices discourage this type of knowledge, particularly by devaluing knowledge that depends more on connectedness than on separateness, and by undermining the necessary confidence in self-knowledge. In the context of a predominantly female teaching community, this is hardly gender-neutral (Johnston, 1992).

Technological thinking pervades our problem solving as well as our language, trapping us in glass walls of transparent assumptions. For example, when school districts invest enormous effort in revising report cards, the usual outcome is a larger sheet of paper with more (sometimes fewer) boxes, some of which are different from the previous ones, and with different labels alongside the number (or letter) grades. Assumptions of uniformity, standardization, and quantification are most prevalent, but we begin by assuming that report cards are necessary. In order to examine this assumption, we might ask, What are the functions of the report card? How many ways can we accomplish these without a report card (e.g., portfolios, voice-mail)? Do any of these functions require grades?

We assume all report cards must be sent home at the same time,ensuring that most are out of date by the time they are read. The more detailed the reporting, the more damaging the assumption. How about five per week? Similarly, we assume that all teachers in the school (or district) must use the same report card. In the spirit of external assessment, we assume that teachers must write all of the report card. But both parents and students are capable of contributing to the report cards and learning in the process. Believing in the clarity of quantification, we assume that most people understand what a grade (or score) means, particularly when it is carefully labeled. Get a group of people (parents, teachers, administrators) together and ask them to write on a piece of paper what a particular grade or score (B, E, 82%) means. Surprise! Think out loud onto a tape recorder as you compose report card grades.

If we are to make real progress in assessment, we will have to rethink assessment as a problem of learning and responsibility. I will devote a subsequent column to exploring this matter; however, several points seem important. First, we will need to know reading and writing better. If nothing else, this will require us to both read and write ourselves, and to talk about our reading and writing with one another. The more complex reading and writing seem to us, the less likely we are to feel comfortable framing children's learning normatively.

Second, we will need to know our students better. This will require almost daily individual contact with them in which we observe, and encourage them to teach us about, their reading and writing. Engaging our colleagues in serious study of individual children's development and valuing the diverse perspectives that they bring will also be important both for depth of understanding and for error correction. The basis of classroom assessment is diverse and deep case knowledge.

Third, our responsibility involves reflectiveness, and reflection requires record keeping and time. It also requires understanding that there is no single correct way to assess or to teach. A teacher who believes otherwise will not be reflective because of either insecurity or arrogance. Just as with books, there is no certifiably "right reading" of a student's literate development. Thus, we are not responsible for having it. We are, however, responsible for checking on the consequences of our assessments and seeking alternative perspectives. Individually, we can never have the expertise of the community, particularly when it involves studying our own practice.

Unfortunately, it is these critical and reflective aspects of responsible assessment that are most vulnerable in a context of high profile accountability testing. These conditions make it easy to become defensive and insecure about our knowledge and practice, and difficult to engage openly with colleagues and to question our practice

publicly. They make it easy to place blame rather than confront and solve problems, and they make it very difficult to view divergent understandings of teaching, literacy, and children in a positive way.

References

Field, J. (1991). *Educators' perspectives on assessment: Tensions, contradictions and dilemmas.* Unpublished doctoral dissertation, University of Calgary/ Victoria, Canada.

Johnston, P. (1992). *Constructive evaluation of literate activity.* White Plains, NY: Longman.

Johnston, P., Afflerbach, P., & Weiss, P. (1990). *Teachers' evaluation of teaching and learning of literacy* (Technical Report). Albany, NY: State University of New York at Albany, Center for the Learning and Teaching of Literature.

Keller, E.F. (1985). *Reflections on gender and science.* New Haven, CT: Yale University Press.

Leslie, C., & Winger, P. (1990, January 8). Not as easy as A, B or C. *Newsweek,* pp. 56-58.

Paris, S., Lawton, T., Turner, J., & Roth, J. (1991). A developmental perspective on standardized achievement testing. *Educational Researcher, 20*(5), 12-20.

Smith, M.L. (1991). Put to the test: The effects of external testing on teachers. *Educational Researcher, 20*(5), 8-11.

Looking at the Ideal and the Real in Large Scale Reading Assessment: The View from Two Sides of the River

Reprinted from *The Reading Teacher* (1994), *47*, 578-580

Barbara Kapinus, Editor

Recently, there have been major changes in large scale reading assessment in response to concerns that have been repeatedly raised about the quality and effects of high stakes reading assessments. Concerns focus on problems such as assessment tasks that bear little or no resemblance to those encountered in good instruction or the world beyond the classroom; decontextualized reading passages and trivial questions; multiple choice items that allow little opportunity for students to respond according to their own interpretations or to make personal connections with reading; and activities that do not engage students as meaning makers. So newer assessments are being developed in U.S. states such as California, Arizona, Kentucky, and Maryland and in national efforts such as the National Assessment of Educational Progress to respond to these concerns and to improve assessment.

However, as assessments evolve, they are accompanied by new concerns. As teachers and school administrators begin to use the newer assessments, they discover the nature and effects of those assessments and find themselves involved in an almost continuous process of evaluation and revision. To illustrate, I will relate a story about how two groups of teachers came to know one of the new assessments.

A Different Type of Reading Assessment

At the center of the story is a statewide reading assessment, used to assess schools' performance, that contains some of the changes that reading educators have been demanding. The assessment, developed by teachers and administered to all students in Grades 3, 5, and 8, uses texts drawn unabridged and unedited from children's publications such as *Cricket*, literature anthologies, and trade books. The assessment items are all open-ended questions. Reading and writing are integrated with each other and with science and social studies, so some of the items are actually scored two or three times using different scoring guides to assess performance in each of the content areas. The science and math components contain hands-on experiments, such as exploring

the forces that affect the flight of a model plane, and the social studies component includes group simulation activities, such as deciding what to do about a community problem. One reading task asks students to choose one of three or four stories to read; the open-ended questions that follow can be answered by considering any of the stories. Tasks on the assessment are integrated and designed to include group work and hands-on components that demand considerable time to administer: 1 hour and 45 minutes a day over 5 days.

The purpose of the assessment is to provide one piece of information on school performance, along with other indicators such as attendance and parent involvement. Results are reported for schools and districts but not for individual students. Thus, the assessment carries high stakes for schools and districts but not for individuals. One teacher described students' positive reactions to the assessment:

> My students were challenged, but they generally enjoyed the testing. That's right; they enjoyed it. Actually, they enjoyed "the doing" and the working in groups and the activity and the cutting and the pasting and the getting to choose their own reading and lots of other aspects. I think they were telling us a lot about how they wish we'd teach them.

The Ideal Versus the Real

Recently, I had the opportunity to describe the assessment to a group of reading educators across the river in a nearby state. They saw the assessment as the answer to their own woes caused by state and district use of traditional multiple choice assessments. Several teachers expressed the wish that their state would move more quickly to adopt a similar assessment. Back on my side of the river, educators' response to assessment, while warm in some areas, was not unqualified enthusiasm.

Administrators and teachers who have actually worked with the assessment were asked to review it as part of a study being conducted by the National Reading Research Center. Some of these people were involved in the development or scoring of the assessment, so they were acquainted with its realities from several perspectives. Their views about the assessment, although a little surprising, pointed out the values, beliefs, and difficulties involved in trying to change and improve reading assessment. The following are some of the areas where the responses of educators on the two sides of the river varied as they viewed the ideal and real aspects of the assessments from their different perspectives.

Authenticity. The teachers on the other side of the river were impressed by the authenticity, or the degree to which assessment tasks reflected real life reading and writing situations. They applauded the content area integration that they struggle to achieve in their own classrooms and curriculum guides in order to prepare students for real life applications of content and skills. They liked the notion of group activities and peer response to writing. They were impressed that students could take extended amounts of time to read and respond to the passages on the assessments and take a piece of writing through various stages of drafting, peer response, and revision. They recognized an effort to model assessment activities on good instruction by providing contexts or settings for the activities and activating relevant prior knowledge.

On my side of the river, although teachers appreciated the authenticity of the assessment activities, some educators were concerned that the activities were too difficult, requiring sustained engagement and more effort than many students could put forth. Some complained about the length of the assessment; they wanted it to be shorter with fewer items. They saw the assessment as intruding on classroom time. Some found it bothersome to deal with the logistics of the activities for peer response, collaboration, and context setting, which required following a complex script.

Items. Teachers on the two sides of the river viewed the items differently. Teachers on the other side of the river saw the open-ended items that including writing long responses, writing short responses, completing graphic organizers, and drawing pictures as major improvements over the multiple choice and fill-in-the-blank items on the assessments they were using. Teachers on my side of the river were very concerned that writing fluency might confound reading scores: Would students who wrote slowly and meticulously be able to provide enough in their responses to demonstrate their comprehension of and responses to the texts they read? Teachers liked the idea of open-ended responses in general, and neither they nor their students were held individually responsible for scores; nevertheless, teachers felt the pressure for their schools to do well.

Reporting: Student vs. school level. Teachers on the two sides of the river also responded differently to the issue of reporting assessment results. Because the purpose of the assessment is to determine whether schools are successful, results are reported only for schools and districts as percentages of students reaching each of 5 levels of achievement. Individual student scores are calculated and used to determine school scores, but they are released only to the local districts, which can then decide whether to release them to schools. Most districts have not done so.

In fact, state guidelines caution against using scores to compare, diagnose, or place students in specific programs or groups. This is because each student receives only one part of the three different parts to the assessment. Scores on all three parts are pooled to obtain a school score, but individual student scores are not really comparable, so their use for individual diagnosis and placement is inappropriate. Teachers are encouraged to use their own classroom assessments and professional expertise to determine the progress and needs of individual students.

The teachers on the other side of the river saw this as an acknowledgment of teachers' professionalism. They were glad to see the purposes of the large scale assessment separated from those of classroom assessments, and they appreciated the increased importance of teachers' classroom observations. Teachers on my side of the river viewed the assessment as a waste of time if individual scores could not be reported and used for diagnosis. They wanted this one assessment tool to serve both accountability and diagnostic purposes. Again, differences were apparent between the teachers who saw the ideal and those who experienced the reality.

The Ideal and the Real

These differences in perceptions of teachers on the two sides of the river point out some of the difficulties when the ideals of new approaches to reading assessment are translated into realities. Two additional difficulties have arisen in developing reading assessments that reflect the authenticity and congruence with good instruction that recent literature has proposed as characteristics of good reading assessment (Jett-Simpson, 1990; Valencia, McGinley, & Pearson, 1990).

Good instruction and good assessment. Members of the general education community, as well as reading and measurement experts, have called for assessments that are almost seamlessly connected with instruction (Wiggins, 1992). Good assessment should look like good instruction by providing contexts for activities, allowing for social interaction, providing time for reflection, and engaging students' interests and motivation. However, some aspects of large-scale assessment activities differ from instruction. The need for some standardization on large-scale assessments limits the spontaneity and support that the teacher can provide. Time limits may frustrate teachers who would rather let students take whatever time is necessary, as they would in regular classroom activities.

In addition, the desire to integrate large-scale assessment with instruction can lead to poor models of instruction. For example, teachers often want to review concepts or ideas before assessing them. In one instance, eighth-grade teachers developing a large-scale assessment task wanted to be sure students could deal with questions about metaphors used in a passage, so they included a minilesson on metaphors as part of the assessment activities. But the lesson was followed immediately by the assessment—a teach-then-test model that is not supported by the instructional theory, which suggests that students need opportunities to practice applying concepts or skills before being tested on them. Thus, an effort to provide scaffolding like that provided in the classroom without the classroom opportunities for practice and learning can lead to large-scale assessment tasks that reflect poor instructional models.

Reliability. Reliability refers to the likelihood that students will receive similar scores with successive administrations and scorings of the assessment. Since the assessment is an important indicator of school performance in the state accountability program described here, less than acceptable reliability in the scores can be a serious flaw, a source of limitations and difficulties. For example, tension exists between wanting rich performance tasks and not wanting to devote the time required to have students complete enough work to yield reliable scores. Do administrators and teachers therefore discount the concern with reliability, because it is considered an old-fashioned measurement trait? Should they observe students reading in fewer situations? Or should they conclude that measuring students' proficiency in reading using fewer passages would be a less than adequate look at students' reading proficiency? Such a narrow set of reading tasks contradicts the suggestion that our measures of reading should be multifaceted and should try to encompass the varied aspects of reading.

My Perspective

Regardless of the problems, many teachers on my side of the river are convinced that the new assessment supports sound instruction. This support, however, is not without its price. Teachers have discovered that they must give up some valued instructional time for the new assessment, which can disrupt the school routine. They see that the longer, more challenging assessments require effort and abilities that they are not sure their students are ready to demonstrate. Their perceptions are important and need to be carefully considered in revising the assessment.

Not all of the responses of educators who have administered the assessment are critical. In fact, many offer words of encouragement. One principal wrote:

> We finally have a "test" that we should be "teaching to." We must focus more on the learning process to gather, organize, and interpret information rather than the memorization of content facts. And this assessment program...is a step in the right direction. Continue to emphasize futuristic needs: don't be pushed into backing up...

The enthusiastic encouragement received from colleagues inside and outside the state, as well as their constructive criticism, helps the writing team to keep working on improving the assessment and to keep reflecting on what we want students to be able to do as readers. We continue to ask questions. How can we observe and measure high-level reading performance? How can we teach students so they can demonstrate rich, thoughtful reading? How can the large-scale assessment serve all of us—students, teachers, administrators, parents, and the public? The new reading assessment is providing a rich context for ex-

ploring both our goals for students as readers and the means of reaching those goals in literacy education.

References

Jett-Simpson, M. (Ed.). (1990). *Toward an ecological assessment of reading progress.* Schofield, WI: Wisconsin State Reading Association.

Valencia, S.W., McGinley, W., & Pearson, P.D. (1990). Assessing reading and writing. In G.G. Duffy (Ed.), *Reading in the middle school* (pp. 124-153). Newark, DE: International Reading Association.

Wiggins, G. (1992). Creating tests worth taking. *Educational Leadership, 49, 26-33.*

Some Limits of Assessment

Reprinted from *The Journal of Reading* (1993), *36*, 44-48

Walter H. MacGinitie

To guide what we do in helping students learn, we assess what they already know and what they need to know. So assessment is an important part of teaching. Unfortunately, it is not a part of teaching that we are able to do particularly well. Human nature and the kinds of things we must assess set limits on the accuracy and effectiveness of school assessments.

Normal Biases in Human Judgments

Because our assessments entail human judgments, they can take into account all kinds of significant observations. The teacher has a fair idea of how hard Vicki worked on this paper. The teacher saw Ichiro strike out at recess just before taking this test. But because our assessments entail human judgments, they also suffer from human frailties. And it is not just that to err is human but that to be biased is human—to err *systematically* is human.

Human judgment, subject to both random and systematic errors, plays an obvious part in performance and portfolio assessments. But test scores, too, are subject to errors of human judgment, since a test score typically has little meaning until someone makes a judgment about it. Someone will decide that Shelby's percentile rank of 58 is encouraging, or disappointing, or neither.

There is a vast literature on the errors of judgment that people make. Although many of these studies were originally addressed to questions in person perception, reasoning, category formation, probability estimation, and other areas, they have implications for classroom judgments. A few examples can illustrate how important it is for us to be tentative in our assessments and ready to reconsider our decisions.

Assimilation and Contrast

In a typical experiment (Jones, Rock, Shaver, Goethals, & Ward, 1968), groups of adult observers watched while an unknown adult male attempted to solve a series of 30 reasoning problems. Unknown to the observers, the problem solver was actually a confederate of the experimenters, and he solved or failed to solve the problems in a prearranged sequence. The confederate always solved 15 of the problems correctly, but some groups of observers saw the confederate solve more of the earlier problems and fewer of the later problems, while other groups saw the confederate solve fewer of the earlier problems and more of the later problems.

The observers who saw the confederate solve more of the earlier problems rated him as more intelligent than the observers who saw him solve more of the later problems. Thus, the observers made their assessments of the confederate's ability early on and did not change them. They *assimilated* subsequent evidence to their earlier impression. This conclusion is reinforced by the observers' distorted recall of the number of problems the confederate solved. Although the confederate always solved 15 problems, the observers who

had seen the confederate do well at first remembered seeing him solve more problems than the observers who had seen the confederate do well later in the series. We have a general tendency to ignore later evidence and base our assessment on early evidence whenever we assume that we are observing a stable characteristic (Jones & Goethals, 1972).

And we are aware that many educational achievements are quite stable. For example, we know that a good reader or writer doesn't usually turn into a poor reader or writer next week—or even next year. But reading ability or writing ability *can* change. In addition, any student's performance in reading or writing will vary considerably from task to task and from time to time. Even a good ballplayer makes errors; even a mediocre one makes a great play occasionally. Yet many of our assessments of reading ability and writing ability are likely to be biased in favor of first impressions.

This tendency to assimilate—to make our later judgments fit our earlier ones—is just one of many tendencies that can bias our assessments. We also have a tendency to *exaggerate the difference* between early evidence and late evidence. This *contrast* effect is likely to occur when we assess a series of products that we regard as completely independent as when they are done by different students (Jones & Goethals, 1972). Thus, a piece of poor work is likely to seem worse if we see it after seeing another student's good work. And a piece of good work is likely to seem better if we see it after seeing another student's poor work.

Negativity Bias

Our human judgments are also subject to *negativity bias*, first formally demonstrated by Asch (1946). Asch asked people to form an impression of a person who was described by a list of traits. For example, to one group of people the person was described as "intelligent, skillful, industrious, warm, determined, practical, and cautious." To another group the person was described as "intelligent, skillful, industrious, cold, determined, practical, and cautious." The simple substitution of the word *cold* for *warm* created large differences in people's impressions of the person. Asch found that certain negative adjectives had disproportionate effects on the impressions that were formed.

Subsequent experiments showed that negative information is typically much more potent in swaying assessments than is positive information (Kanouse & Hanson, 1972). Clearly, we must be wary of letting occasional disappointing information distort our assessments.

Category Bias

Assimilation and negativity bias are often combined in the effects of the categories we use. Once we have put a person in *any* category—young or old, male or female, bright or slow, good reader or poor reader—the stereotypic content of the category is likely to influence our assessment (Fiske & Taylor, 1984). The occupation of a student's parent, for example, can bias our belief about the student's home environment. In one study, people saw a videotape of a woman eating dinner with her husband. People who were told that she worked as a waitress were more likely to remember seeing her drinking beer and owning a television than were people who were told she worked as a librarian. But those who were told that the woman worked as a librarian were more likely to remember her as wearing glasses and owning classical records than were the others (Cohen, 1981).

Thus, when we put someone in a category, we tend to deprive that person of some of his or her individuality. And we certainly do put children in categories: dyslexics, Chapter 1 students, free-lunch kids, underachievers, latchkey kids, LEPs, good readers, LD kids, emotionally disturbed—the list could go on and on. If you knew only that some child belonged in one of these categories—latchkey kid, for ex-

ample—wouldn't you sometimes be tempted to think that you already knew *other* things about that child?

Confirmation Bias

Clearly, once we get an idea in our heads, we tend to ignore other possibilities. One reason is that people tend not to test their beliefs. This *confirmation bias* (Evans, 1989) appears in remedial work, for example, when we decide that a student's problem has one particular cause and then fail to look for contrary evidence—for evidence of additional or different causes.

And we are even biased in assessing our assessments: We tend to be overconfident about our assessments; we overestimate how much we know and how often we are right (Evans, pp. 97-99, 103). That's not surprising: Since we infrequently test our beliefs, we seldom discover that our judgment has been wrong.

The Measurement Selection Problem and the Validity Dilemma

Assessments are also limited by the difficulty of choosing what to assess and how to assess it—*the measurement selection problem*. There is so much that we hope students will learn and there are so many ways we might attempt to assess each of those learnings.

How many significant aspects of reading ability are there, for example? Fifty? Fifty thousand? Using a matrix of strategies, rhetorical types, subject matter, semantic structures, and purposes for reading, one can easily develop a list in the thousands (MacGinitie, 1990). Which aspects should we choose to measure?

A response to this problem that is now frequently recommended is to keep many samples of a student's work in a portfolio. Some appear to claim that portfolios solve the measurement selection problem in reading assessment by measuring everything—that they can furnish "a *complete* picture of a student's literacy abilities" (Valencia, 1990, p. 340; emphasis in the original). But portfolios cannot really provide for a measure of everything; portfolios do not solve the measurement selection problem, but they do illustrate the validity dilemma.

The *validity dilemma* refers to the observation that often, as we try to increase the validity of assessments, we reduce their reliability. However, if an assessment is to be valid—if it is to measure well what it is supposed to measure—it must also be reliable, that is, it must measure *something* reasonably consistently.

Reliability is often a problem for portfolio assessments. How can impressions of the many items in a portfolio be combined? Is a rater simply to look at the entire contents and assign a total score based on whatever items are remembered until the end of the perusal? Two raters are likely to notice different items and to rate corresponding items differently, and thus to produce quite different total valuations. The resulting low reliability limits the validity of portfolio assessments made in this way.

An alternative way of assessing a portfolio is to assign a rating to each of the items and then combine the ratings systematically. But how should those ratings be combined? Are some items twice as important as others? Ten times as important? Are some items more important for some students than for other students? On what basis could answers to these questions be justified? Different sets of weights could give very different valuations to the same student's work.

A solution to this problem might be for all the teachers to use the same weights. But then only those items that had been as-

signed a weight would be included in evaluating the portfolio. Indeed, it is often advised that only a preselected, standard set of items in the portfolio be rated in judging each student's reading development: "It is important to be *selective* about what should be included in the portfolio" (Valencia, 1990, p. 339).

But when selection occurs, a portfolio can no longer even appear to provide "a *complete* picture of a student's literacy abilities." For example, a student's spontaneous explanation of how he or she worked on an assignment or interpreted a passage or solved a problem can be one of the most revealing items in a portfolio. But that kind of information would not even be considered if the assessment is based on a preselected, standard set of materials. Thus, trying to solve the validity dilemma by using a standard set of weights brings us right back to the measurement selection problem.

Another common, though unnecessary, limitation on the validity of "reading" portfolios is imposed when they include many writing samples—"pieces of writing at various stages of completion" (Valencia, 1990, p. 339). Reading and writing are closely related, of course, but they are not the same. Some students who are excellent readers are relatively poor at expressing their thoughts, and writing samples can be very misleading for assessing reading ability.

Portfolios *can* be very useful in assessment. They can relate assessment closely to instruction. They serve the particularly important function of encouraging the teacher and student to record significant observations of the student's successes, difficulties, or ways of working that might otherwise be forgotten or ignored in planning instruction. But if portfolios are to be used to arrive at a rating or score, a great deal of time and knowledge must be devoted to planning and assembling the collections and to designing and carrying out the procedures for scoring them.

The Meaning of the Assessment to the Student

We may hope to influence students with our assessments, but we cannot be sure what our assessments will mean to them. We assess a student's work according to what we, as teachers, are looking for, but the student may judge that work by different standards. Gordon (1990) studied the criteria that teachers and sixth-grade students use when rating the quality of short stories written by other students. While the study is limited by a very small sample of teachers, the results are intriguing. The students agreed fairly well among themselves on the criteria for a good story: A good story should be imaginative, exciting, and have a well developed plot. The teachers, on the other hand, had criteria that varied considerably from teacher to teacher, and some had criteria that were very different from the students' criteria.

Thus, a student may be proud of something we fail to notice, or be dissatisfied with something we find acceptable. To the student, our assessment may be perplexing, or disappointing, or, most happily, perhaps, just irrelevant. "The spectator's judgment," says William James (1962), "is sure to miss the root of the matter. ...The subject judged knows a part of the world of reality which the judging spectator fails to see" (p. 114). Our assessments cannot encompass a student's private joys and griefs, or a mind's own secrets from itself.

Reflecting on the limits of assessment, we discover that no matter how careful we are, we will be biased in many of our judgments; that we cannot hope to assess many things that are important; that our assessment procedures, however realistic we try to make them, will have limited validity; and that we can never be sure what our assessments will mean to the students who are assessed.

Since our assessments are fallible and limited, the decisions based on them should

be tentative. There are not many decisions about students that *need* to be *final.* Nearly every decision should be reconsidered periodically. A program that seemed right at one time should eventually be reevaluated. A diagnosis that once seemed correct should be reexamined. Above all, a student who didn't make it on one try should have another.

We should stop thinking of assessment as a way of making categories and start thinking of assessment as a way of making opportunities. If our assessment tells us that a student needs help with some school task, that is an opportunity for us to help and for the student to grow. If our assessment tells us that a student has reached some remarkable level, that is an opportunity for us to share the joy and for the student to explore new paths to fulfillment. To use assessment for making opportunities, we will need to change some political and administrative policies as well as our own ways of thinking. Knowing the limits of assessment can help us achieve those changes.

References

Asch, S. (1946). Forming impressions of personality. *Journal of Abnormal and Social Psychology, 41*, 258-290.

Cohen, C.E. (1981). Person categories and social perception: Testing some boundaries of the processing effects of prior knowledge. *Journal of Personality and Social Psychology, 40*, 441-452.

Evans, J. (1989). *Bias in human reasoning: Causes and consequences.* Hillsdale, NJ: Erlbaum.

Fiske, S.T., & Taylor, S.E. (1984). *Social cognition.* Reading, MA: Addison-Wesley.

Gordon, C.J. (1990). Students' and teachers' criteria for quality writing: Never the twain shall meet? *Reflections on Canadian Literacy, 8,* 74-81.

James, W. (1962). *Talks to teachers on psychology and to students on some of life's ideals.* New York: Dover. (Original work published 1899).

Jones, E.E., & Goethals, G.R. (1972). Order effects in impression formation: Attribution context and the nature of the entity. In E.E. Jones, D.E. Kanouse, H.H. Kelley, R.E. Nisbett, S. Valins, & B. Weiner (Eds.), *Attribution: Perceiving the causes of behavior* (pp. 27-46). Morristown, NJ: General Learning Press.

Jones, E.E., Rock, L., Shaver, K.G., Goethals, G.R., & Ward, L.M. (1968). Pattern of performance and ability attribution: An unexpected primacy effect. *Journal of Personality and Social Psychology, 10,* 317-340.

Kanouse, D.E., & Hanson, L.R., Jr. (1972). Negativity in evaluations. In E.E. Jones, D.E. Kanouse, H.H. Kelley, R.E. Nisbett, S. Valins, & B. Weiner (Eds.), *Attribution: Perceiving the causes of behavior* (pp. 47-62). Morristown, NJ: General Learning Press.

MacGinitie, W.H. (1990, March). *What's the score in reading assessment?* Paper presented at the Texas Testing Conference, Austin, TX.

Valencia, S. (1990). A portfolio approach to classroom reading assessment: The whys, whats, and hows. *The Reading Teacher, 43,* 338-340.

A Study of the Differences Between Instructional Practice and Test Preparation

Reprinted from *The Journal of Reading* (1993), *36*, 524-530

Sheila McAuliffe

Recently I had opportunity to watch at length a skilled teacher help at-risk teenagers work well on developing authentic literacy processes. Part way through the year, the students were to take a standardized reading test mandated by the state. Their teacher helped them prepare for the test by working with a similar practice test. The discrepancy between the authentic instruction they had been enjoying and the rigid demands of the reading test were a shock to all involved. It became clear that authentic reading instruction deserves authentic reading assessment.

This ethnographic research study involved an eighth-grade class of 15 readers considered to be at risk. They had been placed together because scores, grades, and teacher recommendations indicated that they were the least able readers at their grade level in that school. This article will compare weekly samples of the students' reading and discussion processes to later samples of their assessment practice sessions, which preceded administration of the state-mandated reading test.

For 25 Friday sessions—the better part of the school year—I joined this class as a participant observer. In the beginning, in September, I described my goal as wanting to learn what helped them most in reading to understand and in reading to learn. I explained that my job was to teach teachers, and that I would be sharing what I learned with teachers.

The original questions for this study were derived from the work of Bruner (1986), Rosenblatt (1985), Vygotsky (1978), and Wertsch (1985a, l985b). These theoretical conceptions of reading gave rise to the social and procedural focus of the following initial questions of this study:

1. How is the teaching-learning situation planned and prepared for?
2. How is it organized and how does it operate?
3. What are the roles of texts?
4. What does the teacher believe about how students learn language and how they use language to learn?
5. Is background knowledge assessed and are the findings used?
6. For what purposes is language used in the classroom? (Read to ... Write to ... Discuss to ... Listen to ...)
7. What is the nature of interaction between and among students?
8. What is the nature of comprehension (literal, inferential, evaluative, appreciative)?
9. What do students see as useful in helping them to read to understand?
10. How is learning being evaluated?

What Helps Students Read and Understand

After introducing myself and answering student questions about my role as a participant observer, I asked the eighth graders what helped them to read and understand best. They were given the opportunity to respond orally and in writing.

Students gave these examples of what helped them to understand as they read: "When you're reading out loud," "When you take notes," "When I find something interesting," and "When we talk about things in class, yeh, class discussion, ya get all the brain concentration." There was a consensus that class discussion was most helpful, so students were asked whether they liked to discuss before, during, or after they read. They agreed that they liked to "discuss in between reading parts," so they could ask questions about what they had read so far and then finish it up.

When students were asked if they could tell how teachers helped them, they again agreed that teachers who "went over things in the middle of the reading" helped them the most. In contrast, when asked what kept them from understanding what they read, they stated: "When the teacher doesn't listen to you," "When if you ask too many questions at once the teacher will get mad," "When the teacher just gives you a reading assignment and you don't talk it over," and "When the teacher talks too much in class and we always have to read silently at home."

Instructional Planning Incorporates Student Interest and Background Knowledge

Whether the information gained in this first session altered what the classroom teacher did as she planned throughout the year cannot be determined, but the observed reading instruction reflected what she had learned from her students. Early in September she confided that she had "only a notion of these students' needs and where they might be capable of going." She saw the coming year as a journey. As she got to know these students, she said, she expected the curriculum to unfold.

During the first 2 months the teacher chose selections from the Scott, Foresman reading basal *Moon Canyon* (1985), and several issues of *Read Magazine* that fit her students' interests, background knowledge, and abilities. The general pattern the teacher followed for most lessons was to informally assess and share background knowledge before reading, set purposes, and stop the class at intervals in the text to discuss what had been read.

In November the teacher selected a longer piece for the class to read and discuss. Because these students seemed to identify with having to struggle as learners and had some problems with self concept as learners, the teacher chose Daniel Keyes's *Flowers for Algernon* (Bantam, 1970), the insightful diary of a man of low intelligence who had participated in a medical experiment that attempted to increase his mental ability. Segments were read aloud by the teacher or read silently by the students and discussed. The students were obviously interested and involved as they predicted, inferred, questioned, and enjoyed this text.

Interpersonal Negotiation Encourages Rich Meaning Construction

The following dialogue segments of the December 8 class session illustrate the kinds of reading and discussing that emerged during the work with *Flowers for Algernon* and eventually became routine during the following months when thematically linked, high interest texts were shared. This example, taken from near the middle of the lesson, shows how the students were able to recall or locate pertinent background information from the previous day's reading and discussion, to reflect

upon it with the teacher's guidance, and to make predictions as to what might happen next before they returned to reading.

T: We have been reading something. Can someone tell me what we have read?
S1: We've been reading about Charlie Gordon. He took a potion or had an operation or something to make him smart.
T: Was it a potion?
S2: No, it was an operation.
S1: He has had surgery on his brain to make him smart. He had convulsions, sort of.
T: Yesterday, tell me what we read.
S3: He won a race against Algernon. He beat him eight times.
S4: Charlie Gordon is not feeling smarter.
T: Good specific detail. Is he feeling smarter yet?
S4: Well yeh, a little bit, with spelling.
S5: He is getting smarter but not feeling it.
T: A good clarification. He is getting smarter but not feeling smarter. Sometimes you're reading better, but you do not feel that you are reading well yet. What do you think might happen?
S6: He will get smarter.
S4: He's not going to get smarter on the operation but on his own.
S7: The operation might be permanent. ...
T: Yes. Now how does he feel about Algernon?
S8: Jealous.
S12: He kind of likes Algernon.
T: Why?
S5: Why he likes him?
T: Yes.
S5: Because he's a mouse. Because he's had the operation like Charlie.
T: He feels a relationship with Algernon.
S13: He beat him in the race.
S2: A doctor let him hold the mouse and pet him.
T: Does he race Algernon any more?
S8: No.
T: Why?
S10: Because he beat him all the time.
S1: Also because of the cheese. He didn't want to beat him so he wouldn't get his cheese.
T: Yes, that was in reference to their changing the maze.

Reading and Discussion Promote Reflection, Prediction, Inferencing

During the reading of the next two sections of *Flowers for Algernon*, in which Charlie was informed that his IQ was expected to triple from its original measure of 68, students asked what a normal IQ was. The teacher explained and diagramed the IQ scale on the chalkboard. After reading these sections, students reflected on Charlie's reporting of incidents that had taken place with former friends and acquaintances and concluded that his new intelligence had allowed him to feel shame and understand that people had been laughing at him. The students also went beyond the text to speculate on reasons why a person might fear a previously mentally disabled person who had become more intelligent.

Before the class read the subsequent entry in which Charlie was to take another Rorschach Test, the teacher asked if the students could remember what Rorschach Tests were. They were able to find the illustration of a Rorschach ink blot in the diary. The teacher also asked, "Do you think he'll find anything in the blots this time?" There was a mixed chorus of *yeses* and *nos*. When asked why some thought he would find something, they answered, "Because he knows what teasing is" and "Because he is getting smarter."

After reading the entry the teacher guided students' comprehension by asking them to relate what they knew from previous reading and discussion about the relationship between imagination and intelligence. In doing so she made a positive reference to the abilities of the class members.

T: Remember what we said about imagination and low intelligence?
S1: Ink blots aren't really anything.

T:	What is it that people who have higher intelligence have that you all have?
Ss:	Imagination [a chorus of answers]

Readers Share Their Idiosyncratic Comprehending Processes

Lastly in this read and discuss segment, the teacher asked the students to find and read aloud the words in the text that supported their responses to whether Charlie had been misled by the psychologist. Several students thought he had been misled until one student located the following conversation between the psychologist and Charlie. The student read the following passage in support of Charlie's not having been misled:

> "People see all sorts of things in these inkblots. Tell me what it might be for you—what it makes you think of."
>
> I was shocked. That wasn't what I had expected him to say at all. "You mean there are not pictures in those ink blots?"
>
> He frowned and took off his glasses. "What?"
>
> "Pictures. Hidden in the inkblots. Last time you told me that everyone could see them and you wanted me to find them too."
>
> He explained that the last time he had used almost the exact same words he was using now. I didn't believe it, and I still have the suspicion that he misled me at the time just for the fun of it. Unless I don't know any more—could I have been that feeble minded?

As students responded following this passage, it became clear that some still doubted the psychologist's good intentions because he had asked Charlie "not to read up on psychology yet." Although cases were subsequently made for the interpretations that "Charlie might not be quite ready to understand such a complex subject" and that "the doctor might not want Charlie to know about the experiment in which he was involved,"one student still believed that "the doctor didn't want Charlie to read up on psychology because he didn't want him to know that they were misleading him about the ink blots."

This beautiful illustration of students using their idiosyncratic processes to develop possible and probable meanings was closed by the teacher's simple and gentle guiding statement: "Maybe they weren't misleading him. Maybe his intelligence only let him understand what he did at the time."

Engaging Students by Developing High-Interest Themes

After the positive experience with *Flowers for Algernon*, curricular decisions continued to be influenced by responses and interests of the students. Several students in the class had been heard informally discussing community events that appeared to involve racial and ethnic prejudice. Using their concern and interest in this topic and their growing awareness of the prejudices that often challenged the less able, like Charlie in *Flowers for Algernon*, the teacher selected more readings on the topic of prejudice.

The thematic relatedness of the works that they studied encouraged integration and intertextual linking. The works below were chosen to explore and develop themes which seemed to fit the interests and needs of the students in this class: (a) *Reunion* (F. Uhlman, Farrar, Straus & Giroux. 1971)—a story of prejudice and friendship in a boarding school before World War II presented as a flashback to postwar results of persecution; (b) their social studies textbook, *Spirit of Liberty and American History* (Addison-Wesley, 1987), as a reference to causes and events of World War II and Hitler's rise to power; (c) an excerpt from *The Diary of a Young Girl* (Anne

Frank, Random House. 1978) focusing on the personal hardships that resulted from prejudice and persecution; (d) *The Call of the Wild* (Jack London, Puffin, 1983), with themes of social hierarchy and friendship during the struggle for survival; and (e) *The Wave* (Morton Rhue, Dell, 1981) which meshed themes of friendship, survival, importance of self concept, vulnerability to prejudice, and elitism.

During class discussions of these works, as in the above Algernon example, inferential and literal questions followed one another naturally as the teacher engaged the students in making predictions and or responding to text. She listened carefully as they represented their thinking; she used textual information and the responses of other students to guide their negotiation of meaning. The teacher's purposes seemed to be to help them construct rich meanings and to encourage them to reflect upon how they were making sense of the pieces. Inferential, literal, and evaluative questions were woven together to discover what the students were thinking and guide them to focus on pertinent information which they might overlook. During the transaction the teacher provided essential background information (such as the IQ information in the Algernon discussion) which student responses indicated they did not know or were not recalling.

This read and discuss routine seemed to have become comfortable for the students by February, just before the practice for the Illinois Reading Assessment was to begin. Reviewing video tapes and field notes of class sessions confirmed that most students were consistently involved in the reading and discussing. All students showed signs of being increasingly able to actively engage in this process.

Practicing for the Test: Prediction Takes on a New Meaning

On March 3 the productive routine described above was altered as one of five practice assessments was introduced. "Caged, the Last Wild Condor," from the Mock Assessment Instrument for Reading developed by the Lake County Educational Center in 1988, was used with this class.

As students discussed their answers to the Topic Familiarity questions, they soon realized that the prediction process in this assessment setting differed from the kind of predicting and sharing of background to which they had grown accustomed in the instructional setting. Early in this discussion, students tried to support their answer choices by describing the reasoning involved in their prediction making, much as they had done during instruction.

One boy argued that a prediction statement considered acceptable by testmakers was too general. He also shared his insight that different persons might have different, defensible responses and predictions depending on their previous life experiences. However, the nature of student reactions soon deteriorated into a melodrama of unthinking cheers and boos that greeted the news that statements were or were not acceptable. Several students became upset when their choices were found to be unacceptable to testmakers. Instead of volunteering support for their choices, they were heard to murmur such statements as "I hate these questions" and "I can't stand them."

Several operational elements of this practice assessment session had changed from what students had come to expect in the instructional sessions. The role of the text had been diminished to dispenser of information. The testmakers were now the authority on appropriate predictions. Instead of actively making their own hypotheses on what the passage would be about, students were asked to choose the best predictions from the testmakers' list.

The format did not encourage discussion of student responses that differed from those of the testmakers. No matter what was said, the practice test format deemed that the testmaker would be right in the

end. In rationalizing the acceptability of the testmakers' answers and citing the expertise of the "good readers," the teacher who had consistently focused on student understanding during instruction was trapped into seeming to see the students as less than able readers.

An Exercise in Supporting Someone Else's Understanding of Text

On another Friday in March the class was to focus on the Constructing Meaning section of the Mock Assessment Instrument for Reading, "Worldgame." The teacher wanted to involve students in finding textual support for the multiple choice answers, but the students reacted with an unusual degree of negativity.

For the first 15 minutes the teacher tried to engage the students. When the "Worldgame" booklets were distributed a student commented, "Oh no, not that again." When the teacher asked why they might be pulling it out again the replies were "Because we did poorly?" and "For practice for the real one." Then four students chorused their frustration. The statements "I'm confused," "I'm busted," and "I'm sunk" rapidly succeeded one another.

The teacher asked what they thought the problem was. They said they had not read it well because it was confusing. She suggested they review the questions to see if they could find textual support for their answers which were marked correct, as well as textual support for the answers they needed to correct.

The teacher's directions stated "Go through and find (for questions 14, 15, and 16) where you found the answer or information that told you ideas for the answer. Find where in the story you got the answer. Write in pencil, actually on the test. Write 14, for example, on the place or places in the test where you find the information that fits with question 14." Within 10 minutes, five students had asked if they were really supposed to write on the test itself.

These students who had been accustomed to actively negotiating their own meaning from texts during their regular instruction were now being asked to find support for questions and multiple choice answers that represented the skeleton of someone else's understanding of text. Is it any wonder that they had difficulty engaging or believing that they were being asked to violate the text of the test by marking on it? They had already learned that their own idiosyncratic processes for making sense of text were not welcome in this format.

The test practice situation lacked several supports that had helped these at-risk students to perform with increasing proficiency as they had read and discussed sophisticated texts in regular class sessions. The test texts had not been chosen to fit this group's interests; nor had time been spent sharing and building background knowledge for the pieces. Even though several studies have indicated the importance interest and background can play in comprehension (Asher, 1980: Baldwin, Peleg-Bruckner, & McClintock, 1985), especially in the case of reluctant readers (Asher, Hymel, & Wigfield, 1978; Belloni & Jongsma, 1978), this support was not part of the practice assessment format. Intertextual linking of thematically linked texts, another factor known to enhance comprehension (Crafton, 1983), had supported their instructional reading but was not part of this process.

By the end of this practice in finding support for the testmakers' multiple choice answers, the students understood that the test questions did not fit together in any logical way. Their teacher had praised them for trying to find sequential or otherwise meaningful patterns to the questions, but she had had to explain that in this practice test the questions came in no pattern or order. The more authentic literacy systems they had been developing as they read and discussed in class were again violated.

Practice Questions Call for Lower Level Comprehension and Less Integration of Ideas

During the Algernon instructional segment earlier on December 8, which reflected the literacy routines of this classroom, 20 questions were asked and answered. An analysis of the comprehension level of these questions found that 14 were inferential, 2 were applied, and 4 were literal.

More important than the percentage of higher order questions was the meaningful interweaving of the different types of questions during the informal discussion of text. Inferential, applied, and literal questions flowed together naturally as students and teacher actively tried to make sense of text by negotiating meaning.

The questions from the Constructing Meaning section of the "Worldgame" practice test were also analyzed using the same criteria as had been used with the Algernon discussion questions. This analysis indicated it was necessary to choose 10 factual multiple choice responses and make 21 inferences to answer the testmakers' questions correctly. No application questions appeared in the "Worldgame" practice assessment.

Thus the percentage of higher level comprehension questions (inferential and applied) was greater in the instructional setting (80%) than in the practice assessment session (68%). More important, the test format had actually blocked their attempts to integrate pieces of information into meaningful patterns.

Conclusions

This comparison of instructional reading to practice assessment reading indicated that students were actively involved in more authentic literacy processes as they negotiated meaning in the supportive instructional context. They became a community of learners in the instructional setting. They took risks and used their idiosyncratic processes, as they attempted to make sense of the text and relate it to their lives. Students explored the text's messages in the light of their own responses and the responses of others. They related the text being read to other texts.

In contrast, during assessment practice they did not seem to be trying to figure out text but seemed to be trying to choose the "right" answer. Practicing for the Illinois Reading Assessment appeared to move students away from the empowered stances they were developing during instruction. The practice test format asked them to read to find support for someone else's understanding of the piece. Worse yet, the question format did not present the testmakers' understanding of the piece in a meaningful, connected way.

Aside from the issue of time lost to assessment practice from more authentic reading instruction is the question of the value of the information resulting from standardized tests. Since study outcomes indicate dissimilarity between the reading process that occurs during theory-based instruction and that which occurs during the practice assessment and, one would assume, during the actual assessment on which the practice assessment is patterned, test results can not be expected to reflect what is possible in the instructional setting.

Results of this comparative study support the need for further work in building a more useful and authentic assessment model. Such a model might involve trained educators in qualitative assessments of reading instruction. Videotapes of representative instructional sessions could be reviewed to assess the frequency and quality of student transaction with texts. Questions like the ones that guided this study would be useful in developing guidelines for such an assessment model.

Continued progress toward an authentic model for reading assessment is necessary to support more transactive reading instruction that reflects the way students will want and need to read in the real world.

References

Asher, S.R. (1980). Topic interest and children's reading comprehension. In R.J. Spiro, B.C. Bruce, & W.F. Brewer (Eds.), *Theoretical issues in reading comprehension* (pp. 525-534). Hillsdale, NJ: Erlbaum.

Asher, S.R., Hymel. S., & Wigfield. A. (1978) Influence of topic interest on children's reading comprehension. *Journal of Reading Behavior*, 10, 35-47.

Baldwin, R.S., Peleg-Bruckner, Z., & McClintock, A. (1985). Effects of topic interest on children's reading comprehension. *Reading Research Quarterly*, 20, 407-504.

Belloni, L.F., & Jongsma, E.A. (1978) The effects of interest on reading comprehension of low achieving students. *Journal of Reading*, 22, 106-109.

Bruner, J. (1986). *Actual minds, possible worlds*. Cambridge, MA: Harvard University Press.

Crafton, L.K. (1983). Learning from reading: What happens when students generate their own background information? *Journal of Reading*, 26, 586-592.

Rosenblatt, L.M. (1985). The transactional theory of the literary work: Implications for research. In C.R. Cooper (Ed.), *Researching response to literature and the teaching of literature* (pp. 33-53). Norwood, NJ: Ablex.

Vygotsky, L. (1978). *Mind in society*. Cambridge, MA: Harvard University Press.

Wertsch, J. (Ed.). (1985a). *Culture, communication, and cognition*. London, England: Cambridge University Press.

Wertsch, J. (Ed.) (1985b). *Vygotsky and the social formation of mind*. Cambridge, MA: Harvard University Press.

A Guide to Books on Portfolios: Rafting the Rivers of Assessment

Reprinted from The Reading Teacher (1994), 48, 180-183

Harry Noden
Barbara Moss

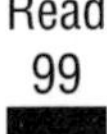

Traveling through the world of reading/writing portfolios is like rafting on a remote tributary of the Amazon River. Both journeys create anxieties for the inexperienced. Fortunately, for those who have yet to make this journey and those already navigating the river rapids, several exciting guides have been published in the last 3 years. Targeting different audiences, these guides address the following categories of travelers' requests: (a) Take me to a rowboat and show me what an oar looks like; (b) Teach me to pilot a river boat; and (c) Let me hear those old weathered captains share tales of adventure.

In the first category are three excellent books for teachers just starting with portfolios and in need of an oar: *Writing Portfolios: A Bridge from Teaching to Assessment* by Sandra Murphy and Mary Ann Smith (1991), *Portfolio Assessment: Getting Started* by Allan A. DeFina (1992), and *Portfolio Assessment and Evaluation* by Janine Batzle (1992). All three books outline portfolio basics in fewer that 125 pages. All take the reader step by step from the rationale for portfolio assessment to the in-class problems of practical portfolio management. Each of these three portfolio books, however, has different strengths.

Writing Portfolios: A Bridge from Teaching to Assessment by Sandra Murphy and Mary Ann Smith.

The Murphy and Smith book resembles a cross between a scholarly lecture and a prime time comedy show. Its strength lies in the authors' ability to combine essential information with a vibrant, entertaining writing style. The voice of this work resonates from each page with comments like these:

On the logistics of portfolio management: "Portfolios do not have to be shipped via freight cars or moving vans to central locations to languish in warehouses. Nor does a school need to convert the baseball field into a holding tank for portfolios. Portfolios belong in the classroom where they'll do some good" (p. 85).

On the nature of testing: "Karen's teacher has reason to be sympathetic. When she was in school, all tests came on Fridays. All reckoning happened on Friday. On that day, students went to school to fill in and match and check. They were steeped in the paraphernalia and rituals of tests: number two pencils, answer keys, bell curves, points, make-ups, posted results. Once in a while they wrote essay exams. These were shot-gun affairs, timed precisely to the number of minutes in the class period, the topic sprung on the students at the last minute as their pens and pencils hovered over blank paper. Always on Fridays. Always returned with the grammar corrected and the grade in place" (p. 10).

Writing Portfolios is a book to relax with on a weekend, a book that lures rather than lectures. It's a teacher-to-teacher text with numerous examples of student portfolio entries and a number of insightful guidelines. The chapter on reflection provides one of the best published explanations of this often overlooked component of the portfolio process. Students learn by reflecting on both product and process. While many books touch theoretically on this concept, Murphy and Smith give concrete classroom examples of reflection strategies in action. They also caution against reflection as another form of "drill and kill," and present detailed explanations of ideas such as the "portfolio audit" and the use of "reflective letters" to enhance the metacognitive process. Presented through the eyes of two secondary English teachers, *Writing Portfolios* is not only a useful guide, but a good read.

Portfolio Assessment: Getting Started by Allan A. DeFina.

In 66 pages DeFina provides an easy-to-read, quick introduction to the basics of portfolio assessment. He begins with a chapter on"Understanding Portfolio Assessment," which presents essential perspectives for implementing portfolios. DeFina points out the importance of involving students in evaluating their own work, and describes how portfolios can be effectively divided into several compartments: "one section for works in progress, another for notes and comments about the collected works, and one to showcase the best works" (p. 16).

Each chapter in DeFina's book attempts to present a brief but definitive capsulization of a key concept. "Getting Started," for example, provides an excellent catalog of the specific types of writing that might go in a portfolio, such as essays, letters, poems, problem/solution papers, response logs, journal entries, interviews, art work, collaborative works, peer reviews, and teacher checklists. The chapter on "Dealing with Possible Portfolio Problems" troubleshoots problems teachers experience when administering portfolios.

The appendix, an essential part of this book, contains 15 ready-to-use checklists—forms such as the "Student Attitude Survey About Reading," the "Student Reading Record," the "Student Self-Reflection Activity Sheet," the "Student-Teacher Conferencing Checklist," and the "Metacognitive Strategies Checklist." For teachers who like to organize with checklists, DeFina offers many useful models, especially for assessing reading. At the conclusion of the book, DeFina adds a well-chosen bibliography for future reading.

Portfolio Assessment and Evaluation by Janine Batzle.

While the Murphy/Smith and the DeFina texts could be used by teachers at any grade level, *Portfolio Assessment and Evaluation* by Janine Batzle targets the K-6 classroom. Its large print format and numerous illustrations help teachers visualize the types of papers, record keeping, and metacognitive evaluation that characterize portfolios in the elementary classroom.

Batzle's book emphasizes "how to," focusing on the day-to-day tasks of managing a portfolio classroom. Her book is designed for the teacher who has already decided to use portfolios but seeks "hands-on materials" to get started. Consequently, both the internal text and the concluding bibliogra-

phy contain limited scholarly references. However, Batzle's lack of references does not indicate a lack of scholarship. Her knowledge of theory is subtly apparent in the comprehensive coverage of critical concepts, which includes samples of everything from a reader response journal to an emergent reader inventory.

One of Batzle's more powerful chapters, "Portfolio Assessment and a Balanced Literacy Program," emphasizes the importance of the classroom environment to a portfolio approach. In this chapter, Batzle provides activities across the curriculum, presents key explanations of concepts such as the Writing Center, the Creation Station, and the Author's Chair, and illustrates several classroom floor plans to help beginning portfolio users [to] get started. For the teacher who wants to begin portfolio assessment with a minimum of anxiety, Batzle's book contains all the essentials.

For those teachers who seek a more comprehensive look at portfolios, two books provide the deluxe river boat training: *Portfolio Assessment in the Reading-Writing Classroom* by Robert Tierney, Mark Carter, and Laura Desai (1991), and *Portfolios and Beyond: Collaborative Assessment in Reading and Writing* by Susan Glazer and Carol Brown (1993). Both works contain complete step-by-step explanations of the entire portfolio process with many examples of alternative possibilities. Both contain excellent checklists and guidelines to help teachers immediately implement portfolio assessment. However, each has a slightly different focus.

Portfolio Assessment in the Reading-Writing Classroom by Robert Tierney, Mark Carter, and Laura Desai.

The work by Tierney, Carter, and Desai derives its richness from practical suggestions of K-12 teachers experimenting with portfolios. In their work with four Ohio school systems—Columbus, Westerville, Upper Arlington, and Bay Village—the authors tested, revised, and honed the strategies they advocate. Consequently, their suggestions communicate a voice of experience. For example, teachers interested in encouraging metacognition with their students would find the following list of reflective questions a good model:

> A Single Piece of Writing
>
> Why did you select this piece of writing?
>
> What do you see as the strengths?
>
> What was especially important to you when you were writing this piece?
>
> What things did you wrestle with?
>
> If you could work on this further, what would you do?
>
> What were some of the reactions you received?
>
> How is this the same or different from your other pieces? (p. 115)

Divided into three sections, the Tierney, Carter, and Desai book explores concepts of (1) assessment in the classroom, (2) using portfolios, and (3) portfolios in context. The opening chapter teases the reader's curiosity with a transcription of a roundtable discussion reminiscent of a somewhat scholarly faculty lunch discussion. The discussion entices the reader by addressing many of the questions teachers ask when first experimenting with portfolio assessment, such as "How does a teacher manage time with portfolio assessment?" "What are the options for portfolio designs?" and "How do teachers grade portfolios?"

The heart of the book elaborates and clarifies the answers to these and many other critical portfolio concerns. Chapters touch on an array of issues ranging from "standardized testing versus portfolio evaluation" to "teacher versus student ownership." In 195 pages, the authors systematically and thoroughly explore each aspect of portfolio rationale and implementation, showing readers numerous options

for developing effective programs. One of the few comprehensive treatments of portfolio assessment, *Portfolio Assessment in the Reading-Writing Classroom* is a "must read" for teachers planning to make portfolios an integral part of their language arts classroom.

Portfolios and Beyond: Collaborative Assessment in Reading and Writing by Susan Glazer and Carol Brown.

Much like the Tierney, Carter, and Desai text, *Portfolios and Beyond* by Susan Glazer and Carol Brown includes a detailed guide to organizing and developing classroom portfolios. *Portfolios and Beyond,* however, emphasizes a slightly different set of concepts. First, some excellent insights into classroom environments are presented in a chapter by Lyndon W. Searfoss. Depending on the environment, the character of portfolios can range from an interactive assessment guide for instruction to simply a folder of student writing samples. Searfoss notes that just as language learning theory has changed,

> the classroom environments in which children learn, assess, and are assessed must also change. The surroundings in which children learn must be environments where they are assessed. Classrooms must be the contexts in which the process of students' language growth is observed and assessed with the products displayed and shared. (p. 11)

Furthermore, Chapter 5 entitled "Assessing Comprehension Processes" presents unique insights into using think-alouds, an area given only a cursory examination in other portfolio texts. Glazer and Brown demonstrate the diversity of the application of think-alouds by showing student examples from first grade, fourth grade, and seventh grade. Similarly, they explain how to transform teacher comments on think-alouds into narrative progress reports.

Chapter 6, "Assessing Comprehension Products," distinguishes the postreading activity of retelling from during-reading activity of think-alouds. Glazer and Brown explain how both work as complementary tools for assessing comprehension processes and products. Nearly one third of the 163 pages of content deal with these two concepts. Although this may appear to be an uneven emphasis on reading, Chapter 4 on "Assessing Writing" balances the work's perspectives. Consequently, teachers will find this work a useful guide to both reading and writing portfolio assessment.

For teachers who have already navigated the rivers of portfolio assessment described in the previous books, two additional titles—*Portfolios: Process and Product* and *Portfolio Portraits*—offer another journey: They invite readers to reflect with the experts. Like river travelers home from an adventure, the teachers and scholars included in these edited collections share fascinating observations of life along the portfolio tributaries.

Portfolios: Process and Product edited by Pat Belanoff and Marcia Dickson.

Belanoff and Dickson describe their edited collection as "practitioner lore," a depiction of how various academic communities have approached portfolio assessment. If Peter Elbow and Pal Belanoff's work on the first large-scale writing-portfolio proficiency project in the country interests you, you can gain insights here. If you wonder how Christopher Newport College met the state of Virginia's mandated criteria for writing competence using portfolios, this work contains the details. If you want to learn how Jeffrey Sommers distinguishes between the "artist's portfolio" and the "holistic portfolio," this collection includes that and much more.

This is not a book for the novice or first-time portfolio traveler. It's a work for experienced professionals, curious about innovations, experiments, and designs. Articles range from topics such as "The Development in British Schools of Assessment by Portfolio" to "A Portfolio Approach to Teaching a Biology-Linked Basic Writing Course." To help the reader understand the relationship of these ostensibly diverse selections, Belanoff and Dickson have organized their book into four sections: (1) Portfolios for Proficiency Testing, (2) Program Assessment, (3) Classroom Portfolios, and (4) Political Issues. As with all edited collections, each article in the collection stands alone; however, viewed collectively, the articles in *Portfolios: Process and Product* reflect the philosophy of scholars such as Emig, Britton, Murray, and Elbow, all of whose work has spearheaded the whole language movement.

Portfolio Portraits edited by Donald H. Graves and Bonnie S. Sunstein.

Portfolio Portraits showcases diversity. Graves and Sunstein take us everywhere from first-grade classrooms to university seminars. Ideal for exploring the options of portfolio applications. *Portfolio Portraits* takes an inside look at teachers who approach portfolios with different purposes and designs. As the authors explain, "*Portfolio Portraits* does not attempt to offer definitive answers...[but instead, offers] glimpses into portfolios through the eyes and words of real portfolio keepers in schools" (p. xi). Graves and Sunstein do not argue for a specific portfolio approach, but simply open classroom doors, allowing the reader to look in on teachers using portfolios. Representing teachers at Grades 1, 5, 8, college, and graduate school, Graves and Sunstein invite the reader to view the spectrum of portfolio problems and solutions.

Notably, the authors include a number of key studies, many previously published in article form. For example, Linda Rief's article "Eighth Grade: Fining the Value of Evaluation," which originally appeared in *Educational Leadership* in 1990, has been a frequently cited source for scholars analyzing the rationale for portfolio assessment.

Similarly, Jay Simmons's article "Portfolios for Large Scale Assessment" elaborates on research he first described in an article in *Language Arts* in 1990. In this update, Simmons shares some extremely significant research. Contrary to the timed-test design of most district-wide writing assessments, Simmons demonstrates that self-selected samples of students' best works provide more accurate estimates of student writing achievement. Also, he contrasts the frequency of modes of discourse (narrative, description, exposition, argumentation, poetry) used in writing tests to the modes of discourse used when students choose their own topics. With the national shift toward using writing tests for large scale assessment, the implications of Simmons's research should compel evaluators to re-examine several common practices.

So, for novices entering the portfolio waters without a life jacket or experienced practitioners with river algae strewn in their hair from riding the rapids, a recent publication awaits those ready at the helm.

Books Cited

Batzle, J. (1992). *Portfolio assessment and evaluation.* Cypress, CA: Creative Teaching. 125 pp. [No ISBN]

Belanoff, P., & Dickson, M. (Eds.). (1991). *Portfolios: Process and product.* Portsmouth. NH: Heinemann. 315 pp. ISBN 0-86709-275-0.

DeFina, A.A. (1992). *Portfolio assessment: Getting started.* New York: Scholastic. 88 pp. ISBN 0-590-49183.

Glazer, S.M., & Brown, C.S. (1993). *Portfolios and beyond: Collaborative assessment in reading and writing.* Norwood, MA: Christopher-Gordon. 172 pp. ISBN 0-926842-25-0.

Graves, D.H., & Sunstein, B.S. (Eds.), (1992). *Portfolio portraits.* Portsmouth, NH: Heinemann. 202 pp. ISBN 0-435-08727-4.

Murphy, S., & Smith, M.A. (1991). *Writing portfolios: A bridge from teaching to assessment.* Markham, ON: Pippin. 96 pp. ISBN 0-88751-044-2.

Tierney, R.J., Carter, M.A., & Desai, L.E. (1991). *Portfolio assessment in the reading-writing classroom.* Norwood, MA: Christopher-Gordon. 200 pp. ISBN 0-926842-08-0.

Learning to Listen

Reprinted from *The Reading Teacher* (1993), *46,* 606-608

Elizabeth A. Nolan
Martha Berry

For 8 years Mardy (Martha) had been making significant changes in her language arts program and had moved from basal instruction to a program based on students' selection of literature from a well-stocked library. Her fourth graders wrote to her in dialogue journals, participated in large and small literature response groups, independently kept track of what they read, and conferred with her. She surveyed parents in the beginning and end of the school year, asking them how they understood their children as readers and writers and what they would like to see happen as their children made their way to June. She had come to see that the less she got in the way of her students, the more they seemed to achieve what she had hoped they would: a thirst for reading, the ability to select literature of merit independently, and the desire to talk about what they read. Mardy knew the children were progressing in lasting ways, but she kept hearing the same questions and concerns from parents, colleagues, and supervisors like:

- I'd like to try that in my classroom, but I have so much curriculum to cover.
- How can I know if they under stand the books they read if I haven't read them?
- How do I know my child is learning from this?
- This is great, but test scores count and the kids need to know how to take them.

She felt these concerns needed to be taken seriously and wanted a collaborator to help address them. She asked if I, Elizabeth, as the reading teacher, would be interested in joining her in her research project. I was delighted as I had known her students since they had started second grade and was familiar with their classroom work, experiences, and families.

We began by scheduling biweekly meetings during which we talked about what we were observing and various theories of language arts instruction. For our part, we resented how the district's standardized tests intruded on class time, created an atmosphere of anxiety, and failed to reflect the complexity of the literate learning, the quality and presentation of text, or the conditions of collaboration and discussion that are valued in Mardy's classroom. Now that literate learning in Mardy's classroom had become more complex, how could children's progress be communicated to parents familiar only with tests, book reports, and work sheets? How could Mardy satisfy the accountability concerns of administrators who might not share her perspective? How could she establish that the standardized test was not the only, or even the best, indicator of growth? What kinds of data would provide the motive and direction for revising teaching practice? What kind of assessment would help children deepen their understanding of their literacy? In other words, we wanted the assessment to be a form of curriculum inquiry for all of the stakeholders.

We began by planning surveys of the parents and interviews with the children. In September the parents were invited to complete a questionnaire asking them to describe their child as a reader and to tell us what growth in literate learning they hoped to see. At the end of the year, we would ask them to reflect on their child's

progress and to describe him or her as a reader and writer once more. The students were to be interviewed every 8 school weeks on topics ranging from the reading and writing processes to their classroom experiences. We wanted to learn about the students' understandings of reading and writing and of their own literate development.

After two of the student interview sessions, we had the sense that some students were hesitant to speak freely whereas others reveled in this one-on-one encounter and had plenty to say. We felt that conversations among peers might open more options for students to talk comfortably about literate matters. Thus, to supplement the interviews and to open a window on more complex literate learning in the classroom, we scheduled whole-class literate conversations in which every student had an opportunity to participate. In addition, to ensure the thoughtfulness of these discussions, we told the students what the topic would be on the day before the discussion.

We called these "circle discussions," and the children took them very seriously. They were able to engage in a group dialogue for close to an hour. They remembered accurately what others had said in earlier discussions and had the confidence to challenge each other respectfully. Many students expressed views more freely in this context than they had in the interview sessions. We tape-recorded these discussions, and the district's teachers' institute funded their transcription through a small grant.

The circle discussions took on a life of their own and became an integral part of Mardy's curriculum. We admired the sophistication with which the children talked about literature. Often one child's observations would begin a chain of responses, as a second or third child picked up where the others left off. A recurring concern for one group of students was the identification of elements that made a story or book difficult to read. Some said it was vocabulary. For others it was the length of the book. Jeff so often intoned "longer doesn't mean harder" that it became his signature statement. Ultimately, Steve thought out loud and combined aspects of his classmates' theories with ideas of his own, stimulated from eavesdropping on conversations at home. He commented:

> When you said, "Do books get harder?", yes, because...the story gets more complicated and what I'm trying to say is...I heard my parents talking to my brother about all these complicated stories, and so it doesn't matter if it's long or if the words are hard. It's a lot harder if the story is complex.

The opportunity to talk about the complexity of a story as distinct from its text level characteristics presented itself. Like the noiseless, patient spider of Whitman, the students were sending out filaments to bridge together their ideas about literature and writing. These focused discussions were opening up a complex curriculum. At the same time, the tapes were making the complexity of students' understanding available for reflection.

Another example of this bridge building is found in the transcripts from our second year of conversations. We chose to have the students discuss Mildred Taylor's *Mississippi Bridge* (1990), which Mardy had read aloud to them. One boy remarked about Taylor's decision to set the story in the midst of a steady, heavy rain:

> In the beginning of the story when...it was raining, I kept forgetting it was raining because everything was okay and stuff, and then when the bus...When Josias got kicked off the bus and...the people died, it was sad, and I remembered it was raining.

We needed only to agree with him that Taylor's choice to use the rain helped evoke our emotions as we read the story. It was a chance to point out how powerful writing results from such decisions. This student may not have been able or willing at age 9 to devote the time and energy needed

to discuss this in a literacy log entry. The demands of writing about literature are different from those of talking about literature, and the circle discussion provided him a way of communicating his knowledge that could otherwise have gone unexpressed.

Mississippi Bridge also prompted a dialogue about the character motivation and the ethics of the driver and passengers on the bus. The driver had expelled the black passengers to make room for white ones. No possibility was left unexamined, from those who vehemently declared that the driver and white passengers were irredeemably prejudiced to those who wanted to find some rational explanation for why people would treat others so poorly. The next three statements serve as illustration:

> The bus driver is really the one that did something. ...Everybody else, they just got seats on the bus, it wasn't their fault.
>
> Just because you're a white bus driver doesn't automatically mean you're prejudiced. It might mean you're trying to follow the rules and make sure you keep your job, and if you have a family, to support your family.
>
> My point was that...the white people had to be prejudiced if they were wanting the seats, 'cause why should [they expect] the black people [to] get kicked off the bus?

The transcripts allowed us to consider the class as a whole and to identify forces at work that might have gone unrecognized. We noticed patterns of gender domination and the stance of approval-seeking that students frequently adopt when discussing ideas when adults are present. It was disturbing to us that these forces existed with real strength. During the first year of our assessment efforts, the circle discussions began in March and concluded in June. In all of them, boys dominated the conversation, both in the number of students who spoke and in the amount said. In the second year, this pattern reemerged, checked only by the strong voice of Rachel. She was eager to please the adults, and she would look for approbation after making strong and generally contrary statements. Nonetheless, as time passed, the girls became more vocal, confident, and original in their statements. By the end of the year, they were the dominant participants.

Some children of both sexes chose to listen more than talk. This was unsettling at first because we feared the discussions would add little to our understanding of the quiet child. No significant change in the behavior of our "listeners" was noted in the first year, but in the second, the students who at first listened and observed talked more freely after a few months. One student remained reticent throughout the year, but even he began to ask us to return to him rather than forfeit his opportunity to speak by saying "'pass."

The circle discussions were worth the time they took. Children initially less comfortable or experienced in discussing the reading process or literature in this manner were now better able to because of their participation in the whole-class dialogues. We began to understand listening as an active rather than a passive stance, and we are careful now to take a long view when we summarize the experience of students. We also have data through which we can help other stakeholders understand literate learning in more complex ways than they are used to.

The responses in the student interviews improved as well. Mardy spent time in class meetings discussing our expectations for the interviews. Some had likened them to a test. We assured them we were not looking for "right" answers, but were curious about their ideas and observations. Combining these "minilessons" with whole-group discussions made the interviews more productive for the teachers and students alike.

By continually integrating subject areas, Mardy has been able to balance the changes initiated in her classroom practice with the curriculum demands set forth

by the state and district. Now many read alouds are books of historical fiction related to the colonial era. She also reads science trade books aloud. During the time reserved for quiet reading, the children can select from a range of books purchased because they illuminate or expand the social studies and science program objectives. While the circle discussions have as a focal point a specific book that was read aloud or a question related to the reading and writing processes, the children are encouraged to make connections with whatever else they have seen, heard, read, or otherwise experienced. The children also refer to the content of the conversations as they proceed with their content area studies.

Some parents and teachers have been curious about how we gauge a child's understanding of a book that we have not read. We begin by asking for a retelling, which generally reveals the literal understanding of the story and by which we can determine the child's grasp of characterization, sequence of events, causal relationships, and so forth. These are surface level features of a story. Beyond these, we are after the child's personal response to the text because, as Flannery O'Connor points out:

> The meaning of a story should go on expanding for the reader the more he thinks about it, but meaning cannot be captured in an interpretation. ... Too much interpretation is certainly worse than too little, and where feeling for a story is absent, theory will not supply it. (Fitzgerald, 1979)

Looking back on this process of curriculum inquiry, or assessment, Mardy sees that her curriculum planning has become an ongoing enterprise. The expectations of students and parents are considered in addition to the mandates of the state and district. The same is true for her assessment of student progress. It has become more complex and thus more accurate. A handful of parents have more confidence than Mardy or me in the grade-level reporting that emanates from standardized tests. But more and more parents are seeing the merit in a complex definition of literate learning that is significantly different from that which underlies the tests. All of the parents appreciate the description of their child's growth that encompasses both the home and school environments and respects the collective insight of child, parent, and teacher.

The parent surveys have been particularly helpful in this endeavor. Mardy points out in reporting conferences how the parents' insights have affected her instructional decisions. One parent wrote in an initial survey that she hoped her daughter would read such classics as *Heidi* and *The Wizard of Oz*. Mardy was able to find out what the mother valued about these books, and Mardy was able to address the ways in which the books of contemporary authors that her daughter was choosing provided similar richness and challenge. Another parent had observed in September that her child "was an excellent reader; however she shies away from books that look difficult by virtue of their thickness. I would like her to choose a book before the TV." In June the same parent said that her daughter now enjoyed reading at home, and what she thought to be impossible "had become a fact! She reads on her own and frequently prefers a book to TV."

Feeling pressured for time and having to assign grades doesn't have to preclude incorporating interviews, parent surveys, or discussion groups into a teacher's practice. Grading classwork that is subjective in nature is not a new dilemma and is not unique to classroom programs designed like Mardy's. The move toward portfolios is in response to the inadequacies of reducing assessment to letter grades or averages. Mardy now includes quotes from the children and parents in her compilation of student work.

Mardy dreads the time sacrificed each year to standardized tests. Time in school is precious enough, and having to forsake any for something that provides little in-

formation is an annoyance. Some say the tests help identify the students having difficulty. Most teachers already know who's struggling, and the tests may only serve to confirm their knowledge. Mardy conducts test preparation in the manner prescribed in the manuals accompanying the tests. General strategies are discussed, and a practice test is given the day before the "real" test. That's it.

We're continuing our research for a third year, joined by a third-grade teacher. This will allow for curriculum inquiry over two grade levels. We are hoping to integrate more thoroughly the diverse subject areas and to expand our sources of data, and we think it would be interesting to host a circle discussion for the parents so that they might understand what has become a central experience for their children. Along the way, Mardy and I have become better observers and questioners and will undoubtedly continue to grow in these skills. We always learn a thing or two about ourselves as well.

References

Fitzgerald, S. (1979). *The habit of being: The letters of Flannery O'Connor.* New York: Farrar, Straus & Giroux.

Taylor, M. (1990). *Mississippi bridge.* New York: Bantam-Doubleday-Dell.

Accountability: Assessing Comprehension During Literature Discussion

Reprinted from *The Reading Teacher* (1991), *45,* 8-17

Edward E. Paradis
Barbara Chatton
Ann Boswell
Marilyn Smith
Sharon Yovich

Accountability, the ability to demonstrate that learning has taken place, has become a popular concept in schools (Costa, 1989). Teachers struggle with external systems including standardized and textbook tests that seek to measure language learning and reading ability; however, these provide little help for teachers and students (Valencia, McGinley, & Pearson, 1990). Teachers who use literature-based reading programs rather than basal reading series are especially concerned with accountability as they seek to convince parents and administrators that children in their classrooms are learning to read and comprehend (Goodman, 1989). This article describes the frustrations and successes of seeking student accountability through the assessment of comprehension in literature discussions.

The five of us, two university faculty members and three elementary school teachers, are experienced in literature-based projects, having worked together for 6 years on various aspects of instruction. We had successfully made the transition from basals to literature (Paradis, 1984), begun assessing children's growth in literature (Yovich, 1985), and resolved problems dealing with the daily management of literature-based classrooms (Boswell, 1987).

Ann, a fifth-grade teacher, Marilyn, a first-grade teacher, and Sharon, a third-grade teacher, worked in the same school and supported each other throughout successive changes in their classroom practices. Their instructional styles differed, but their literature-based programs were similar. They all used literature rather than basals with heterogeneous discussion groups of five to ten children. The room environments were filled with speaking, listening, writing, and reading. Special efforts were made to emphasize the reading-writing connection.

Accountability became a growing concern as the five of us questioned whether standardized test scores reflected the comprehension level children demonstrated in group discussions. Each year we encountered children with low standardized test scores who contributed significantly during discussions of books. We considered the discussions critical for assessment, as this was the time children shared their understandings of the story, verified meaning, and demonstrated higher levels of thinking. We believed the discussions were a better measure of comprehension than the test scores. Our concern for the validity of the standardized test scores was supported by Valencia and Pearson (1987) who questioned the use of standardized tests and recommended reading assessment be reexamined.

In recent years, authorities have increasingly recommended informal assessment because the evaluation occurs during normal reading instruction (Cambourne & Turbill, 1990; Chittenden & Courtney, 1989; Goodman, 1985). A term used frequently in recommending changes for assessment is "authenticity" (Pearson, 1990; Valencia, McGinley, & Pearson, 1990). Authentic assessment occurs during actual reading for real purposes (Edelsky & Harman, 1988). For us, book discussions were authentic tasks with real purposes. Because we believed the discussion comments were truer indications of children's ability than test scores, we decided to examine various informal assessment options for small group discussions.

The teachers were already using some informal assessment tools in their classrooms. Ann and Sharon had been using student reading logs (Mickelson 1987; Youngblood, 1985) for several years to learn about children's reading interests and understandings of text. All three teachers kept portfolios of children's writing (Mickelson, 1987) from which they were able to see progress in conventions of writing, use of literary structures, and allusions to books shared in class. In addition, all three teachers had used a QASOR-type modified miscue inventory (MacLean, 1980) to check children's progress. Ann and Sharon had attempted anecdotal records (Mickelson, 1987), but felt that their recording techniques were sporadic and inconsistent.

As we reviewed the literature on informal assessment, we looked particularly for efficient means of keeping anecdotal records and for a nondisruptive method of recording children's contributions in small group book discussions. We found the Group Comprehension Matrix (see Figure 1) developed by Wood (1988) valuable because it focused on evaluation during reading discussions. The matrix is similar to the more systematic assessment records the school administrators were accustomed to reviewing. We believed we would have more credibility with administrators if we collected and presented information in a manner familiar to them.

We also found the matrix appealing because the underlying philosophy was consistent with the teachers' beliefs on assessment. Wood, who drew from the work of Feuerstein, Rand, and Hoffman (1979), summarized the philosophy in four recommendations: (a) active teaching should occur during the assessment process, (b) interaction should occur between child and teacher during assessment rather than using a scripted monologue, (c) peaks, rather than initial levels of performance, should be sought, and (d) the focus should be on process rather than product.

The emphasis on process rather than product was particularly important to us. An examination of items in the matrix illustrates the focus on the comprehension process. Items such as "Makes predictions about story," "Can read 'between the lines'" and "Possesses broad background knowledge" target whether a child is a strategic reader constructing information. In contrast, the product of reproducing information by answering questions is assessed by the single item, "Answers questions at all levels."

Beginning with the Comprehension Matrix

We prepared for the assessment during the summer by reproducing the group matrix and setting up detailed, tabbed notebooks for recording anecdotal information. After using the Group Comprehension Matrix in September, problems surfaced. We first used the matrix as if it were a list of comprehension skills rather than aspects of the comprehension process. Moreover, we found ourselves calling the items "skills" and watching for children to demonstrate these skills. Ann, Marilyn, and Sharon had been recording information while simultaneously participating in literature discussions, but if they attended to children's contributions to evaluate reading compre-

hension, they could not interact naturally with the children. They were uncomfortable with an assessment system that turned them into outside evaluators rather than equal participants in discussions.

After 1 month, Ann had modified the matrix, and Marilyn and Sharon had stopped using it altogether. The matrix did not fit comfortably with their ideas about reading. Individually, they had to examine their own beliefs about reading and determine items for new matrices based upon what was important in their respective classrooms. They had to develop recording systems that worked for them.

Development of an Accountability System

To record the development of their accountability systems, Ann, Marilyn, and Sharon kept journals and met monthly with Barbara and Ed. The evolution of one of the accountability systems is best shown through Marilyn's journal entries. Her journal was particularly detailed and reflective, in part because this was her first major participation in a cooperative research project and because she had been using literature-based instruction for a shorter period than Ann and Sharon. We all agreed Marilyn's journal was representative of Ann's and Sharon's journals in portraying the difficulties and ultimate success in using and adapting the matrix.

When school started in September, all three teachers began using the matrix. Ann had the least trouble, although she did encounter difficulties. She observed that some items on the matrix did not appear in her group discussions. She was also concerned that she either focused too much attention on the matrix or forgot it altogether as she talked with children. Sharon stopped using the matrix very early as she believed it interfered with discussions. Marilyn had the same problem. In the journal entry below she described the difficulty of participating in discussions and recording information at the same time.

> A problem that I see is remembering what I wanted to document. By the time I had a chance to write my impressions of someone or something, the thought had escaped me—how to find a way to keep these thoughts until I have a chance to write? So often it is in the middle of working with the group that I get these thoughts. I don't like to stop and jot down even a reminder—I'd lose the teaching moment. It seems as if it would interrupt. (9/21/88)

Anecdotal records continued to be a problem for all three teachers. A reflective comment written in January summarized our early difficulties: "I was gung-ho on anecdotal records—got all organized, made about 3 entries per kid, then stopped on Sept. 28, for most of the kids."

By October, the teachers realized that a single comprehension matrix did not work for three different grade levels. Sharon stopped using the matrix. Marilyn and Ann began revising the group comprehension matrix, selecting the items judged appropriate for their grade levels and adding items not already on the matrix.

In her journal Marilyn expressed concern about the appropriateness of the matrix for first-graders.

> I feel I need some general guidelines in what to look for. I need to combine entries pertinent to 1st grade from the group matrix into a matrix that is applicable/usable. (10/8/88)

At this point, Ann began the first of a series of matrix revisions. Her group discussions resulted in continuous reexamination of the matrix items. Marilyn had more difficulty. In November she reported her frustration and explained why she did not complete the revision.

> I've been frustrated in looking back over the past 2 months. I feel i've made little progress in finding a way to assess comprehension

Figure 1

Wood's Group Comprehension Matrix

Story: *The Mandarin and the Magician* Date: October 14th

Genre: Narrative (Realistic) Fantasy
Poetry
Plays
Exposition

Grade: 4th

*New student — Oct. 1st

	Kelly	Ryan*	Marti	Tonya	Jason	David	Teresa
Makes predictions about story	S	+	—	S	—	+	—
Participates in the discussion	S	+	S	S	—	+	S
Answers questions on all levels	—	+	S	S	S	+	S
Determines word meanings through context	—	+	—	—	—	S	—
Reads smoothly and fluently	+	+	+	S	—	+	S
Can retell selection using own words	S	+	+	S	S	S	—
Can read "between the lines"	—	S	S	—	—	S	—
Possesses broad background knowledge	S	S	—	—	—	S	—

Comments: *The students had much difficulty comprehending the story until I provided much more background information. Their predictions were not as accurate and abundant as usual—largely due to their lack of knowledge of Chinese dynasties. Jason remains very quiet unless asked specific questions. He is much more responsive one-to-one. While his recall is good, his oral reading is very choppy. Teresa is always willing to volunteer any answers although her recall is on the literal level. Ryan may need to move up another level—will test individually.*

Often	+
Sometimes	S
Seldom	—
Not observed	N

Words to review:
dynasty
Mandarin
queue

> informally. I'm letting the holidays divert my attention. The complete reorganization of my reading program has taken time away from my focus on assessment. I have felt lost—like I don't know what to do or where to go next. I have decided to take my list of things (behaviors) that I consider show comprehension and make a checklist for each child. When I see the specific behavior I will check the appropriate item and date it. (11/1/88)

This entry indicates our reluctance to abandon the checklist conception of assessment. We all felt the tug of old habits. Checklists were the way we had typically recorded assessment information. A reflective comment written by Marilyn in January describes her mood and exemplifies the severity of problems we had encountered: "I didn't modify the matrix like I'd planned—in fact, I quit making any attempt to assess."

Overcoming Difficulties, Making Changes

Throughout the fall we met monthly. Although the discussions included sharing of concerns, we outwardly downplayed them. As December began, however, we acknowledged a major problem. We met to reexamine our original plans and decided what had to be changed.

First, we operationally defined comprehension. We previously had agreed upon a general notion, but by January we needed a definition that allowed us to define more precisely what children should do to demonstrate comprehension.

Ann, Marilyn, and Sharon each developed a list of items showing comprehension in their respective rooms. In early discussions we called these "skills" but quickly realized they were not skills in the traditional sense of the word. Eventually we called them *indicators* of meaning: if children did these things, they indicated comprehension.

In comparing initial drafts, we found that, although the teachers had similar beliefs about the comprehension process, they listed different indicators they expected to see in their rooms. Nevertheless, in spite of the variation across teachers, three aspects of comprehension were listed by everyone: predicting, inferring, and summarizing.

Figure 2 shows a matrix Marilyn drew using her list of indicators.

Because we wanted a record of how we solved problems, we enlisted a TV crew to videotape Ann, Marilyn, and Sharon as they assessed children's comprehension and our team conferences where we discussed assessment. An example of problem solving occurred at a January taping session where Marilyn expressed frustration that her matrix was unwieldy. She had used the matrix by selecting one of the indicators and watching for children to demonstrate it. This procedure was similar to her past use of basal checklists in which she had selected a specific skill and tested a group of children on the skill. Now, however, the procedure was not working.

In a videotaped team conference, Marilyn described her frustration in not being able to remember which children demonstrated the indicator. She recounted that her observations focused on children, not indicators. Her natural inclination was to share in the book discussion and enjoy it while minimizing special attention to comprehension. Following the book discussion, she was able to recall what children said and the indicators they demonstrated. The difference in Marilyn's observation was subtle, but crucial. She was not able to have an indicator as the focal point and recall children who demonstrated it; she was, however, able to have children as the focal point and then recall the indicators they demonstrated.

February was a turning point. Although we were struggling, we were progressing toward accountability systems.

Marilyn's journal describes her struggles. Previously, she had been trying to document information during instruction. In early February, she indicated her frustration with recording information while teaching.

> I can't document and interact in a group effectively at the same time. But I can assess. Should I start taping the groups? Should I not try to assess during the discussion but wait until I can reflect on the discussion and then document? (2/2/89)

Marilyn now knew she could use her indicators to guide assessment. The problem was how to recall information because she could not write if she participated in discussions.

Ann and Sharon had experienced the same problem of being unable to document during book discussions. They began using audiotape recordings as an aid to recalling information. Ann decided to tape several sessions to verify the information recorded daily on the matrix. Although this was time-consuming, Ann felt that it gave her an accurate picture of children's comprehension. Sharon began taping occasional discussions and typing up transcripts. Using these transcripts and her list of comprehension indicators, Sharon was able to add information to her anecdotal records. Marilyn, however, rejected the use of audiotaping.

> I am too involved in the group discussion to document it and after the discussion there are 17 other kids to look after. Will I be able to reflect on the discussion and document specific things maybe hours after the discussion was held? Or will I end up taping the discussions and replaying them the way Ann does? I feel that I don't want to spend that "extra" time listening to tapes and documenting. It would be better for me if I could recall a discussion later in the day when I had a few minutes to reflect on it, then document the comprehension indicators. Now what? (2/12/89)

Toward the end of February Marilyn found a way to document information without tape recording.

> I don't believe I will have to tape the discussions. If I can sit down for 5 minutes immediately after a discussion and use my checklist of indicators and write down everything I remember from the discussion, I think I will be able to document the kids' comprehension. Later in the day I can then record what I saw or each child on their separate sheets. It worked very well today. I asked the kids to give me 5 uninterrupted minutes—they did their seatwork—it worked great! Now, how will I end up organizing the individual sheets? (2/22/89)

Figure 3 shows Marilyn's recording for the group.

By the end of February, Ann, Marilyn, and Sharon had each devised a recording system for the group instruction. Now their attention turned to records for individual children. Ann compiled data from the matrix recorded in discussions and from audiotapes. Sharon used transcripts of audiotapes to develop notes for anecdotal records. Marilyn developed yet another system.

> I didn't document during the discussion but took 5 minutes and recorded after the discussion was over. Later I made a page for each kid and started recording what they said specifically. (2/29/89)

Figure 4 shows the comments for one child.

In mid-March, with the recording system in place, the teachers had a new concern described in Marilyn's journal.

> My concern now is that I'm not documenting from discussions often enough. How often is often

Figure 2

Matrix of Indicators

	apply literature	assoc.	quest. asked	character quality	picture discuss.	logical pred.	humor	inference	summarize	author's purpose	reason for title
Andy											
Erin											
Jane											
Barry											
Lindsey											
Jake											

All names are fictitious.

> enough? I don't know. If I could have had my documentation procedure set up at the beginning of the year I wouldn't have this question now. It would have been all worked out. But I needed this year to develop a way to document. (3/14/89)

At the end of the school year, Marilyn decided specific documentation once a month would be sufficient; each child would then have nine individual records. Ann and Sharon were transcribing tape recordings from the final sessions of book discussions. They did this at least once each marking period. Although each teacher believed she had sufficient information to evaluate the children, the issue of how much assessment information was needed remained a concern.

By the end of March, Marilyn's assessment procedure was working. Nevertheless, she was still debating using audiotapes.

> I'm still considering audiotaping the reading group discussions. I feel I am missing a lot by relying on my memory. I hesitate to start doing this because of the time it would take. Sharon and Ann are

Figure 3

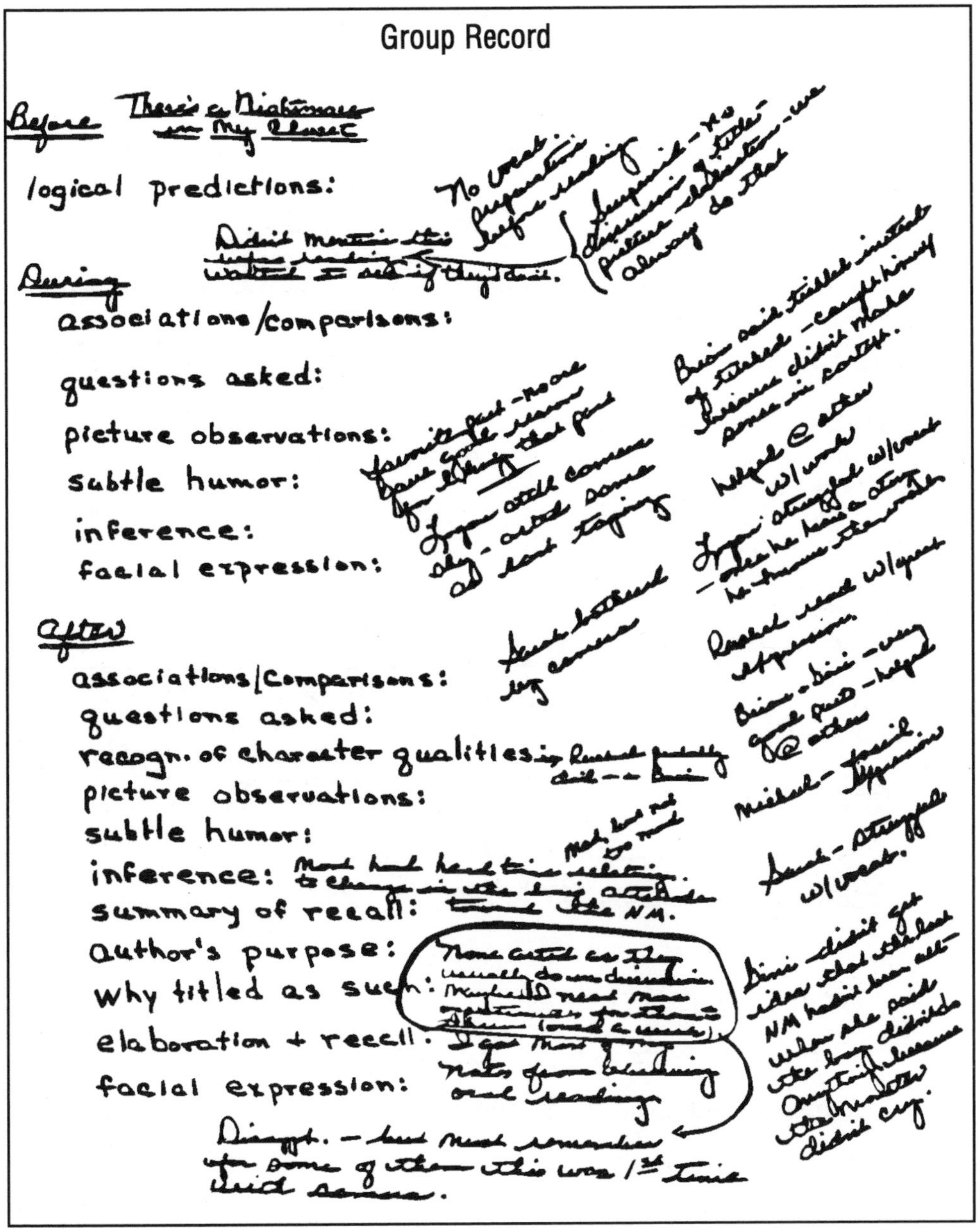

Group Record

Before There's a Nightmare in My Closet

logical predictions:

During

associations/comparisons:

questions asked:

picture observations:

subtle humor:

inference:

facial expression:

After

associations/comparisons:

questions asked:

recogn. of character qualities:

picture observations:

subtle humor:

inference:

summary of recall:

author's purpose:

why titled as such:

elaboration + recall:

facial expression:

All names are fictitious.

both doing this now. I'm still balking. (3/29/89)

Marilyn did not audiotape any lessons. She did, however, plan to tape a discussion the following September to determine the value of audiotapes.

By the end of April, Ann, Marilyn, and Sharon had refined their list of comprehension indicators and were reasonably satisfied with their record keeping. One school year had passed before they had accountability systems they could use with confidence. They now felt prepared to implement an assessment system for discussion during the next school year.

Figure 5 shows the form Marilyn developed to be used in the fall.

Figure 4

Individual Record

Before *There's a Nightmare in My Closet* Jason

logical predictions: 1st time reading + discussing a book oral

During

associations/comparisons: during oral reading w/partner 2-3 times used context clues to figure out information word

questions asked:

picture observations: partnered very well with Gini

subtle humor:

inference:

facial expression: I can see him think

After

associations/comparisons: not swayed easily by others' ideas → took time to analyze the questions + organize his thoughts before answering – does this all the time – confident

questions asked:

recogn. of character qualities: – good job here – recognized the change in characters feeling

picture observations:

subtle humor:

inference:

summary + recall: – did well

author's purpose:

why titled as such:

elaboration + recall:

All names are fictitious.

Summary and Conclusions

This article describes three teachers moving toward systems of accountability which will work smoothly for them and yet reflect children's learning. Their journal entries and discussions present a picture of a year of both frustrations and successes.

Kid watching is not easy and documenting what we see is even more difficult.

What have we learned about accountability in literature discussions? We learned we could not implement a procedure developed by someone else. Only the teachers knew what children should do in their

Figure 5

Final Form

Informal Assessment of Comprehension Indicators/Criteria

Student Name: ______________________ Week of: ______________

Main idea

Summarize ______________________

Author's purpose ______________________

Understands purpose of title ______________________

Association/comparison

Can recognize and discuss

- Plot ______________________
- Setting ______________________
- Characters ______________________

As they relate to own experiences.

Elaboration

Prediction ______________________

Subtle humor ______________________

Inference ______________________

Questions asked ______________________

Recall ______________________

Picture observation ______________________

Reaction

Body language ______________________

Facial expression ______________________

Application

Applies literary pattern to own writing and speaking

____

____

Comments:

____

____

____

classrooms to demonstrate comprehension. Each teacher had to decide the specific indicators for that classroom. The day has passed of telling a teacher, "This is the list of skills to be mastered for comprehension."

We also learned that the teachers must decide how to effectively record assessment information. Based upon our experience, the record keeping varied considerably.

A simple solution to accountability such as a new test or assessment procedure would be welcomed. Unfortunately we found nothing simple about accountability—but with work, reflection, and perseverance, we saw progress. We continue to refine the accountability systems. The information gained is important to teacher, child, and parent and is critical to the promotion and success of literature-based reading programs.

References

Boswell, A. (1987). Managing a fifth grade classroom literature program. In B. Chatton (Chair), *Managing a literature-based classroom reading program.* Symposium conducted at the annual convention of the International Reading Association, Anaheim, CA.

Cambourne, B., & Turbill, J. (1990). Assessment in whole-language classrooms: Theory into practice. *The Elementary School Journal, 90,* 337-350.

Chittenden, E., & Courtney, R. (1989). Assessment of young children's reading: Documenting as an alternative to testing. In D.S. Strickland & L.M. Morrow (Eds.), *Emerging literacy: Young children learn to read and write* (pp.107-120). Newark, DE: International Reading Association.

Costa, A.L. (1989). Re-assessing assessment. *Educational Leadership, 46,* 3.

Edelsky, C., & Harman, S. (1988). One more critique of reading tests—with two differences. *English Education, 20,* 157-171.

Feuerstein, R., Rand, Y., & Hoffman, M.B. (1979). *The dynamic assessment of retarded performance.* Baltimore, MD: University Park Press.

Goodman, K.S. (1989). Preface. In K.S. Goodman, Y.M. Goodman, & W.J. Hood (Eds.), *The whole language evaluation book* (pp. xi-xv). Portsmouth, NH: Heinemann.

Goodman, Y.M. (1985). Kidwatching: Observing children in the classroom. In A. Jaggar & M.T. Smith-Burke (Eds.), *Observing the language learner* (9-18). Newark, DE: International Reading Association.

MacLean, M. (1980). QASOR: A framework for qualitatively analyzing silent and oral readers. In M.L. Kamil & A.J. Moe (Eds.), *Perspectives on reading research and instruction: Twenty-ninth yearbook of the National Reading Conference* (pp. 276-282). Washington, DC: National Reading Conference.

Mickelson, N.J. (1987). *Evaluation in whole language.* Victoria, BC: University of Victoria, Centre for Whole Language.

Paradis, E.E. (1984). Thematic units to increase comprehension. In S. Kucer (Chair), *Thematic unit development: Facilitating comprehension as an ongoing process.* Microworkshop conducted at the annual convention of the International Reading Association, Atlanta, GA.

Pearson, P.D. (1990, May). Who's at risk? Our students, our schools, our society? A research and policy perspective. Paper presented at the annual convention of the International Reading Association, Atlanta, GA.

Valenica, S.W., McGinley, W., & Pearson, P.D. (1990). Assessing reading and writing. In G.G. Duffy (Ed.), *Reading in the middle school* (pp. 124-146). Newark, DE: International Reading Association.

Valencia, S.W., & Pearson, P.D. (1987). Reading assessment: Time for change. *The Reading Teacher, 40,* 726-732.

Wood, K.D. (1988). Techniques for assessing students' potential for learning. *The Reading Teacher, 41,* 440-447.

Youngblood, E. (1985). Reading, thinking and writing using the reading journal. *English Journal, 74,* 46-48.

Yovich, S. (1985, May). Assessing a literature-based program in a third grade classroom. In E. Paradis (Chair), *Documenting growth in a literature-based reading program.* Symposium conducted at the annual convention of the International Reading Association, Atlanta, GA.

A Framework for Authentic Literacy Assessment

Reprinted from *The Reading Teacher* (1992), *46,* 88-98

Scott G. Paris
Robert C. Calfee
Nikola Filby
Elfrieda H. Hiebert
P. David Pearson
Sheila W. Valencia
Kenneth P. Wolf

Assessment is fundamental to the improvement of education; it provides measures of success for students' learning, for educators' leadership, and for continuous evaluations of instructional programs. Many researchers and educators have argued that traditional psychoeducational tests are no longer adequate for these diverse assessment purposes (e.g., Resnick & Resnick, 1990; Valencia & Pearson, 1987). The proposals offered to improve literacy assessment include a wide variety of suggestions from new national tests based on performance measures to classroom assessments of individuals based on portfolios of work samples. It is unlikely that a single test or alternative assessment will meet the needs of all stakeholders, but it seems clear to us that the efforts are stimulating many new and useful approaches to assessment.

The purpose of this article is to describe a framework for literacy assessment that can be adapted to suit the assessment needs of particular schools and districts. The framework involves five phases of decision making that policymakers should consider as they revise assessment practices. Because the decisions about what outcomes are valued, how to assess literacy achievements, and how to use the data directly affect teachers, parents, and students, we believe that the decision making should be shared among the various stakeholders. In this manner, all the participants are informed about the goals and criteria of assessment, and they are motivated to participate fully in assessment. Although this article describes a process of decision making about authentic literacy assessments that was created by the authors for an external program evaluation, we encourage educators to emulate this process in schools and districts because it can establish an informed consensus among local stakeholders about the literacy outcomes and processes that will be assessed and valued in each community.

Our team was assembled as a group of consultants to the Far West Laboratory for Educational Research and Development charged with designing a framework for the evaluation of literacy achievement in the Kamehameha Elementary Education Program (KEEP). The overall evaluation, conducted by the Southwest Regional Educational Laboratory, is part of a U.S. federally funded project designed to assess the effectiveness of the K-3 KEEP literacy curriculum and to compare the achievement of KEEP students at the end of third grade to similar students in other classrooms in Hawaii. What began as a program evaluation of a "whole literacy" curriculum grew into the creation of alternative literacy assessments because of the limitations of

standardized tests to capture critical aspects of the curriculum objectives of both KEEP and the Hawaii Department of Education (DOE) curricula (Giuli, 1991). The situation provided a unique opportunity for our team to work together on a specific practical problem. We believe that both the process and the outcome can serve as models for others to design authentic literacy assessments.

The Hawaiian Context of KEEP

KEEP began in 1972 as an experimental project at the Kamehameha School to foster literacy among native Hawaiian students (Tharp & Gallimore, 1988). It is now disseminated in eight schools throughout the islands of Hawaii and serves annually approximately 3,000 students in K-3 classes. The curriculum has recently been extended to some grade 4, 5, and 6 classrooms also. The KEEP curriculum has been revised several times and may be described most appropriately as a dynamic rather than static set of guidelines for curriculum, instruction, and assessment. For example, the KEEP *Literacy Curriculum Guide* (Au, Blake, Herman, Oshiro & Scheu 1990) describes instruction that includes language experience and whole literacy activities relevant for native Hawaiian children.

The *Guide* also describes a portfolio assessment system of observations and checklists that teachers can use to assess students' progress against developmental benchmarks. The checklists summarize children's literacy in four broad areas: ownership and voluntary reading, reading comprehension, writing processes, and emergent literacy (Au, Scheu, Kawakami, & Herman, 1990). Although the *Guide* provided us with valuable information about the goals of the KEEP curriculum and assessment, our suggestions for authentic assessments were not constrained by extant practices. The portfolio system described by Au et al. is used primarily by paraprofessional aides for diagnostic purposes although teachers are gradually learning about the system so that they can record similar observations. In contrast, the assessment system that we were charged to create will be used by external evaluators to make quantitative comparisons between the achievements of KEEP and nonKEEP students.

The *Language Arts Program Guide* (Hawaii Department of Education, 1988) describes an integrated language arts curriculum that is similar to the KEEP framework but less oriented to whole language instruction and the sociocultural backgrounds of native Hawaiian children. Learner outcomes for each grade level and domain of language arts are specified in more detail than the KEEP benchmarks, but the objectives of both curricula are generally congruent. It is important to note that we used the curricular goals and activities of both KEEP and the Department of Education (DOE) to determine which aspects of literacy are emphasized in daily instruction and which outcomes are valued.

The assessment problems in Hawaii are similar to those faced by most school districts, that is, how to create assessments that (a) measure critical features of the curriculum, (b) are consistent with instructional practices, (c) motivate students, and (d) provide measures of accountability (Winograd, Paris, & Bridge, 1991). The traditional practice in Hawaii has been to test all students above second grade every spring with the Stanford Achievement Test which does not measure many of the goals in the KEEP and Hawaii DOE curricula. Many teachers spend months preparing their students for the Stanford with materials and activities that are inconsistent with their regular curriculum. Likewise, many students regard the Stanford as the goal of literacy learning and the pinnacle of the academic year. Administrators report a "canyon effect" of low motivation for the last month of school following the Stanford. The Stanford results have been used historically to evaluate the KEEP program without regard for the variable time that teachers and students have participated in actual KEEP classrooms or for the

misalignment between the Stanford and the curricula.

Given these problems, it is not surprising that evaluations of KEEP using scores from the Stanford and the Metropolitan Achievement Test (Yap, Estes, & Nickel, 1988) revealed poor performance of KEEP students and frustrated KEEP staff. There was a clear and compelling need to design alternative assessments to measure literacy development in KEEP classrooms. The assessments needed to measure reading and writing proficiency as well as students' literacy ownership, habits, attitudes, and strategies in a manner that reflected the interactive, collaborative, and constructive nature of learning in Hawaiian classrooms. This is the problem we tackled.

Negotiating a Framework for Alternative Assessment

We began meeting in January 1991 as a group, met periodically during the year, collected pilot data, and corresponded regularly about the framework. As with many new projects, we realized the shape of the task and the solutions only after being immersed in them for many months. In the end, we can identify five discrete phases to our decision making that may be a heuristic for others.

Phase 1: Identifying Dimensions of Literacy

Our discussions about alternative assessments always hinged on issues of curriculum and instruction because we all agreed that "authentic assessment" must reflect daily classroom practices and goals. Thus, the initial task was to decide which aspects of students' literacy development are important to measure in Hawaiian schools and, correspondingly, which aspects are not assessed by current procedures. We began by considering various taxonomies that included elements such as knowledge, skills, and attitudes or reading, writing, listening, and speaking. None of these were satisfactory because they failed to capture the interconnectedness and the psychological characteristics of motivated literacy that were central to the curricula. From discussions with educators from KEEP and the DOE, as well as our observations and knowledge of KEEP, we gleaned a list of 5-10 dimensions that were the basis for continuing discussions. We subsequently identified seven critical dimensions of literacy, described in Table I, that we considered to be at the core of both curricula. These dimensions embody a view of literacy that is interactive, social, constructive, metacognitive, motivated, and integrated with functional language uses. The assessment of these dimensions transcend the Stanford scores and traditional emphases on basic reading skills.

The results of this phase of decision making included both a product and a process. The process of examining the curricula, observing classroom instruction, and operationalizing the objectives of "whole literacy" took several months and involved brainstorming, clarifying values, and building consensus among our team. We also discussed our assessment proposals with Kathy Au and Chuck Giuli at KEEP and with Betsy Brandt at the DOE. It was remarkably illuminating to negotiate the alignment of curriculum and assessment, and we were all struck by the value this process can have for teachers and administrators. Indeed, students who understand the connections between daily activities for learning and assessment might also become more informed about the purposes of assessment and the criteria for success. Knowing what counts in literacy performance in the classroom can help create a shared vision for teaching and learning.

Phase 2: Identifying Attributes of Literacy Dimensions

As we identified potential dimensions we also discussed the kinds of literate performance that distinguish skilled from less skilled students on each dimension. These attributes could be described at general or specific levels. For example, in the dimension of Engagement With Text Through

Table 1

Critical Dimensions and Attributes of Literacy

1. **Engagement with text through reading**
A critical aspect of literacy is the extent to which readers and writers interact with the ideas conveyed in text. They need to relate their background knowledge and experiences to new textual information and integrate the ideas. Thoughtful engagement with text implies that readers construct meaning sensibly, that they employ strategies as they read, and that they reflect on the meaning and style of the text. Comprehension is a key element of engagement, but the dimension also includes the demonstration of thinking strategies and personal responses to text that extend the basic interpretation of text.

2. **Engagement with text through writing**
Writing is a constructive expression of ideas that are communicated coherently and accurately. Students' involvement with writing and reading should provide mutual support for effective literacy strategies, habits, and motivation. Writing should be embedded in everyday activities and based on genuine communicative purposes. It should allow students to compose their ideas on a variety of topics with different genres and styles. Students' writing should include their personal opinions, reflections, and elaborations to texts they have read. The message and voice should be clear. The technical aspects of writing such as spelling, word choice, punctuation, grammar, and organization should be appropriate for the students' grade level.

3. **Knowledge about literacy**
Students should understand that language can be expressed through reading and writing according to literacy conventions and that adherence to these conventions helps people to understand each other through written communication. For example, effective readers and writers understand the different purposes and structures of various literary genres and know how strategies can be used while reading and writing. Their knowledge about literacy also includes their metalinguistic understanding of the nuances of language, such as ambiguity and figurative language, as well as their understanding about the connections among reading, writing, listening, and speaking.

4. **Orientation to literacy**
Reading and writing require more than engagement with text and the construction of meaning. They also require motivation so that children can read, write, and learn independently. Learners must set appropriate goals for literacy and persevere in the face of difficulty. Motivated readers seek challenges in what they read just as motivated writers extend themselves to compose more text, to write in various genres, or to write creatively. A positive orientation to literacy also includes feelings of confidence, optimism, enjoyment, and control so that children regard their achievements with pride and satisfaction.

5. **Ownership of literacy**
Good readers develop independent reading habits, identify their favorite topics and books, and monitor their own progress and achievements. In this sense, they develop "ownership" of their reading that reflects pride in their accomplishments and their enjoyment in recreational reading. Likewise, good writers engage in writing independently, read their own compositions, and develop preferences for writing about some topics or writing with particular genres. This sense of ownership fosters lifelong literacy habits and is evident in children's preferences for reading and writing, their independence, and their initiative for literacy.

6. **Collaboration**
Reading and writing are not always private activities; they often involve discussion and cooperation so that meaning can be negotiated among individuals. The social construction of meaning is especially important in school where instructional activities may involve shared reading and writing, cooperative learning, and peer tutoring arrangements. Effective readers and writers can work with others in "communities of learners" to create meaning, revise compositions, present and share their ideas, and solve problems while they read and write. Frequent participation with other students in school is one mark of collaboration; social respect for others and mutual benefits for learning are also desirable consequences of collaboration.

7. **Connectedness of the curriculum**
Reading and writing are pervasive activities in school and are fundamental for learning across the entire school curriculum. It is important, therefore, that children read and write in order to learn in subjects such as social studies, science, and mathematics and that the skills, motivation, and collaboration evident in literacy instruction are reinforced in content areas. It is also important for children to understand the connections among reading, writing, listening, and speaking so that they regard language arts as integrated, purposeful, and pragmatic. Literacy also needs to be connected between school and home so that families can support school-based literacy skills and habits and so that teachers can be sensitive to the unique backgrounds and talents of each child.

Reading, we discussed how good readers are constructive, strategic, reflective, and evaluative. For each of these general attributes, we generated three specific literacy indicators that could be verified empirically from students' performance, such as using appropriate strategies for monitoring comprehension or making inferences. Each of these indicators is described in Table 2 and provides a tangible referent point for evaluating students' literacy. These indicators lie on continua, but anchored descriptions are provided only for the high and low ends. More detailed standards and scoring rubrics can be generated for each indicator.

One virtue of this activity for educators in general is that the participants share their theories of literacy with each other so that ideas about literacy development are reconsidered within this collaborative context. We believe that this exercise is extremely valuable for groups of teachers, administrators, and parents who design assessment. A second virtue of identifying specific attributes of literacy is that it forces us to consider jointly the questions "What is important?" and "How can we measure it?" Although the ease and economy of measurement are important, we need to ensure that new forms of assessment are aimed at critical aspects of students' learning and development and not just those skills that are readily tested. Of course, the dimensions, attributes, and indicators are interrelated, so they all must be negotiated together. We often expanded and reduced the lists we produced because there appeared to be an imbalance in the level of detail or emphasis. We cannot emphasize too strongly the importance of the *process* of negotiating what is important to assess because it allows local stakeholders to create a shared set of values and concepts about literacy development.

Evaluating Literacy Performance

The next three phases in the design of alternative assessments translate the values and specific attributes identified in phases 1 and 2 into assessment procedures. There are several options available to decision makers at this point for gathering evidence about students' learning, including conventional tests, checklists, structured lessons, observations, etc. We chose to analyze students' ordinary literacy artifacts and activities rather than their responses to specific instruction or uniform content for three reasons. First, we wanted the literacy assessment to reflect authentic activities in classrooms, including the variety and quality of students' literacy experiences. Second, we wanted to design a prototypical assessment model based on students' work samples that could be used flexibly and adapted by other educators. Third, the overall KEEP evaluation plan includes several other assessments of children's literacy development that are not based on students' daily performance.

Phase 3: Methods for Collecting Evidence About Literacy Proficiency

Work that students produce in class every day reveals their usual learning and motivation. Such work samples are authentic performance measures that reflect instructional opportunities afforded in classrooms as well as achievements of students. Ordinary work samples, therefore, are not pure ability measures, but they can provide illuminating evidence about students' typical and best work in class. Conversely, a paucity of outstanding work samples may indicate a lack of opportunities in the classroom, an "instructional deficit," rather than some kind of deficit in the student. Additional information about students' achievements, including their perceptions, understanding, and self-assessment, can be gained when students are given opportunities to reflect on their strengths, weaknesses, and progress. The method of reflective interviews about work samples is consistent with portfolio approaches, but it is an equally fair assessment in classrooms where portfolio systems are not used.

The method we devised was to collect all literacy work samples produced in one week by children who represented a range of achievement levels in each classroom. The artifacts included reading logs, journal entries, letters, essays, spelling lists, worksheets, and book reports. In the pilot project, teachers collected work samples from four students in each class who were then interviewed about their work as well as their literacy habits and attitudes. In our pilot project with four teachers and 16 third graders, there was an abundance of diverse materials that reflected the curricular units and literate activities occurring in each classroom.

At the end of the week, an interviewer discussed the materials with students individually for 20-30 minutes. Approximately 20 questions were assembled in a structured yet conversational interview, described fully in Wolf et al. (1991), that was designed to yield information about the attributes and indicators of each dimension so that a score could be assigned. For example, students were asked questions such as:

- Here is a sample of your writing that you did this week. Are you finished with it? What do you like about this piece? What would you change to make it better? Did other students in the class help you to write or revise it?
- What book have you read this week? Tell me about it. How did it make you feel? Was there anything surprising in the book?
- Do you think you are a good reader and writer? What makes someone a really good reader? When you think of your self as a reader, what would you like to do differently or better?

The interview was tape recorded and transcribed later so that we could discuss the students' answers as we created the scoring system. In the future, we anticipate that trained interviewers can score the students' reflections and work samples during the interview so that the process is speedy and efficient.

Phase 4: Scoring Students' Work Samples

The next phase in our project was to score the pilot data from 16 students to determine if the system could yield reliable and informative measures of differences among students. We gathered the data in May and discussed whether the data should be scored at the level of indicators (the 42 "a, b, c" items in Table 2) or at the level of attributes (the 14 subcategories in Table 2, e.g., "Reading is constructive") or at the general level of dimensions (the 7 major entries in Table 2, e.g., "Engagement With Text Through Reading"). We settled on an intermediate level of attributes as most appropriate for the holistic, quantitative judgments that we wanted to make. However, teachers who use a similar system may elect a more holistic evaluation or choose to record narrative comments rather than quantitative scores.

The scoring procedure involved reading the transcript of the student's interview, examining the work samples, and assigning a score of l-4 for each attribute. The four-point scale was anchored at both ends with descriptions of the attributes (e.g., "Integrates new ideas with previous knowledge and experiences"; see Table 2) which aided the judgments considerably because they were tangible examples of students' knowledge, attitudes, or behavior for each attribute. The scores can be aggregated across the two attributes per dimension (values range from 2-8) and across the seven dimensions (values range from 14-56) to give summary scores about the literacy performance of individual students. As we evaluated different students' work samples, we achieved greater consensus in scoring. Although the evaluations were conducted by our team, we are optimistic that trained and knowledgeable teachers can use this holistic scoring procedure to obtain trustworthy assessments of students' literacy development.

An example might help to illustrate the scoring procedures. Alice's collection of work included nearly 20 pages of her own

Table 2

Performance Indicators for Each Attribute and Dimension of Literacy

ENGAGEMENT WITH TEXT THROUGH READING

Low engagement	High engagement
Reading is constructive	
a. Fails to build on prior knowledge	a. Integrates new ideas with previous knowledge and experiences
b. Few inferences or elaborations; literal retelling of text	b. Exhibits within text and beyond text inferences
c. Focus is on isolated facts; does not connect text elements	c. Identifies and elaborates plots, themes, or concepts
Reading is evaluative	
a. Fails to use personal knowledge and experience as a framework for interpreting text	a. Uses prior knowledge and experience to construct meaning
b. Is insensitive to the author's style, assumptions, perspective, and claims	b. Is sensitive to, and may even question, the author's style, assumptions, perspective, and claims
c. Fails to examine or go beyond a literal account of the ideas in the text	c. Expresses opinions, judgments, or insights about the content of the text

ENGAGEMENT WITH TEXT THROUGH WRITING

Low engagement	High engagement
Writing is constructive	
a. Writes disconnected words or phases with few identifiable features of any genre	a. Writes well constructed, thematic, cohesive text that is appropriate to the genre
b. Fails to use personal knowledge as a base for composing text	b. Draws on personal knowledge and experiences in composing text
c. Little evidence of voice, personal style, or originality	c. Creative writing reveals a strong sense of voice, personal style, and originality
Writing is technically appropriate	
a. Writing includes numerous violations of the conventions of spelling, punctuation, and usage.	a. Displays developmentally appropriate use of the conventions of spelling, punctuation, and usage
b. Inappropriate or inflexible use of grammatical structures	b. Writing exhibits grammatical structures appropriate to the purpose and genre
c. Limited and contextually inappropriate vocabulary	c. Rich, varied, and appropriate vocabulary

KNOWLEDGE ABOUT LITERACY

Low knowledge	High knowledge
Knowledge about literacy conventions and structures	
a. Unaware of the functions of print conventions and punctuation in written communication	a. Understands the functions that print conventions and punctuation play in written communication
b. Unaware of text structures and genres	b. Can identify and use several specific text structures and genres
c. Unaware of the subtleties of language use; does not understand or use connotative meaning, ambiguity, or figurative language	c. Understands that words have multiple meanings; can use and understand ambiguity and figurative language
Knowledge about strategies	
a. Unaware of the strategies that can be applied while reading and writing	a. Knows strategies that can be applied before, during, and after reading and writing
b. Limited understanding of how strategies can be applied while reading or writing	b. Can explain how strategies are applied or might be used
c. Naive about the value of strategies; does not use strategies selectively	c. Understands how and when strategies can be used and why they are helpful

(continued)

Table 2, Continued

Performance Indicators for Each Attribute and Dimension of Literacy

ORIENTATION TO LITERACY

Low orientation	High orientation
Motivation for reading and writing	
a. Goals for literacy are task completion and extrinsic rewards	a. Goals are intrinsic and mastery oriented
b. Gives up easily in the face of difficulty	b. Persists when confronted with obstacles or difficulties
c. Chooses tasks where success or failure are certain	c. Chooses challenging tasks on the edge of current abilities
Attitudes about reading and writing	
a. Negative attitudes about reading and writing	a. Exhibits enthusiasm for reading and writing
b. Exhibits embarrassment, passivity, and insecurity about self as a reader or writer	b. Exhibits pride and confidence about self as a reader or writer
c. Views literacy events as under the control of others	c. Views self as in charge of own literacy and feels that others respect contributions

OWNERSHIP OF LITERACY

Low ownership	High ownership
Interests and habits	
a. Expresses little or no preference for different topics, genres, and authors	a. Exhibits clear preferences for topics, genres, and authors
b. Avoids reading and writing as free choice activities	b. Voluntarily selects reading and writing as free choice activities
c. Does not choose texts to read or topics to write about appropriately	c. Chooses appropriate texts to read and topics for writing
Self-assessment of reading and writing	
a. Rarely evaluates own work, learning, or progress	a. Frequently assesses own work, learning, and progress
b. Shows little initiative in evaluating own work	b. Takes initiative to review and monitor own performance
c. Uses single, vague, or unclear criteria in assessing own work	c. Employs appropriate criteria to evaluate what has been read or written

COLLABORATION

Low collaboration	High collaboration
Cooperation among peers	
a. Little participation with others; engages in isolated activities	a. Frequently engages in collaborative literacy activities
b. Unwilling to engage in the collaborative construction of meaning	b. Initiates discussion, dialogue, or debate about text meaning
c. Reluctant to give or seek help; does not encourage the literacy development of peers	c. Provides positive support, affect, and instructional scaffolding for peers
Community of learners	
a. Does not share goals, values, and practices with others	a. Shares goals, values, and practices with others
b. Does not participate, or plays only a limited array of roles, in the learning community	b. Plays a variety of roles (performer, audience member, leader, supporter) within the learning community
c. Is unaware of the contribution others can make to one's own literacy development	c. Values the contributions of others; respects others' opinions and help

(continued)

Table 2, Continued

Performance Indicators for Each Attribute and Dimension of Literacy

CONNECTEDNESS OF THE CURRICULUM

Low connectedness	High connectedness
Within school	
a. Views reading and writing as decontextualized activities	a. Understands that reading and writing are tools for learning and personal insight
b. Views reading, writing, speaking, and listening as independent of each other	b. Views reading, writing, speaking, and listening as mutually supportive activities
c. Sees little relation between reading and writing and other content areas	c. Understands that what one learns in reading and writing is useful in other content areas
Beyond school	
a. Rarely engages in reading and writing outside of school	a. Reading and writing are part of daily routine activities
b. Views the school literacy curriculum as unrelated to one's own life	b. Connects school literacy activities with reading and writing in daily life
c. Feels discouraged and unsupported for reading and writing outside of school	c. Feels encouraged and supported to read and write outside of school

writing, including poems, a response journal, and a long story entitled "Ghost Dad." During her interview, Alice told how she liked to choose her own journal topics and how she chose her best poems to include in a portfolio. She also identified her favorite books and described how she enjoyed reading frequently. These remarks, coupled with the tangible evidence, earned her a score of three out of four points for the attribute of "Interests and Habits" within the dimension of "Ownership" (see Table 2). The other attribute in that dimension, "Self Assessment," only received two points because Alice said that her writing goal was to write faster, a negative piece of evidence that was offset modestly by her discussion of choosing her best poem. In a similar fashion, Alice's comments and reflections, coupled with a review of her work samples, were used to determine scores for each of the 14 attributes.

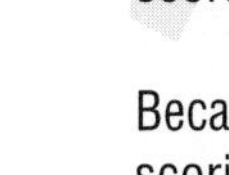

Because this was a pilot project and the scoring system was generated and refined as we examined students' work, we do not have numerical indices of the validity and reliability of the performance assessments. However, we believe that this model yields data that are authentic and trustworthy because the work samples are derived from daily curricular activities and interpreted by students (cf., Valencia, 1990). Traditional notions of reliability, based on the similarity of scores from tests to retest, may no longer apply to performance assessments that provide opportunities for reflection and learning. Indeed, low test-retest reliability may be desirable if students benefit from the process of assessing their own literacy.

Assessments grounded in performance may provide dynamic descriptions of students' rates of learning and degrees of change. Furthermore, Linn, Baker, and Dunbar (1991) have suggested that performance-based assessments be judged by expanded notions of validity that include concepts such as the consequences of assessment, the fairness of tasks and scoring, the generalizability of results, and the quality and complexity of the content of the assessments. We think that evaluations of students' work samples like we've done will encourage teachers and students to produce complex, high quality, diverse, and fair collections of literacy artifacts. The consequences of such assessment will stimulate motivated learning by students

as well as effective instruction by teachers that is aligned with curricular objectives.

These brief comments about reliability and validity illustrate the need to expand traditional psychometric definitions. We believe that various assessment models, such as the one we designed for KEEP, should be examined against standards of validity and reliability, but we also recognize that those psychometric constructs are being redefined as new kinds of assessment are created. Revisions of assessment and criteria for evaluating assessment are intertwined, so we encourage researchers to substantiate the usefulness of new assessment procedures against a wide variety of criteria.

Phase 5: Interpreting and Using the Data

We have not yet had an opportunity to implement the system and use the data derived from the interviews and work samples. However, the framework we created was guided by certain intended uses of the data, and we strongly believe that stakeholders must consider the uses and consequences of assessment *before* creating alternative measures. The data derived from the interviews and artifacts can be reported in several ways. One option is to report the scores for each attribute or dimension. These can be compared directly across students, classrooms, or programs. Another option is to report the percentage of students meeting some criterion (e.g., a "High orientation" see Table 2), on each dimension. A third option is to aggregate the data across dimensions and report single scores for each student, although this mixes evaluations from quite different dimensions of literacy. A fourth option is to record students' achievements with narrative comments rather than numerical scores, noting areas of particular talent or weakness.

Regardless of the format of the data, the results of authentic assessments can serve a variety of purposes, all of which can improve opportunities for students to learn. First, alternative assessments can provide richer diagnostic information about students' development because the assessments are tied directly to the curriculum objectives and to instructional procedures and goals in the classroom (Calfee & Hiebert, 1990). In this model, assessment and instruction become overlapping and symbiotic activities. A second use of the data is to inform parents about their children's progress as well as the curriculum objectives and instructional practices. We believe that parents can become more involved in their children's literacy when they understand how they can support and extend instructional efforts at school. Third, authentic assessments help students to engage in monitoring and evaluating their own work, to reflect on their efforts and accomplishments, and to gain insights into the processes of learning that will help them in future tasks (Tierney, Carter, & Desai, 1991). Fourth, we think that authentic assessments can yield summative data for administrators who must provide quantitative indicators of accountability. These multiple functions can be served by authentic assessments when they are designed with these purposes in mind.

Modifying and Applying the Framework

The strength of the five-phase framework is that it can serve as a dynamic, flexible system for any district or state revising or creating alternative assessments of educational progress. Our project illustrates the feasibility of the framework for large-scale literacy assessments. We see the coherence, flexibility and local control as strengths of the process. For example, a district might identify different dimensions of literacy than we did, but the process of identifying what is valued in a curriculum and building consensus among stakeholders clarifies what needs to be assessed. The specification of characteristics and attributes of literacy can also be negotiated to reflect the level of specificity desired for different purposes. Teachers who want fine-grained assessments to use diagnostically may use the evidence in a different manner than administrators who may need only general descriptions; however, the same kinds of dimensions and evidence undergird both assessments. For example, a teacher who reviews a student's work in an interview may notice that the student is unaware of text structures, genre, and specific comprehension strategies suitable for expository text. The teacher might design specific projects involving documents and library research skills to improve the student's knowledge about literacy. An administrator who notices low scores on this dimension across many students may look for concomitant low reading scores in social studies and science and may suggest instructional strategies for content area reading.

There is also flexibility in the ways that evidence is collected and scored. We believe that a broad array of evidence is needed to augment traditional test scores, evidence that should include students' daily work samples collected periodically throughout the year. The collection of evidence need not be disruptive nor undermine the curriculum if assessment, instruction, and curricula are mutually supportive. Local decision makers can choose to score students' work quantitatively or qualitatively. In our project there was a need for quantitative data to make yearly comparisons among programs so the data could serve summative evaluation purposes. If the data are used primarily for formative purposes, then qualitative descriptions might suffice.

We consider the local control and implementation of assessment reform to be essential, but at the same time, we see a need for districts to generate coherent frameworks to guide their decision making. As districts move away from using "off-the-shelf, one-size-fits-all" commercial tests of literacy, they need to clarify what they value, what they measure, what standards will be used for evaluation, how they will collect the evidence, and how the data will be used. Our framework for creating alternative literacy assessments provides a starting point that can be expanded and revised to fit the needs of any district. We are enthusiastic about the opportunities that exist today for designing new kinds of educational assessment, not just new tests, but whole new systems of assessing teaching and learning in schools. Creative solutions to longstanding problems of assessment hold great promise for enhancing students' learning, motivation, and achievement.

References

Au, K., Blake, K., Herman, P., Oshiro, M., & Scheu, J. (1990). *Literacy curriculum guide.* Honolulu. HI: Center for the Development of Early Education, Kamehameha Schools.

Au, K.H., Scheu, J.A., Kawakami, A.J., & Herman, P.A. (1990). Assessment and accountability in a whole language curriculum. *The Reading Teacher, 43,* 574-578.

Calfee, R., & Hiebert, E. (1990). Classroom assessment of reading. In R. Barr, M. Kamil, P. Mosenthal, & P.D. Pearson (Eds.), *Handbook of reading research* (2nd ed.) (pp. 281-309). New York: Longman.

Giuli, C. (1991). Developing a summative measure of whole language instruction: A sonata in risk-taking. *The Kamehameha Journal of Education, 2,* 57-65.

Hawaii Department of Education. (1988). *Language arts program guide.* Honolulu, HI: Office of Instructional Services.

Linn, R.L., Baker, E.L., & Dunbar, S.B. (1991). Complex, performance-based assessment: Expectations and validation criteria. *Educational Researcher, 20,* 15-21.

Resnick, L., & Resnick, D. (1990). Tests as standards of achievement in school. *The uses of standarized tests in American education* (pp. 63-80). Princeton. NJ: Educational Testing Service.

Tharp, R.G., & Gallimore, R. (1988). *Rousing minds to life: Teaching, learning, and schooling in social context.* New York: Cambridge University Press.

Tierney, R.J., Carter, M.A., & Desai, L.E. (1991). *Portfolio assessment in the reading-writing classroom.* Norwood, MA: Christopher-Gordon.

Valencia, S.W. (1990). Alternative assessment: Separating the wheat from the chaff. *The Reading Teacher, 44,* 60-61.

Valencia, S., & Pearson, P.D. (1987). Reading assessment: A time for change. *The Reading Teacher, 40,* 726-733.

Winograd, P., Paris, S., & Bridge, C. (1991).

Improving the assessment of reading. *The Reading Teacher, 45,* 108-116.

Wolf, K., Filby, N., Paris, S., Valencia, S., Pearson, D., Hiebert, E., & Calfee. R. (1991). *KEEP literacy assessment system.* Final report from the Far West Laboratory for Educational Research and Development.

Yap, K.O., Estes. G.D., & Nickel, P.R. (1988, September). *A summative evaluation of the Kamehameha elementary education program as disseminated in Hawaii public schools.* Northwest Regional Educational Laboratory, Evaluation and Assessment Program.

Soon Anofe You Tout Me: Evaluation in a First-Grade Whole Language Classroom

Reprinted from *The Reading Teacher* (1991), *45*, 46-50

Linda J. Pils

Last year, on the last day of first grade, Courtney handed me a small book that she had made as a gift. It read, "First I didn't know how It would be like to have you. But less then one week I had alredy started to like you. First I didn't know how to read very well. Soon anofe you tout me." I had my report card. Courtney had just provided me with all the evaluation that I needed about my efforts to change the way that I had previously taught reading to children.

I had embraced the whole language philosophy because it allowed me to teach children at their levels and enable them to become independent learners. I had abandoned workbooks for journals, Ditto sheets for key words, and basal readers for trade books and reading/writing workshops. I still taught phonics, strategies for decoding, and comprehension, but they would be only one lane on the literacy highway, and often there were many detours along the way. Meaning and natural language became the basis of my curriculum, and literature, oral language, drama, and writing became my major building blocks.

However, during my transition, I struggled with ways to piece all of the parts together to make a snug fit. If I used alternative methods for reading instruction, then I could not rely on the formal assessments which were part of the basal program I used previously. How should I evaluate children's progress and the program itself, and how should I demonstrate to parents and administrators the progress which had been made?

This article is a story of changes: changes in perspective, attitude, and responsibility. In it I describe the assessments that were implemented in my classroom in order to evaluate my students' progress and guide their acquisition of literacy abilities. First, I describe my classroom and the literacy events that occur in it. Next, I share the new perspective on evaluation that I have acquired and various special ways I gather and respond to information about my students.

My Classroom

I have always believed that children should be surrounded by good literature, so the jump from the classroom with lots of read-aloud time, literature follow-up activities, and sustained silent reading to a literature-based/whole language classroom was not a broad one. But as I read articles, attended conferences, and shared ideas with colleagues, my understanding of why these activities were important changed. I came to realize that these activities were not the fluff but the substance of the reading program. I changed my basal reading program to one which included a wide variety of literacy activities. These be-

gan with our class meeting and continued with reading, writing/sharing, and read-aloud blocks (see daily schedule figure). Thematic units were implemented to integrate the subjects of math, science, and social studies. The following is a brief description of some of these literacy activities.

- *Key words and sentences.* I use a key word program based on Sylvia Ashton-Warner's work as described by Johnson (1987). Three to four times a week the children dictate words which I write on tagboard strips. The children copy their words into a key word booklet, draw a picture, and write a story. These words are also used as a resource for writing and reading.
- *Daily news.* As we complete our calendar activities, I ask the children for sentences about yesterday, today, and tomorrow. I write down the today sentences on a piece of large, lined story paper. I use these daily news stories in various ways, for example, as a source of words for decoding lessons.
- *Buddy reading.* In this time, children select their reading material and sit alone or with a buddy and read. Initially I assigned buddies, usually a strong reader with a child of lesser ability. Now we alternate between assigned and self-chosen buddies.
- *Reading workshop.* In reading workshop, small groups of children look at and talk about books that have been placed in a large container. There are books of varying levels and interests in each container, multiple copies of books that have been read aloud, and others that the children have selected.
- *Writing workshop.* Working in pairs or alone, the children write about themselves and the world around them. They write fiction and nonfiction; they write humorously and poignantly. I model the writing process with a class story. Parent helpers, trained in process writing, assist in the publishing stage, and the published books are kept in our class library.

New Forms of Assessment

In the past, I would rely on basal tests to assess my students' growth in reading, but in my new environment, those tests were not useful. Instead, I began to examine students' work. For example, I would analyze the children's journal entries and make some judgments about their word identification abilities. For instance, Kristi wrote in her journal, "I wis I had a hamsdr his name is cdls. I wd pl wt hma" (I wish I had a hamster. His name is Cuddles. I would play with him.). This told me Kristi could formulate a complete idea in a paragraph; she was aware of syntax, spacing between words, beginning and ending sounds, and some medial vowels and consonants; she used some standard spellings; and she understood the components of sentence structure and was beginning to capitalize and use periods appropriately.

In contrast, Bobby's entry on the same date was "IWTOM" (I went to Madison). He understood that writing is a meaningful activity and that letters are the basis for written communication. He relied on beginning sounds and understood the left-to-right convention in written language.

The information from these journals gave me a much richer picture of these two very different children. How I assisted them was determined by where they were in the reading/ writing process. In working with Kristi, I began stressing vowel sounds and word families in her key words; in her journal writing we talked about how to expand her story and about the possibility of making a "Cuddles" chapter book. In planning for mini-lessons, I included different uses of capital letters, for if Kristi were ready to expand her knowledge, there were other children who could also benefit from such a lesson.

Bobby was ready for other things. Bobby was selected to be our song leader during our morning meeting. He pointed to the words as we sang them, which made him aware of the spaces between words and the need for them. In our big book lessons,

I used a variety of cloze activities. I covered up the ends of words with small sticky notes, sometimes covering the entire word and, at other times, just the endings of specific words. Bobby could predict which words were appropriate and then check his predictions as individual letters were shown. This activity stressed the ends of words and involved him in the process. When I assisted Bobby with his journal, I encouraged him to write all of an unknown word with the use of boxes to designate each letter. He usually knew the first letter, and we worked together to formulate the rest.

Clipboards and Labels

My classroom paraphernalia now includes a clipboard with strips of blank mailing labels attached. Each morning I date several of these labels and write names and observations that I make as I walk around the room discussing each child's work, progress, and problems. At the end of the day, I place the labels on sheets of paper in a three-ring binder which is divided into sections for each child in my class. As I reread these anecdotal records, it is easy to spot patterns of behavior, problems that I need to address, and recent achievements. My anecdotal records take many forms:

- 8-30 Ben: Rarely raises hand during meeting, but always attentive.
- 9-30 Ben: "I like doing daily news because it's so easy sometimes."
- 10-30 Ben: Tells story of The Three Little Pigs to Chris.
- 10-30 Ben: "Look, *at* is in my last name."
- 8-23 Amy: Very interesting story in journal, re: eagles nesting; good beginning and ending sounds.
- 10-17 Amy: Running record taken of daily news, self-corrected *monkeybars*. Says she read three books at home that we've read in school.
- 10-30 Amy: "Eleven minus seven equals four, it's a rhyme!"

- 9-24 Stacy: "I can read *Hop on Pop* all by myself."
- 10-5 Stacy: Stacy and Alan very good buddies, Stacy helps Alan with words. She read all of helper chart when she selected her job.

What do I learn as I meander around the room observing students and taking notes? On October 2, I learned that Danny said, "Oh, goody!" when I announced that it was buddy reading time. This was from a boy who cried daily for the first month of school and said "I can't" to every new activity or lesson. On November 20, I learned that Richard read *Noisy Nora* by Rosemary Wells perfectly; he held the book up as I do to show the pictures, even though no one was listening. I learned that Crystal was reading the song that we had learned at Halloween, a song put on sentence strips. She sang aloud as she pointed to each word with the pointer.

These observations, made on a daily basis, gave me a clear picture of the progress these children were making. All teachers observe children, but now I am using my observations in a more coherent, organized way.

Portfolios

As a means to assemble and analyze the large amount of data I began to gather on my students, I initiated literacy portfolios for each student. I placed a variety of materials in these literacy portfolios, including the following:

Writing samples. At the beginning of the year after we had brainstormed ideas, I asked each child to write a story about what she or he did during the summer. I compared these initial stories to other writings done later on during the year. I analyzed the stories for sentence structure, number of known words, punctuation, and content. Some children could write one sentence in invented spelling about what they had done over the summer. Bobby wrote "I W Rg A The P" (I went raking at the park). Other children like Brian and Shan-

non could only draw what they enjoyed during the summer.

Some children develop their understanding of the code in great leaps. Others make minute but steady steps. For example, it took a month for Danny to change from "I can't" to initiating his own drawing and dictating the story. It took another month to write "I" every day on the first line of his journal. On November 20 after making the illustrations for his first book, Danny asked me to write the words: "I am learning to read." By December, Danny was writing his own stories independently. By gathering and analyzing Danny's writing samples, I was able to guide his development as a writer.

Number of words read aloud in one minute. In September, each child was asked to read aloud an excerpt from *Frog and Toad All Year* by Arnold Lobel. The selected passage was long enough so that no child could finish reading it in less than a minute (Kramer, 1990). I calculated the number of words read aloud in one minute. The children read the same selection again in January and May, and the results were tabulated. This assessment, which took less than an hour to administer to all 24 children in the class, provided important feedback to both me and my children regarding their developing competence as readers.

Ten-minute writing sample. I also keep track of how many words each child can write in a 10-minute period at 3-month intervals throughout the year. The children and I compare these totals, giving us evidence of their development as writers.

Lists of books read and to be read. Each child keeps a list of books read during buddy reading time. As we confer, this list is a starting point for our talks, and it assists me in making suggestions for interesting or challenging follow-up titles. We also keep a list of books or authors that each child would like to read. These often are titles that other children have mentioned in reading workshop, in sharing time, or during read alouds.

Challenge Cards. Lists of unknown words and their sources are placed on Challenge Cards. These are discussed at reading conferences. I examine these words for miscue patterns and initiate mini-les-

Daily Schedule

Class meeting
8:10-8:40: Calendar, weather report, class business, poetry helpers (we read 2-3 poems), music, and daily news

Reading block
8:40-9:30: Shared reading (big books), skill follow-up on a book previously read, daily news independent work, key words, story mapping, small group or individual conferences.

Writing/sharing block
9:45-11:05: Buddy reading, writing workshop, journals, publishing center, reading workshop, formal and informal dramatics, sharing time.

Read alouds
11:45-12:15: Read alouds and silent reading.

Math, science, and social studies
12:15-2:45: Large and small group, centers, special classes, end-of-the-day meeting.

sons as needed for individuals or groups of students.

Conference records. In reading and writing conferences, the children and I discuss what interests them in their readings, how books or themes are alike or different, and what they are currently writing about. They read favorite passages and talk about authors. They discuss problems and how to solve them. We keep a check list that contains items such as "I use capital letters at the beginning of sentences," and "I can write from left to right."

Conclusion

In previous years, I was in charge of the learning and the evaluation that occurred in my classroom. Now the children share responsibility for their learning, and they participate in its evaluation.

Parents also participate. For instance, at a fall conference with Laura's parents, we discussed what kinds of growth they could expect to see, what stages would probably come next. They read her journal and her book list and listened to a tape of Laura reading. I learned about Laura's interests and hobbies from the completed parent survey. They did not hear about what Laura could not do; we discussed what she *could* do.

At first my evaluation was episodic. There was a flurry of activity prior to each conference or reporting period. Now assessments are done every day. This makes me more aware of my students' development and any possible problems. We can work on a difficult area immediately, individually or in a small group. The children do not need to stop their reading or writing to be evaluated. Their reading and writing *is* the evaluation; it is not a separate phenomenon.

In *Leo the Late Bloomer* by Robert Kraus, Leo's father watches Leo for signs of blooming.

> "Are you sure Leo's a bloomer?" asked Leo's father. "Patience," said Leo's mother, "A watched bloomer doesn't bloom." So Leo's father watched television instead of Leo. ...Then one day, in his own good time, Leo bloomed! He could read! He could write! ...He also spoke. And it wasn't just a word. It was a whole sentence. And that sentence was ..."I made it!"

In a whole language classroom, kids bloom just like Leo, and the reason that they bloom is that we trust them to learn. Teachers bloom in such classrooms, too, not because they are super teachers but because teachers can rely on themselves and not the faraway editors of standardized tests to legitimize observations of children.

I am trusted to observe and evaluate. Yetta Goodman (1989, p. 5) states it succinctly when she writes, "Once teachers begin to take account of what they know about learning, language, and conceptual development ...their reflective thinking grows and takes on new dimensions."

Move over, Leo.

References

Goodman, Y.M. (1989). Evaluation of students. In K.S. Goodman, Y.M. Goodman, & W.J. Hood (Eds.), *The whole language evaluation book* (pp. 3-14). Portsmouth, NH: Heinemann.

Johnson, K. (1987). *Doing words.* Boston: Houghton Mifflin.

Kramer, C.J. (1990). Documenting reading and writing growth in the primary grades using informal methods of evaluation. *The Reading Teacher, 44,* 356-357.

Anecdotal Records: A Powerful Tool for Ongoing Literacy Assessment

Reprinted from *The Reading Teacher* (1992), *45*, 502-509

Lynn K. Rhodes
Sally Nathenson-Mejia

A great deal of attention is being paid to the assessment of process in addition to product in reading and writing. Observing the process a student uses provides the teacher with a window or view on how students arrive at products (i.e., a piece of writing or an answer to a comprehension question). This allows the teacher to make good decisions about how she or he might assist during the process or restructure the process in order to best support more effective use of strategies and students' development as readers and writers. Anecdotal records can be written about products or can include information about both process and product. As process assessment, resulting from observation, anecdotal records can be particularly telling.

Observations of students in the process of everyday reading and writing allow teachers to see for themselves the reading and writing and problem-solving strategies students use and their responses to reading and writing. Genishi and Dyson (1984), Jaggar (1985), Pinnell (1985), Y. Goodman (1985), Galindo (1989), and others discuss the need to observe children while they are involved in language use. Goodman notes:

> Evaluation provides the most significant information if it occurs continuously and simultaneously with the experiences in which the learning is taking place.... Teachers who observe the development of language and knowledge in children in different settings become aware of important milestones in children's development that tests cannot reveal. (Goodman, 1985, p. 10)

When teachers have developed a firm knowledge base that they can rely on in observations of students' reading and writing, they usually prefer recording their observations in anecdotal form. This is because the open-ended nature of anecdotal records allows teachers to record the rich detail available in most observations of literacy processes and products. The open-ended nature of anecdotal record taking also allows teachers to determine what details are important to record given the situation in which the student is reading/writing, previous assessment data, and the instructional goals the teacher and student have established. In other words, what is focused on and recorded depends upon the teacher, the student, and the context, not on the predetermined items on a checklist.

Taken regularly, anecdotal notes become not only a vehicle for planning instruction and documenting progress, but also a story about an individual. The definition of an anecdote is "a short narrative (or story) concerning a particular incident or event of an interesting or amusing nature"

(*The Random House Dictionary of the English Language,* 1966). A story is "a way of knowing and remembering information—a shape or pattern into which information can be arranged.... [Story] restructures experiences for the purpose of 'saving' them" (Livo, 1986, p. 5). Anecdotes about events in the reading/writing life of a student tell an ongoing story about how that child responds to the classroom's literacy environment and instruction. Since stories are how we make sense of much of our world, anecdotal records can be a vehicle for helping us make sense of what students do as readers and writers. In addition, teachers find that telling the story accumulated in anecdotal records is a natural and easy way to impart information about students' literacy progress to parents and others who care for the children.

In short, anecdotal records are widely acknowledged as being a powerful classroom tool for ongoing literacy assessment (Bird, 1989; Cartwright & Cartwright, 1974; Morrissey, 1989; Thorndike & Hagen, 1977). In this article we will provide information about techniques for collecting and analyzing anecdotal records. In addition, we will review uses of anecdotal records including planning for instruction, informing parents and students, and generating new assessment questions.

Techniques for Writing Anecdotal Records

Reflecting about techniques for writing anecdxotal records can positively affect both the content of the records as well as the ease with which they are recorded. Thorndike and Hagen (1977) suggest guidelines for the content of anecdotal records that teachers may find helpful:

1. Describe a specific event or product.
2. Report rather than evaluate or interpret.
3. Relate the material to other facts that are known about the child.

We have found these points particularly helpful if teachers feel that the content of

their previous anecdotal records has not been useful to them. Below we have included an example of an anecdotal record for a first grader, Eleanor. Note how Eleanor's teacher uses detailed description to record how Eleanor is starting to understand sound/letter relationships but is still confused about word boundaries and sentences.

Eleanor

STRDAIPADENBSNO
(Yesterday I played in the snow)
STRDA = yesterday
I = I
PAD = played
EN = in
B = the (said "du" and thought she was writing "D")
SNO = snow
Showed her how to stretch her words out like a rubberband—doing it almost on own by SNO. E does have a fairly good grasp of sound/letter relationships. However, has a hard time isolating words and tracking words in sentences in her mind. That may hold up progress for awhile. Asked her—at end—what she did in writing today that she hadn't done in previous writing. She said, "I listened to sounds." Told her to do it in her writing again tomorrow.

Instead of recording the descriptive detail found in Eleanor's anecdotal note, the teacher might have written, "Eleanor sounded out words in writing for the first time today and will continue to need lots of help to do so." A general conclusion such as this is not as useful to instructional planning or to documenting progress as the detailed description in the note written by Eleanor's teacher. However, we believe that Thorndike and Hagen's points should be treated as guidelines, not as strict rules. We find that it is sometimes helpful to evaluate or interpret what has been observed.

For example, read the sample anecdotal record below written about Katie, a fourth grader.

Katie

I asked if I could read more of the poetry book she had written at home over the last two years. (She had read selected poems to her classmates earlier.) She showed me a poem she didn't want to read to the class "because they wouldn't understand." (It's quite serious and deep.) Poetry doesn't look like poetry though she reads it as poetry—could use a formatting lesson.

The teacher's comment, "could use a formatting lesson," in Katie's note provides useful evaluation and interpretation as long as it is supported by a description of the event or product itself. The comment "Poetry doesn't look like poetry though she reads it as poetry," is the description that supports the interpretive comment.

Observational guides can be valuable complements to anecdotal recording because they serve to remind teachers what might be observed. If teachers find an observation guide helpful, they may want to post for themselves a list of the kinds of observations that might be recorded anecdotally. The table illustrates such a guide resulting from teachers' brainstorming. The list is displayed in a place in the classroom where the teachers can easily consult it, especially when they feel they need to improve the content of their notes.

In addition to increasing the content value of anecdotal notes, teachers also are concerned about increasing the ease with which anecdotal notes can be recorded. In part, ease of recording emanates from the classroom environment the teacher has established. Classroom routines that encourage students to be increasingly independent and responsible as readers and writers enable teachers to more easily record anecdotal records than classrooms in which literacy tasks are more teacher directed. Once students are familiar with and secure about the structure and behaviors demanded in routines such as Sustained Silent Reading, Author's Circle, Literature Circles, Writers' Workshop, and Readers' Workshop, teachers can find the time to work with and record observations of individuals or groups.

In addition to encouraging student independence and responsibility in literacy situations, it is easier to write anecdotal notes as teachers discover recording techniques that fit their styles and busy classroom lives. It is useful to carry a clipboard to a variety of classroom settings, using such complementary recording tools as sticky notes to transfer information to a notebook sectioned off by students' names. Teachers can take notes on a prearranged list of children each day, labeling sticky notes with the date and the names of students to be observed. This technique makes it possible to take notes on every child a minimum of once a week in each curricular area in which notes are taken. Students can keep records too. Following a conference, the teacher might ask the student to record a summary statement of what they worked on together, what the student learned, or what the student still had questions about or wanted help with. Students can use sticky notes too so that their notes may be placed in the notebook along with the teacher's notes.

Teachers can take notes on groups as well as on individuals. For example, in working with a group of Chapter I students, one teacher noted that all five students were having difficulty putting the information they were gathering from books into their own words as they took notes. Instead of writing the same information five times, she wrote it once and put the note in a spot in her notebook reserved for notes about the group. When a note is taken in a group, but applies only to selected students in the group, the note can be photocopied for the file of each student to whom it applies.

Analyzing Anecdotal Records

Good techniques for recording anecdotal notes must be matched with good tech-

Teacher-Generated Observation Guide

- Functions served in reading/writing
- Engagement in reading/writing
- What appears to impact engagement in reading/writing
- What aspects of text student attends to
- Interactions with others over reading/writing
- Interactions with materials
- Insightful or interesting things students say
- Hypotheses students are trying out in reading/writing
- Misconceptions students have
- Miscues students make while reading
- Changes students make in writing
- How students use text before, during, and after reading
- How a lesson affects students' reading/writing
- Comparisons between what students say and what they do
- Plans students make and whether/how plans are amended
- How, where, and with whom students work
- What students are interested in
- What students say they want to work on in their reading/writing
- What students say about reading/writing done outside of school
- How students generate and solve problems in reading/writing
- Ideas for reading/writing lessons and materials
- How students "symbol weave" (use multiple symbolic forms)
- How students theorize or talk about reading/writing
- How one reading/writing event relates to another
- How students use a variety of resources in reading/writing

niques for analyzing those notes if the potential for anecdotal records is to be realized. Effective analysis techniques include making inferences from the notes, looking for developmental trends or patterns within individuals and across children, identifying both strengths and weaknesses in learning and teaching, and making time for analysis.

Making inferences. Teachers continually make inferences about students' reading and writing on the basis of observations. Looking back at the sample anecdotal record on Eleanor, you can see that Eleanor's teacher made one of her inferences explicit: "E does have a fairly good grasp of sound/letter relationships." Because the teacher observed that Eleanor was able to consistently produce letters that matched the sounds she heard, she was able to infer that Eleanor had developed knowledge of sound/letter relationships.

Katie's teacher doesn't explicitly infer anything in the first anecdotal record but it is possible for us to hypothesize that Katie may think she is different from many of her classmates with regard to what she thinks and writes. An analysis of other anecdotal records on Katie may lead the teacher to uncover a pattern in Katie's responses that confirms her hypothesis.

Identifying patterns. Patterns of behavior can be uncovered for individuals and groups by reading and rereading anecdotal records looking for similarities and differences. For example, the following two notes were taken during a reading period in a second-grade classroom in which the majority of the students elect to read in pairs or small groups. What pattern of behavior do you see?

> Brooke & Larry reading a *Nate the Great* story together—switching off at each paragraph. Brooke

> jumps in to correct Larry or give him a word at the slightest hesitation.
>
> Aaron & Shawn reading—switching off after every 2 pgs. Shawn loves the story—keeps telling Aaron the next part will be funny & chuckling as he reads aloud. Shawn is the leader in this situation. He interrupts with immediate help when Aaron hesitates with a word.

In recording and reviewing these notes, the teacher noticed that she had observed the same problem in both pairs of readers: one reader would take over the responsibility for working out words from the other reader. Since she had notes on only two pairs of students, however, the teacher interviewed the class the next day, focusing on what they did to help classmates who encountered difficult words to find out whether the pattern she had uncovered in these two situations was a more general problem. Differing patterns in language use, both oral and written, can be seen through regular anecdotal record keeping.

To illustrate with another example, a second-grade teacher, one of our practicum students, was concerned about Raul, who was new to the United States. She felt he was gaining more control over written and oral English, but she had nothing to document his progress. Moreover, she did not want to push him too hard if he wasn't ready, or cause him to lag behind. The following are excerpts from anecdotal records Sally took as the practicum supervisor while observing Raul working with his peers, none of whom spoke his native Spanish. These notes demonstrate not only his interaction with print, but also his use of oral language.

> The boys begin reading through the questions. Raul looks at the book and says, "Que es esto?" (What is this?). No one answers him.
>
> They are sitting next to a chart that has all their names on it. They proceed to copy each others' names from the chart. Raul says to the group, "You can get my name from the chart."
>
> T [the teacher] comes over to see what they are doing. She asks which question they are on. Raul replies, "Where do they live? Water." T reminds them to write the answer in the appropriate square.

Using these and other notes, the teacher was able to see patterns in Raul's use of language on two levels, interacting with print, and interacting with peers. Getting no response when he initiated interaction in Spanish, Raul proceeded to use English to read from the chart, read from the book, speak to his classmates, and respond to his teacher. Together the teacher and Sally were able to plan for how his use of English could continue to be encouraged in context-laden situations without worrying about pushing him too fast.

Identifying strengths and weaknesses. Anecdotal records can be analyzed for both strengths and weaknesses in students' reading and writing. Katie's anecdotal record, which we discussed already, reveals that she writes poetry for herself outside of school and that she has a sense of audience. These are strengths. The record also reveals an area in which Katie can grow—formatting the poetry she writes. A look back at Eleanor's note also reveals strengths and weaknesses. For example, the teacher discovered that Eleanor has graphophonic knowledge not previously revealed in her writing and that she could verbalize what she learned during the conference with the teacher. The teacher also discovered that Eleanor had previously been using random strings of letters in her writing because she had such difficulty tracking words in sentences in her mind.

Finding time for analysis. Finally, just as it is important to find time to *record* anecdotal records, it is important to find time to *analyze* anecdotal records. Some analysis occurs concurrently with recording

anecdotal notes and is recorded along with a description of the event that was observed. However, other analysis follows the recording of notes. We recommend that teachers try two things to make time for such analysis. First, use the start of each instructional planning period for an analysis of anecdotal records for individuals and groups. This will serve to focus planning time so that it may be used more efficiently. Second, if teachers meet on a regular basis with other teachers, analyzing anecdotal records can be a fruitful part of the meeting. For example, if a classroom teacher and Chapter I teacher both take anecdotal records on the same child, they can analyze both sets of notes together by comparing individual notes and looking for shared patterns and trends. If a group of teachers from the same grade level meets regularly, an analysis of one another's notes may uncover a great deal to talk about, including how best to adapt teaching to students' needs.

Uses of Anecdotal Records

Analysis of anecdotal records allows teachers to find patterns of success and difficulty for both individuals and groups of students. Students who have a need for particular information or for particular kinds of reading and writing opportunities can be grouped together and provided with the information or opportunities meeting their needs. In addition to instructional planning, the records also can be used to inform students and parents about progress and the value of various instructional and learning contexts. Finally, anecdotal records can help teachers generate new assessment questions.

Instructional planning. To extend what Genishi and Dyson say about oral language to written language (1984), anecdotal records on children's social behaviors and responses to written language can help teachers plan stimulating situations for the reluctant as well as the enthusiastic reader/writer. Using the set of anecdotal notes taken in the second-grade classroom during buddy reading discussed previously, we will show how the earlier analysis we provided can lead naturally to an instructional plan.

To review, the teacher noted that students in the buddy reading activity were taking reading responsibility away from their classmates when they hesitated or showed any sign of difficulty with reading words. When she interviewed the class the next day to glean more information about why this happened, she found that few students knew any options for helping partners with difficult words except to tell them the words. These assessment data helped the teacher plan lessons to demonstrate how to help readers retain responsibility for figuring out difficult words. For example, she talked to the children about the strategies she used with them—providing plenty of wait time, suggesting that they read on, suggesting that they reread, and so on. Then she demonstrated each of these strategies with a child and made a list of the strategies for the children to refer to. Finally, she ended the next several reading sessions early so that the children could share with her and each other the strategies they used to successfully figure out their own words and to assist peers in figuring out words they didn't know. The children also shared problems they encountered and talked about how to solve them.

During the week the class focused on improving their strategies, the teacher observed pairs as they read, provided individual coaching for some, recorded more anecdotal notes, and used the notes to couch her lessons in detailed examples. In short, though the original anecdotal records and class interview were the basis of her first lesson, the anecdotal notes taken *after* the lessons began became equally important in planning ongoing instruction to further develop the students' strategies and understanding.

Informing. In addition to using anecdotal records for planning ongoing instruction, teachers also may use them to periodically inform others, including the students themselves, about students' strengths, weaknesses, and progress. Reviewing

anecdotal records with students helps them see the growth they have made as readers and writers, and helps them gain a sense of progress over time and learn to pinpoint where improvements need to be made. To illustrate, one Chapter I teacher who involved students in generating instructional goals claimed that the process of writing anecdotal records affected the students' attention to the goals they had set: "The children seem to get more focused faster since I started carrying a clipboard and taking notes. It seems to remind them about the goals they decided to work on."

Anecdotal records also can help teachers create support systems for students outside the classroom. Report cards, parent conferences, and staffings are all situations in which instructional planning can take place on the basis of the teacher's analysis of anecdotal records. Specific examples pulled from anecdotal records help parents or other school personnel see the child in the same way as the teacher who has collected the anecdotal records. They can augment the home or test information provided by others and provide clues about what contexts are and are not supportive of the child's learning in school.

Generating new questions. Analyzing anecdotal records and using them to plan instruction encourages teachers to generate new questions that lead full circle to further assessment of students and of teaching itself. One teacher commented, "As I review kids' notes, sometimes even as I write them, I realize what else I need to find out." Bird (1989) commented that anecdotal records "not only guide [a teacher] in her instructional decision making but also provide her with a frequent opportunity for self-evaluation, enabling her to assess her role as a teacher" (p. 21).

We agree, and find that the use of anecdotal records to inform instruction helps teachers become more aware of how their instruction is interpreted by students. Teachers able to see how they can influence students' interactions with each other as well as with books and other materials through specific instructional practices. To illustrate, below are some assessment questions generated by the teacher who recorded the anecdotal notes on pairs of students who were reading together in her classroom:

- What effect will the planned lessons have on students' interactions over words during reading?
- What other interactions do students have with each other over *ideas* in the story when they read together? (Her notes about Shawn led her to wonder this.)
- Do different pairings during reading make a difference in how readers interact with each other? What kinds of pairings are optimal?
- In what other situations is Shawn a leader? What can be done to further encourage that side of him?

The teacher has come full circle. Her original anecdotal notes were analyzed and used to plan instruction. But the notes also led to more focused assessment of individuals as well as assessment of a wider range of students and incidents. Her analysis and instructional planning led her to consider new assessment questions, questions not only about the students' reading but also about the effect of her teaching on their reading. For this teacher and for others who have realized the potential of anecdotal records, these "stories" are the basis from which they assess both their students' learning and their own teaching.

Conclusion

Anecdotal records are a powerful tool for collecting information on an ongoing basis during reading and writing and for evaluating the products of instruction. Keeping anecdotal records on a regular basis can enhance a teacher's classroom observation skills. Teachers report that they see and hear with more clarity when using anecdotal records, by focusing more intensively on how children say things and how they interact with each other.

Anecdotal records are advantageous not only for planning instruction but for keeping others informed of children's progress in reading and writing and for focusing future assessment. When teachers discover the value of anecdotal records and figure out techniques to embed them in classroom literacy events and planning, anecdotal record keeping becomes a natural and important part of teaching and learning.

References

Bird, L.B. (1989). The art of teaching: Evaluation and revision. In K. Goodman, Y. Goodman, & W. Hood (Eds.), *The whole language evaluation book* (pp. 15-24). Portsmouth, NH: Heinemann.

Cartwright, C.A., & Cartwright, G.P. (1974). *Developing observational skills.* New York: McGraw-Hill.

Galindo, R. (1989). "Asi no se pone, Si" (That's not how you write, "si"). In K. Goodman, Y. Goodman, & W. Hood (Eds.), *The whole language evaluation book* (pp. 15-24). Portsmouth, NH: Heinemann.

Genishi, C., & Dyson, A.H. (1984). *Language assessment in the early years.* Norwood, NJ: Ablex.

Goodman, Y. (1985). Kidwatching. In A. Jaggar & M.T. Smith-Burke (Eds.), *Observing the language learner.* Newark, DE: International Reading Association.

Jaggar, A. (1985). On observing the language learner: Introduction and overview. In A. Jaggar & M.T. Smith-Burke (Eds.), *Observing the language learner* (pp. 1-7). Newark, DE: International Reading Association.

Livo, N. (1986). *Storytelling: Process and practice.* Littleton, CO: Libraries Unlimited.

Morrissey, M. (1989). When "shut up" is a sign of growth. In K. Goodman, Y. Goodman, & W. Hood (Eds.), *The whole language evaluation book* (pp. 85-97). Portsmouth, NH: Heinemann.

Pinnell, G.S. (1985). Ways to look at the functions of children's language. In A. Jaggar & M.T. Smith-Burke (Eds.), *Observing the language learner* (pp. 57-72). Newark, DE: International Reading Association.

The Random House Dictionary of the English Language. (1966). New York: Random House.

Thorndike, R.L., & Hagen, E.P. (1977). *Measurement and evaluation in psychology and education* (4th ed.). New York: John Wiley and Sons.

Assessment of Emergent Literacy: Storybook Reading

Reprinted from *The Reading Teacher* (1991), *44*, 498-500

Elizabeth Sulzby

Early childhood plays a crucial role in human development. The learning that takes place during this period is very complex and, in recent years, educators and researchers alike (e.g., Meisels, 1989) have protested the inappropriateness of turning paper and pencil, multiple choice tests, or other test screening devices into high-stakes decision tools for young children. Nonetheless, as professionals we need to make informed assessments that provide help for children and guidance to their parents, teachers, and other help providers. In emergent literacy, such research-based assessments have begun to be available.

Educators and researchers have learned a great deal about how children become readers and writers long before schooling begins and, as a result, alternative ways of assessing children's learning and development have surfaced. This column will describe one assessment instrument—the Classification Scheme for Emergent Reading of Favorite Storybooks (Sulzby, 1985, 1988)—that began as a research tool describing children's attempts to read emergently. This instrument can be used to track the development of individuals or groups of children over time. Hence it has evolved into a tool for helping teachers understand development —a day-to-day assessment instrument.

As the field of assessment is changing, this storybook classification scheme has begun to be used for accountability purposes. Its most important use, however, is as a tool through which teachers may further develop their abilities to use knowledge about children's performance in day-to-day teaching; thus it is a teacher development instrument. This emergent literacy instrument, along with a number of others, should be used to replace or supplement traditional reading readiness tests.

Theoretical Basis

The storybook classification scheme is based upon a number of theoretical premises (Sulzby, 1985, 1988; Sulzby & Teale, 1987). First, it assumes that children become literate long before they are reading from print and that such emergent literacy can be observed through children's everyday explorations with print. Second, it assumes that emergent literacy is based upon social interactions with important people, such as parents and teachers, and with literary products of people, such as children's storybooks. Third, it assumes that children are acquiring both oral and written language simultaneously and interrelatedly and that children are constantly figuring out the oral and written language relationships used in their particular culture. Finally, it assumes that children emergently acquire all of the aspects of conventional literacy and that they reorganize these aspects into a coordinated, flexible, integrated system which enables them to figure out print independently.

The Instrument

The Sulzby storybook classification scheme was designed to be used with favorite storybooks, books that children request parents read to them again and again

and those in which children often correct their parents' misreadings or omissions. It was particularly designed for the books that children begin to "read" emergently—long before they are reading from print. The instrument consists of a set of descriptions of 11 subcategories, the highest of which is reading independently from print. Figure 1 shows the major categories and subcategories in tree structure format.

Elicitation Techniques

Books. For use in classrooms, books should be selected from storybooks with characters and plots that children respond to enthusiastically over repeated rereadings, (The scheme can be used with some other genres, but not with very brief nonstorybooks—particularly pattern books, such as *Brown Bear, Brown Bear,* which children memorize verbatim.) An indication that such a book has been chosen is that children chime in during the teacher's readings and choose the book to "read" themselves during choice time. Alternatively, the instrument can be used after "planting" several books in the classroom and requesting multiple readings (3-5). Notice these elicitation techniques assume that students have experiences in a print-rich and literacy-rich classroom. If the classroom environment does not typically include many opportunities to read emergently, we will be only assessing children's home literacy backgrounds.

Reading requests. For formal assessment, an adult arranges for a quiet spot away from distractions and asks the child to "Read your book to me." For informal assessment in the classroom, the adult eavesdrops while a child reads to another child or group of children. If the child does not read immediately or says, "I can't read," the adult uses appropriate prompts, such as, "It doesn't have to be like grown-up reading—just do it your own way." If the child still hesitates, the adult suggests that they read together, begins reading, and pauses for the child to complete sentences or phrases. After a few pages of interactive reading, the adult again urges the child to read: "It's your turn now. Read to me."

The child should hold the book and turn the pages. The adult listens attentively and appreciatively, focusing upon the story being shared rather than on the reading performance.

Recordkeeping. Recordkeeping will vary according to the purpose for the assessment, the experience of the teacher or researcher, and the linguistic and literacy backgrounds of the children. The most careful and laborious recordkeeping would involve taperecording the child, transcribing the taperecordings, and then having two judges independently rate the child and compare ratings. This is typically done for research purposes or during teacher inservlce training.

Two intermediate levels of recordkeeping have been used by classroom teachers. The full 11-point scheme and an abbreviated 5-point version (Sulzby & Barnhart, 1990) have both been used by making on-the-spot judgments of the child's reading behaviors. Eventually, teachers get so acquainted with the scheme that they make running record notes using the subcategory labels, for example, "Keshun—*CFS*—verbatim-like, 6/3/90," which translates as "Keshun read *Caps for Sale* in language fitting the subcategory reading verbatim-like story' on June 3, 1990."

Figure 2 contains the simplified version of the Sulzby classification scheme, which can be used or adapted for local purposes. Daycare, pre-school, and kindergarten teachers will find the most use for the simplified version. This scheme also comprises part of the basis for judging children's emergent writing and reading from their writing (Sulzby, 1989; Sulzby, Barnhart, & Hieshima, 1989). However, first-grade teachers will want to focus on the upper ends of the original version, because it enables them to assess how close a child is to becoming a conventional reader.

Figure 1

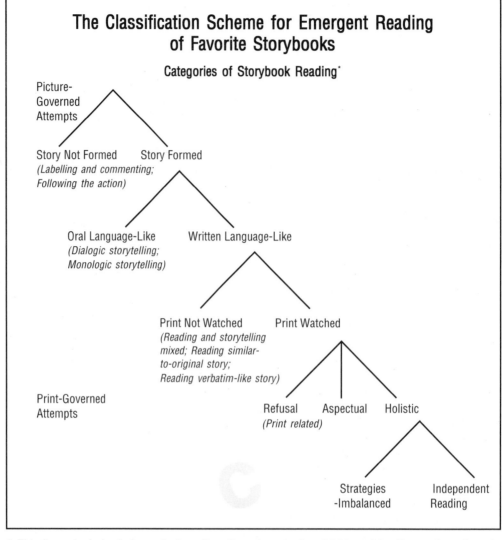

The Classification Scheme for Emergent Reading of Favorite Storybooks

Categories of Storybook Reading*

* This figure includes independent reading attempts only; the child is making the reading attempts without dependence upon turn-taking or interrogation by the adult.

Authenticity and Trustworthiness

The classification scheme described in this column was taken directly from reading behaviors that children show in their homes. Children who are read to regularly typically begin to read emergently; this has been tested with middle- and low-income children, both from Anglo and Hispanic backgrounds (Sulzby & Teale, 1987). The classification scheme is a direct measure of emergent reading and of initial conventional reading. It can be extended into the early conventional period by using other assessment strategies such as informal reading inventories, the Reading Miscue Inventory, and running records.

Our research with the scheme shows that two independent raters can use the scheme reliably. Disagreements are not random or erratic but usually involve fine-grained interpretations of a child's behavior. Children's performances are not static, not

Figure 2

Simplified Version of the Sulzby Storybook Reading Classification Scheme

Broad Categories	Brief Explanation of Categories
1. Attending to Pictures, Not Forming Stories	The child is "reading" by looking at the storybook's pictures. The child's speech is *just* about the picture in view; the child is not "weaving a story" across the pages. (Subcategories are "labeling and commenting" and "following the action.")
2. Attending to Pictures, Forming ORAL Stories	The child is "reading" by looking at the storybook's pictures. The child's speech weaves a story across the pages but the wording and the intonation are like that of someone telling a story, either like a conversation about the pictures or like a fully recited story, in which the listener can see the pictures (and often *must* see them to understand the child's story). (Subcategories are "dialogic storytelling" and "monologic storytelling.")
3. Attending to Pictures, Reading and Storytelling mixed	This category for the simplified version was originally the first subcategory of (4). It fits between (2) and (4) and is easier to understand if it is treated separately. The child is "reading" by looking at the storybook's pictures. The child's speech fluctuates between sounding like a storyteller, with oral intonation, and sounding like a reader, with reading intonation. To fit this category, the majority of the reading attempt must show fluctuations between storytelling and reading.
4. Attending to Pictures, Forming WRITTEN Stories	The child is "reading" by looking at the storybook's pictures. The child's speech sounds as if the child is reading, both in the wording and intonation. The listener does not need to look at the pictures (or rarely does) in order to understand the story. If the listener closes his/her eyes, most of the time he or she would think the child is reading from print. (Subcategories are "reading similar-to-original story" and "reading verbatim-like story.")
5. Attending to Print	There are four subcategories of attending to print. Only the *final* one is what is typically called "real reading." In the others the child is exploring the print by such strategies as refusing to read based on print-related reasons, or using only some of the aspects of print. (Subcategories are "refusing to read based on print awareness," "reading aspectually," "reading with strategies imbalanced," and "reading independently" or "conventional reading.")

at hard and fast stages, yet they have quite a bit of stability. The scheme enables teachers to have *language* to use to describe children's performance and *multiple assessments over time* to use to interpret progress. Finally, teachers have been able to have children keep records of the books which they have read, often with their reactions to the books, and use these records along with the teacher's ratings on the classification scheme as part of a portfolio assessment.

References

Meisels, S.J. (1989). High-stakes testing. *Educational Leadership, 46,* 16-22.

Sulzby, E. (1985). Children's emergent reading of favorite storybooks: A developmental study. *Reading Research Quarterly, 20,* 458-481.

Sulzby, E. (1988). A study of children's early reading development. In A.D. Pellegrini (Ed.), *Psychological bases of early education* (pp. 39-75). Chichester, NY: Wiley.

Sulzby, E. (1989). Assessment of writing and

of children's language while writing. In L. Morrow & J. Smith (Eds.), *Assessment for instruction in early literacy* (pp.83-109). Englewood Cliffs, NJ: Prentice Hall.

Sulzby, E., & Barnhart, J. (1990). The developing kindergartener: All our children emerge as writers and readers. In J.S. McKee (Ed.), *The developing kindergarten: Programs, children, and teachers* (pp. 201-224). Ann Arbor, MI: Michigan Association for the Education of Young Children.

Sulzby, E., Barnhart, J.E., & Hieshima, J.A. (1989). Forms of writing and rereading from writing: A preliminary report. In J. Mason, *Reading and writing connection* (pp. 31-63). Needham Heights, MA: Allyn & Bacon.

Sulzby, E., & Teale, W.H. (1987). *Young children's storybook reading: Longitudinal study of parent-child interaction and children's independent functioning.* Final report to The Spencer Foundation. Ann Arbor, MI: University of Michigan.

Portfolios: A Process for Enhancing Teaching and Learning

Reprinted from *The Reading Teacher, 47* (1994), 666-669

Sheila W. Valencia
Nancy Place

Portfolios have captured the imaginations of educators across the U.S. It would be rare to find teachers or school district personnel who have not heard about portfolios and, in many cases, tried to implement them. These new portfolios represent a redefinition and redesigning of student work folders of the past. The definitions and structures of portfolios vary, but in general, all embrace three major concepts: the alignment of curriculum, instruction, and assessment; student engagement in their own learning and evaluation; and student growth over time.

Although the impetus for portfolios grew out of a desire for more authentic assessment, another advantage of portfolios has begun to receive attention—their potential to enhance both teaching and learning. By engaging in self-reflection and self-evaluation, teachers are encouraged to evaluate their instruction critically and to use portfolio information to make instructional decisions. Similarly, students become more interested in and responsible for their own learning.

The Project

Three years ago, a group of teachers in Bellevue, Washington, joined in a study of literacy learning and assessment. The Bellevue Portfolio Project was designed to (a) improve instruction, (b) improve student learning and ownership for learning, and (c) report to others. Approximately 32 volunteer teachers, kindergarten through high school, from various schools across the district participated. The first year of the project was devoted to exploring the new district Language Arts Student Learning Outcomes and issues of assessment. The next 2 years were spent designing, implementing, and revising literacy portfolios. We have had the unique opportunity to implement portfolios gradually.

We have been able to score portfolios reliably using a scoring rubric to assess eight literacy outcomes (Valencia & Place, in press). We have been able to use portfolios to communicate effectively with parents and to support report card grades and progress reports. But more important, our experiences and interviews with teachers, students, and parents have convinced us that the most powerful aspect of our portfolio work is its positive influence on teaching and learning. However, we also have learned that simply setting up portfolios will not necessarily improve teaching and learning. What ultimately makes the difference is what teachers and students *do* with portfolios and the ways in which they use the information in portfolios to think about teaching and learning.

In this column we focus on four aspects of the project that helped teachers use portfolios effectively: involving teachers in

the development of the portfolio framework; conducting monthly group meetings; using portfolios to describe children; and evaluating portfolios.

Developing a Framework for Portfolios

We approached portfolio development as a group problem solving process. We began with a review of the purposes for our portfolios and of the various portfolio models (e.g., Au, 1992; Chittenden & Courtney, 1989; Tierney, Carter, & Desai, 1991; Valencia, 1990; Wolf, 1989). The challenge was to develop a model to achieve our own purposes. Our composite portfolio consisted of several categories of evidence: (a) work selected by the students and periodic self-reflection/evaluation of their progress; (b) several "common tools," included in all portfolios, which were based on the district learning outcomes; and (c) other work and notes included by the teacher or student that were important to understanding individual students and documenting their learning processes (Valencia & Place, 1994).

Together, the group worked through the process of identifying the purposes for the portfolios and then developed a structure and strategies for meeting those purposes. This process forced us to be thoughtful and deliberate about what we needed and wanted. We tried to guard against a structure that was too formalized or one that would be too idiosyncratic across classrooms. Teachers made individual decisions about issues such as how they were going to organize portfolios, what they would look like, and how to coordinate them with other work folders and classroom procedures. However, other issues had to be agreed upon by the entire group so that we could examine information across students and classrooms.

Establishing the common tools proved to be an important process for the group. Because the tools had to be effective and aligned with district literacy outcomes, we were forced to ask ourselves questions such as: How will I recognize these outcomes in my students? What instructional strategies and activities in my classroom enable students to learn and apply these outcomes? Which of these activities might be included in a portfolio? We looked to good teaching practices and classroom activities that could serve as models for our tools.

For example, we tried out oral and written retelling tools to assess students' construction of meaning. As we listened to a tape of one child's reading and retelling of *Fluffy the Porcupine*, an interesting discussion evolved. Some teachers thought the child had only a superficial understanding of the book and didn't understand the humor and irony of the title. Others suggested that a child at the second-grade level shouldn't be expected to understand the humor. The child's teacher suggested that this child probably didn't know that porcupines had sharp quills. Finally, someone suggested that we needed to check or build background knowledge before we had this child do a retelling or before we could understand her ability to construct meaning. This led to a discussion about prior knowledge, instruction, and expectations for student performance.

As other common tools were developed, reviewed, and revised, we were forced to clarify our understanding of literacy. Although we were trying to develop assessment tools, issues of curriculum, instruction, and student performance had to be addressed if the tools were to be meaningful.

Monthly Group Meetings

We met almost every month, sometimes after school, sometimes during the school day. Most of the teachers remained with the project over the 3 years; however, new members joined each year. The combination of experts and novices provided refreshing ideas for returning members, and it supported and speeded implementation for newcomers. Nevertheless, the process was developmental; the longer teachers participated in the group, the more comfortable they were with the portfolios and the more likely they were to use them to think about teaching and learning.

The meetings were both the carrot and the stick that kept teachers involved and interested. As one teacher commented,

> Being in this group kept me going. There were times when I was too tired or overwhelmed and wanted to give up, but I knew I wanted to come to these meetings and I had to bring portfolios with work in them to share. So, sometimes I would do something the week of the meeting just so I had something to share. It worked. Now [at the end of the year] portfolios are much easier. I can't wait until next year to begin again.

Monthly meetings began with an open time for teachers to raise concerns, tell stories, and share new ideas. Initial meetings focused on logistics: constructing portfolios that wouldn't fall apart, helping students choose work, designing entry slips for students at various grades, and managing portfolio components. These concerns were important. We needed a feeling of control over the logistics before moving on to issues of content and teaching. One primary teacher worried in October,

> It takes so much time to get the common tools in place. And my portfolios are getting very fat. How do you decide what to keep?

The same teacher commented later in the year,

> I can finally see that portfolios are making my life easier. Portfolios keep me organized and accountable. I can see where my gaps were as a teacher. Until portfolios become part of the classroom instruction, not an add-on, one feels overwhelmed. I no longer do.

As the year progressed, the open part of our meetings began to shift to issues of instruction and student performance. For example, at about midyear, several teachers raised concerns about one of the common tools, constructing summaries. Student performance was poor, and teachers believed the summarizing task was artificial. After much discussion and analysis of the tasks and of student performance, the group decided that they needed to learn some new instructional strategies for summarizing and that they needed to integrate these strategies into other facets of their instruction. They asked us to provide professional articles and to teach model lessons. The problem, they discovered, was not simply in the students or in the tools but in the instruction as well.

Using Portfolios to Describe Children

After the first couple of months, we began using samples of children's portfolios to look closely at teaching and learning. These meetings proved to be the most inspiring and most useful. A small group of teachers reviewed a child's portfolio. The child's teacher was a member of that group but could not contribute until the others had discussed their observations. In this way, the initiating teacher judged how well the portfolio represented a particular child. The group addressed four questions:

1. What did you learn about this child?
2. How did the group's description confirm, conflict, or add to the teacher's perceptions?
3. What goals would be appropriate for this child and what instructional strategies might be useful for helping the child achieve those goals?
4. What other things would you like to see in this portfolio to help you understand this child's literacy abilities?

This process of looking closely at students' work provided teachers with a concrete starting place for thinking about instruction and learning. Insights from colleagues often reaffirmed teachers' interpretations of children's strengths and weaknesses

and served as a check that portfolios were capturing each child's individuality. After going through this process, one middle school teacher commented, "I realize what the kids don't have in place and I see where my teaching needs to change." Another teacher shared a strategy which she called "front loading." She explained how she had come to realize that she needed to be clear with herself and her students about what they were learning, why they were learning it, and the criteria for good work. As a result, she reported that she was more deliberate and focused in her teaching and her students were more engaged, successful, and reflective about their work.

Evaluating Portfolios

A subgroup of teachers evaluated the portfolios. We wanted to determine if portfolio information could be aggregated to report to others who were interested in group performance. To do that, we had to develop common scoring rubrics and apply them to the portfolios of children from different classrooms and schools. The process of scoring helped us compare and find common anchors for our expectations for children at various developmental levels. Scoring was tedious and seemed to emphasize efficiency over depth of understanding of teaching and learning. Nevertheless, we did learn that it is critical to establish some benchmarks, criteria, or performance standards for determining what we think students should be able to do. We already had our outcomes; we needed to anchor them in expectations.

We learned the value of the evaluation process, which forced us to use portfolio information to rethink students' capabilities and our own instruction. We concur with an intermediate teacher who noted a "focus on criteria. ... There was lots of debate because the conversation about scoring helps you focus." While the score itself may not provide as much information as the process of describing children's work, the discussions about standards and criteria for good work helped teachers clarify what they needed to teach and anchor their expectations for students.

Conclusions

After 3 years, participation in the portfolio project is thriving—100% of the teachers in the program want to continue, 15 schools have applied to implement portfolios with school teams, and approximately 88% of the students want to keep portfolios again next year. Teachers talk of the "intellectual and professional challenge" of being part of a portfolio group, and students can describe their specific literacy goals for next year and reflect on how they have changed as readers and writers. As one middle school special education student wrote, "I have come so far this year. I have come from Beverly Cleary to Edgar Allan Poe."

We realize that all teachers may not have the district support we have had, but there are other ways to create opportunities to use portfolios to think about teaching and learning. For example, grade level teams could use planning time to design and discuss portfolios, or a portion of each faculty meeting could be set aside to share sample portfolios. Alternatively, any teacher could team up with a colleague to regularly share portfolio work and ask each other the describing questions outlined above. The process will be different depending on the motivation of the people involved, their expertise, and the type of support they receive. The key, however, is to spend time with the portfolios.

Our process changed *portfolio* from a noun, a place to store work, to a verb, a process of looking closely at students' work to help us learn about ourselves and our students. There are no shortcuts here. There is no substitute for involving teachers in the design, development, and discussion of portfolios. The process helps clarify our understanding of the interdependence of curriculum, instructional strategies, learning, and assessment. One

teacher captured this when asked how she had changed since becoming a member of the portfolio project. She wrote,

> I can't begin to say:
> I am more focused;
> I see each child differently
> (as he/she is);
> I teach differently—I am more
> reflective;
> I model more;
> I understand more about reading
> and writing.

Note: Special thanks to the Bellevue Literacy Portfolio Team, who were generous contributors, collaborators, and colleagues throughout the project.

References

Au, K H. (1992, April). *Development and implementation of a whole literacy-based curriculum framework and portfolio assessment system.* Paper presented at the annual meeting of the American Educational Research Association, San Francisco, CA.

Chittenden, E., & Courtney, R. (1989). Assessment of young children's reading: Documentation as an alternative to testing. In D. Strickland & L. Morrow (Eds.), *Emerging literacy: Young children learn to read and write* (pp. 107-120). Newark, DE: International Reading Association.

Tierney, R.J., Carter, M.A., & Desai, L. (1991). *Portfolio assessment in the reading - writing classroom.* Norwood, MA: Christopher Gordon.

Valencia, S.W. (1990). A portfolio approach to classroom reading assessment: The whys, whats, and hows. *The Reading Teacher, 43,* 338-340.

Valencia, S.W., & Place, N. (1994). Literacy portfolios for teaching, learning, and accountability: The Bellevue Literacy Assessment Project. In S. Valencia, E. Hiebert, & P. Afflerbach (Eds.), *Authentic reading assessment: Practices and possibilities* (pp. 134-156). Newark, DE: International Reading Association.

Valencia, S.W., & Place, N. (in press). *Implementing literacy portfolios* (Research Report). Athens, GA: National Reading Research Center, University of Georgia and University of Maryland, College Park.

Wolf, D.P. (1989). Portfolio assessment: Sampling student work. *Educational Leadership, 46(7),* 35-39.

Using Think Alouds to Assess Comprehension

Reprinted from *The Reading Teacher* (1990), *43*, 442-451

Suzanne E. Wade

In a recent issue of *The Reading Teacher* (Squire, 1987), educators have called for changes in reading assessment that would rely less on standardized tests that result in a product—usually a numerical score—and more on informal, process-oriented assessment procedures. Even criterion-referenced tests have been criticized as narrowly defining reading as the mastery of a series of discrete skills. Recent research in comprehension and metacognition suggests that reading is a far more complex process that involves reasoning and problem solving rather than simply the accumulation of skills. As an alternative, process-oriented measures can provide valuable information about learners' cognitive and metacognitive strategies and thought processes—information that teachers can use to focus and evaluate their teaching (Valencia & Pearson, 1987; Wittrock, 1987).

The purpose of this article is to describe an informal assessment procedure that uses think alouds—that is, readers' verbal self-reports about their thinking processes—to obtain information about how they attempt to construct meaning from text. The first sections present an overview of the processes involved in comprehension. The next sections describe the assessment procedure that is designed to gather information about those processes. Next, I present a taxonomy of different types of comprehenders, which can be used to analyze think alouds. Then I describe instructional approaches to use with different types of readers. The final section is an evaluation of the strengths and limitations of the procedure.

Processes Involved in Comprehension

As a result of research since the 1970s investigating the role of background knowledge in comprehension, reading is now viewed as the active construction of meaning (Anderson & Pearson, 1984; Spiro, 1980). In constructing meaning, the reader integrates new knowledge derived from the text with his or her background knowledge in ways that make sense. This background knowledge is referred to as *schemata*—the theories we hold about events, objects, and situations. According to Rumelhart (1980), each schema (singular for schemata) provides a skeleton for understanding incoming data. Thus, schemata determine how new information will be interpreted, causing people to "see" messages in certain ways (Anderson, Reynolds, Schallert, & Goetz, 1977).

When good comprehenders have enough information from the text, they select one or several schemata that make sense of this information, usually from subtle cues in the text. As they read on, they evaluate how well their schema fits with new incoming information—a process similar to hypothesis testing. If it does, the schema enables the reader to make predictions as to what will come next in a text. This *interactive* process between the text and the reader's background knowledge explains how readers can process text so rapidly.

However, if the schema does not account for incoming information, it is either modified or rejected, and the search for a more adequate schema is begun. Thus, a major component of effective reading is comprehension monitoring—self-regulatory mechanisms that include evaluating one's understanding of a text and taking correct action when failures in comprehension are detected (Brown, 1980, 1987; Garner, 1987; Markman, 1981; Paris, Lipson, & Wixson. 1983).

Problems of Poor Comprehenders

What has been described so far is how readers ideally construct meaning from text. Recent research, however, has shown that all readers do not process text in the same way (Spiro & Meyers, 1984). Some, described as bottom-up processors, over rely on the text, thus failing to create a coherent understanding of it. By focusing on decoding and failing to activate or maintain schemata, they make reading far more laborious than is necessary. In contrast, some readers are top-down processors, over relying on their background knowledge. Although they are able to read efficiently and develop a coherent understanding, it may not be the one intended by the author.

In both cases, little cognitive monitoring is occurring. A large body of evidence reveals that many younger and poor readers do not realize when a passage is incomprehensible, do not know that they should check their comprehension, lack strategies for doing so, and fail to make the necessary repairs (Paris et al., 1983).

Think Alouds as a Method for Assessing Comprehension Strategies

How do we get a picture of what is going on in the heads of children as they attempt to construct meaning from text? Verbal report data are an important source of information about cognitive processes that otherwise could only be investigated indirectly; furthermore, verbal reports allow access to the reasoning underlying cognitive behaviors (Afflerbach & Johnston, 1984; Brown, 1987; Ericsson & Simon, 1980; Garner, 1987; Genest & Turk, 1981).

One type of verbal reporting is the think aloud method in which the examiner provides a task and asks subjects to say aloud everything that comes to mind as they are performing it. Only indirect cues are used to elicit information when necessary, such as "Can you tell me more?" These remarks are recorded, usually on audiotape, while the examiner notes nonverbal kinds of information such as signs of anxiety, frustration, proficiency, etc. When used to assess reading comprehension strategies, the examiner usually has students think aloud after reading short segments of a passage (cf., Alvermann, 1984; Garner & Alexander, 1982; Hare & Smith, 1982; Olshavsky, 1976-1977; Phillips & Norris, 1986).

Assessing Comprehension Strategies

Similar to the comprehension methods described above, this procedure has readers think aloud about the meaning of a passage after they have read short segments of it. Like the text used in Phillips and Norris's (1986) study, passages should be selected or written so that readers cannot know for sure what the topic is until they have read the last segment. Thus, readers are required to generate hypotheses during their think alouds about the text's meaning from clues in each text segment. The procedure ends with the reader retelling the whole passage in his or her own words. Table 1 presents a detailed description of the procedure for administering and scoring a comprehesion think aloud.

This think aloud assessment procedure has been used and refined in courses on the diagnosis of reading difficulties at the University of Utah for the last 4 years. The children with whom it has been used ranged in grade level from second to ninth, and all were referred for tutoring by their classroom teachers, who identified them as having difficulty in reading.

Table 1

Procedure for Administering and Scoring a Comprehension Think Aloud

I. Preparing the text

Choose a short passage (expository or narrative) written to meet the following criteria:

1. The text should be from 80 to 200 words in length, depending on the reader's age and reading ability.
2. The text should be new to the reader, but on a topic that is familiar to him or her. (Determine whether the reader has relevant background knowledge by means of an interview or questionnaire administered at a session prior to this assessment.)
3. The text should be at the reader's instructional level, which can be determined by use of an informal reading inventory. Passages at this level are most likely to be somewhat challenging while not overwhelming readers with word identification problems.
4. The topic sentence should appear last, and the passage should be untitled. Altering the text in this way will elicit information about the reader's strategies for making sense of the passage and inferring the topic.
5. The text should be divided into segments of one to four sentences each.

II. Administering the think aloud procedure

1. Tell the reader that he or she will be reading a story in short segments of one or more sentences.
2. Tell the reader that after reading each section, he or she will be asked to tell what the story is about.
3. Have the student read a segment aloud. After each segment is read, ask the reader to tell what is happening, followed by nondirective probe questions as necessary. The questions should encourage the reader to generate hypotheses (what do you think this is about?) and to describe what he or she based the hypotheses on (what clues in the story helped you?).
4. Continue the procedure until the entire passage is read. Then ask the reader to retell the entire passage in his or her own words. (The reader may reread the story first.)
5. The examiner might also ask the reader to find the most important sentence(s) in the passage.
6. The session should be tape-recorded and transcribed. The examiner should also record observations of the child's behaviors.

III. Analyzing results

Ask the following questions when analyzing the transcript:

1. Does the reader generate hypotheses?
2. Does he/she support hypotheses with information from the passage?
3. What information from the text does the reader use?
4. Does he/she relate material in the text to background knowledge or previous experience?
5. Does the reader integrate new information with the schema he/she has already activated?
6. What does the reader do if there is information that conflicts with the schema he/she has generated?
7. At what point does the reader recognize what the story is about?
8. How does the reader deal with unfamiliar words?
9. What kinds of integration strategies does the reader use (e.g., visualization)?
10. How confident is the reader of his/her hypotheses?
11. What other observations can be made about the reader's behavior, strategies, etc.?

In our experience with this procedure, we find that readers typically fall into one, or a combination, of the five categories that are described below. These categories evolved over 2 years as we searched for patterns in the data. The resulting taxonomy was then validated with a group of 52 students who had not been used in the preliminary analyses. Using the typed protocols, two trained raters were instructed to place each student in one of the five categories or in a sixth category labeled "mixed findings?" Interrater agreement was 92%, with disputes settled in conference.

Eighty-one percent of the students were classified as belonging predominantly to one of the five categories; the remainder (mixed findings) were classified as belonging to two or more categories.

In the following section, each category is briefly described along with a portion of a think aloud protocol that exemplifies the category. Examples of think aloud passages are presented in Table 2.

Types of Comprehenders

The good comprehender. The good comprehender is an interactive reader who constructs meaning and monitors comprehension. Notice in the example below how this seventh grader draws on her extensive background knowledge as she reads the passage about snow. She makes reasonable inferences about the topic of the passage, recognizes when more information is needed to confirm her hypothesis, and abandons her original idea in favor of one that more adequately accounts for all of the information in the text. The portion of text the student read is in upper case letters, *S* represents the student's response, and *T* represents the teacher's questions and comments.

IT IS REALLY COLORLESS BUT WHEN LIGHT RAYS REFLECT OFF OF ITS SURFACE, IT LOOKS WHITE.

S: Can I make an early guess?

T: Yes

S: I'm not positive, but I think it's about clouds.

T: What information led you to think that?

S: When it mentioned the color white and talked about light rays, like you have in the sky. But I'm not positive. I guess I better read some more.

SOMETIMES IT CAN TURN BLACK OR BROWN WHEN IT MIXES WITH FACTORY DUST, OR YELLOW WHEN IT MIXES WITH AIRBORNE PINE TREE POLLEN.

S: It could still be about clouds because factory smoke and dust can get inside clouds. So could pollen, I guess, if the wind blew it high enough. But I'm still not sure. Is there more to it?

T: Yes, let's read the next section.

SOMETIMES IT LOOKS LIGHT AND DELICATE. A CUBIC FOOT OF IT MAY WEIGH ONLY 6 POUNDS. BUT WHEN IT IS COMPRESSED, IT CAN WEIGH UP TO 30 POUNDS A CUBIC FOOT, POWERFUL ENOUGH TO CRUSH BUILDINGS.

T: What do you think it's about now?

S: Well, clouds aren't heavy, so it's probably about something else, maybe rain, but I'm not sure. Rain is heavy, but I'm not sure it weighs 6 pounds a cubic foot. I don't think it could crush buildings, either, although a flood of rain could wash it away. Is there more information?

IT IS ONE OF NATURE'S BEST INSULATORS. HOLD A THERMOMETER JUST ABOVE IT AND LOOK AT THE TEMPERATURE. NOW PUSH THE THERMOMETER INSIDE OF IT AND SEE HOW MUCH WARMER IT READS.

S: I know that snow is a good insulator because Eskimos build their houses out of it and they stay warm inside. It's also white and, when you think about it, the bricks they use in their igloos are very heavy, like it said in the story. I guess the snow changes color when it gets mixed with smoke and other stuff in the air, like it said before. So, I think it's about snow.

One-third of the students in our sample were categorized as good comprehenders, yet they all had been labeled as having reading difficulties, as many exhibited poor word attack skills and lacked fluency in oral reading. Their ability to draw on their back-

Table 2

Examples of Assessment Passages

Passage I

It is really colorless but when light rays reflect off of its surface, it looks white.
Sometimes it can turn black or brown when it mixes with factory dust, or yellow when it mixes with airborne pine tree pollen.
Sometimes it looks light and delicate. A cubic foot of it may weigh only 6 pounds. But when it is compressed it can weigh up to 30 pounds a cubic foot, powerful enough to crush buildings.
It is one of nature's best insulators. Hold a thermometer just above it and look at the temperature. Now push the thermometer inside of it and see how much warmer it reads.
Farmers know that snow holds heat in the ground and keeps their seeds from freezing.

Passage 2

The first thing you will want to do is find a big person to help you out. Have the grown-up hold on tight so that everything remains steady while you climb on top.
The grown-up must walk beside you and hold on to make sure you don't fall over. Then you can start going faster and faster.
When you gain speed the grown-up will have to run alongside of you to keep up and still hold on.
When you have peddled up to a good speed and you feel like you can keep your own balance, you can tell the grown-up to let go.

Passage 3

It sat very still not moving its body, just throwing its head this way and that to toss the silk in the right place.
Finally, its home for the winter is done at last.
As it hangs, soft and gray in color, it looks like a dead leaf.
It seems to be dead, but inside something wonderful is happening.
After a brief struggle, a body with folded wings breaks out of the silken shell.
The insect lies still for a moment, its wings damp.
Soon the wings dry out and spread, wide and beautiful.
What was once a caterpillar is now a butterfly.

ground knowledge and their comprehension monitoring strategies may be the reason they were able to understand as well as they did, despite their problems in word recognition.

The non-risk taker. The non-risk taker is a bottom-up processor who assumes a passive role by failing to go beyond the text to develop hypotheses. In some cases, non-risk takers will look for clues from the examiner rather than risk being wrong. When asked to tell what the story is about so far, they often say that they do not know, or they may repeat words and phrases verbatim from the story, an indication that they are not developing a coherent understanding of the text. When they do venture a guess, it is often in a questioning manner. The following excerpt of a second grader reading a story about learning to ride a bicycle is a prototypical non-risk taker response.

> THE FIRST THING YOU WILL WANT TO DO IS FIND A BIG PERSON TO HELP YOU OUT. HAVE THE GROWN-UP HOLD ON TIGHT SO THAT EVERYTHING REMAINS STEADY WHILE YOU CLIMB ON TOP.
>
> T: What do you think this is about?
> S: I don't know.
> T: Can you give me any guesses?

S: (no response)
T: Can you describe for me what is happening?
S: A big person is helping.
T: Can you tell me anything else?
S: (shrugs "no")

THE GROWN-UP MUST WALK BESIDE YOU AND HOLD ON TO MAKE SURE YOU DON'T FALL OVER. THEN YOU CAN START GOING FASTER AND FASTER.

T: Okay, now what do you think it's about?
S: I don't know.
T: Can you describe to me what's going on here?
S: Beside?
T: Why don't you read this part again and then describe to me what's happening?
S: (after reading) A motorcycle?
T: It could be a motorcycle. Can you add anything else? (pause, no response) All right, let's go on to the next part.

WHEN YOU GAIN SPEED, THE GROWN-UP WILL HAVE TO RUN ALONG SIDE OF YOU TO KEEP UP AND STILL HOLD ON.

T: Okay, what is it saying there?
S: A motorcycle?
T: Tell me what clues tell you it's a motorcycle.
S: Speed, still hold on.
T: Speed and still hold on. Can you tell me more about it? (pause) No? Okay, let's go on to the last part.

The non-risk taker appears to be a relatively common problem, especially among younger, poor readers (19% of the students in our sample were placed in this category). These readers either lack or underutilize their background knowledge and over rely on the text to suggest an appropriate schema. As in the preceding example, however, this may never happen. There are several reasons for over reliance on the text (Pearson & Spiro, 1980; Spiro & Myers, 1984). One is a lack of background knowledge; another may be difficulty in accessing an appropriate schema when it is signaled by the text. In addition, many younger and poor readers have the misconception that reading is primarily a textbased process—decoding is all that they are supposed to do (Canney & Winograd, 1979). Finally, laborious decoding could leave few cognitive resources for the processes of meaning-getting and comprehension monitoring (although other children escape decoding problems by over relying on their background knowledge).

The non-integrator. Drawing on text clues and prior knowledge, non-integrators develop new hypotheses for every segment of the text, never relating the new hypotheses to previous ones or to information presented earlier in the text. They represent a curious mixture of bottom-up and top-down processing that leads to comprehension failure. It seems that the schema of the moment guides the interpretation of the text; however, the reader never goes beyond the text to develop an inclusive, integrated understanding.

In the following excerpt, a second grader is attempting to make sense of a passage about the metamorphosis of a butterfly. Notice how he develops a new hypothesis after each sentence, apparently unconcerned that the latest does not fit with earlier information. Notice also the effect of incorrect background knowledge on schema selection.

IT SAT VERY STILL, NOT MOVING ITS BODY, JUST THROWING ITS HEAD THIS WAY AND THAT TO TOSS THE SILK IN THE RIGHT PLACE.

S: Spider!
T: Okay, what clues in the story tell you that it's a spider?
S: Spiders make silk come out of their bodies.
T: Anything else that gives you a clue about it being a spider?
S: Because it stays still.
T: Oh, because it stays still sometimes.

FINALLY, ITS HOME FOR THE WINTER IS DONE AT LAST.

S: A polar bear.
T: Oh, a polar bear. Remember, all of these sentences belong together to make a story. Do you still think that these sentences have anything to do with a spider?
S: No.

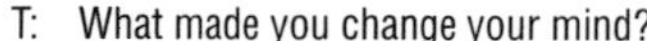

T: What made you change your mind?

S: Because a spider doesn't have a house under the ground.

S: Does the story say anything about houses under the ground?

S: Yes, the polar bear makes a house under the ground to get ready for winter.

T: Okay, are you ready for more?

AS IT HANGS, SOFT AND GRAY IN COLOR, IT LOOKS LIKE A DEAD LEAF.

S: Opossum!

T: Now you think it's an opossum? What makes you think that?

S: Because an opossum hangs from its tail.

T: Any other things that might make you think that it is an opossum?

S: Yes, it looks like a leaf.

Twelve percent of the students in our sample exhibited comprehension breakdowns of this sort. These children may be able to access their schemata effectively but are unable to combine them to fit the needs of a given text. Or, they may have difficulty maintaining an activated schema for an extended amount of time, discarding it prematurely to search for another (Spiro & Myers, 1984). There are various reasons why this may occur. Decoding problems may require that they direct all their attention to the visual analysis of print, leaving little or no cognitive capacity for remembering and synthesizing information into a coherent whole (Pearson & Spiro, 1980), or these readers may have difficulty understanding or remembering the relationship between ideas, especially when they occur in separate sentences (Marshall & Glock, 1978-79).

The schema imposer. The schema imposer is a type of top-down processor who holds on to an initial hypothesis despite incoming information that conflicts with that schema, seemingly unaware of alternative hypotheses. In the following example, notice how the ninth grader reading the passage about the butterfly forces the new information to fit his schema.

IT SAT VERY STILL, NOT MOVING ITS BODY, JUST THROWING ITS HEAD THIS WAY AND THAT TO TOSS THE SILK IN THE RIGHT PLACE.

T: What do you think this could be about?

S: Mmmm. Maybe a cat.

T: Why do you think it's a cat?

S: 'Cause of the silk. You know how cats play with yarn?

FINALLY, ITS HOME FOR THE WINTER IS DONE AT LAST.

S: The cat has to make a home for itself for the winter.

AS IT HANGS, SOFT AND GRAY IN COLOR, IT LOOKS LIKE A DEAD LEAF.

S: Well, it's probably a kitten. Yeah, a kitten.

T: What makes you think that?

S: Kittens are soft and gray and when they're asleep they kinda look like they're dead.

IT SEEMS TO BE DEAD, BUT INSIDE SOMETHING WONDERFUL IS HAPPENING.

S: I know. It's a mother cat with kittens inside her.

Ten percent of the students in our sample were classified as schema imposers. They over rely on top-down processing, maintaining an activated schema when it is no longer useful. They do this by forcing new data to fit the schema, as illustrated above, or ignoring conflicting information. The strength exhibited by these readers is that they see reading as a meaning-constructing process, but you probably should not trust them to follow a recipe.

Over reliance on top-down processing may be related to decoding difficulties in some cases; that is, the reader may escape the laboriousness of text-based processing by guessing at the general meaning of the text and filling in details from prior knowledge. Alternately, the reader may lack (or be unable to use) strategies for comprehension monitoring to check his or her understanding against the text.

The storyteller. Storytellers are extreme examples of top-down processors. They

tend to draw far more on prior knowledge or experience than on information stated in the text. Many seem to identify strongly with a character in a story and make causal inferences based on what they would do. The following reader, who is a second grader, exemplifies this category as he reads the passage about learning to ride a bicycle.

> THE FIRST THING YOU WILL WANT TO DO IS FIND A BIG PERSON TO HELP YOU OUT. HAVE THE GROWN-UP HOLD ON TIGHT SO THAT EVERYTHING REMAINS STEADY WHILE YOU CLIMB ON TOP.

T: Frank, can you tell me what is happening, or what this story is about so far?
S: You are going across the street.
T: Why are you going across the street?
S: To get to the other side. We're going to the store.
T: Why do you think we are going to the store?
S: To get some peanut butter.

While not a common problem (only 8% of the sample were placed in this category), the storyteller is an interesting one. Like other types of top-down processors, they understand that reading is a meaning-based process. However, as in the case above, the meaning they construct from the text can be very different from the author's intended meaning. Their meaning consists primarily of their own elaborations; there seems to be little awareness of any discrepancy on the part of these readers, who fail to check their understanding against the text. Like the schema imposers, this may be due to decoding difficulties or lack of strategies for comprehension monitoring.

Instructional Implications

Understanding whether and how students use their background knowledge in constructing meaning from text and whether they monitor their comprehension has important implications for instruction. Strategies that might be effective for one type of comprehender may be inappropriate for another. For good comprehenders, instructional strategies should draw from their strong comprehension strategies. In many cases this may involve developing rapid, automatic decoding proficiency, practiced in context so that they can use their strengths at top-down processing and comprehension monitoring to facilitate word recognition.

Strategies for bottom-up processors, on the other hand, should focus on using prior knowledge to enhance understanding. Techniques for accomplishing this goal will vary, however, depending on the cause of the problem. For example, if the problem is one of schema availability, emphasis should be placed on developing relevant background knowledge before reading. Those who have difficulty activating the background knowledge they already have need strategies to make reasonable predictions from cues in the text and test them against later information. Some of these readers simply may believe that bottom-up processing is all that they are supposed to do, while other may lack confidence and fear making mistakes. Those who tend to abandon reasonable predictions prematurely may need help in linking ideas together to form a coherent understanding. Learning to visualize and to develop semantic maps showing the relationships among ideas are ways to accomplish this. Finally, many bottom-up processors may need to develop rapid, automatic word recognition skills to free up their cognitive resources for more top-down processing.

In contrast, top-down processors need strategies that emphasize cognitive flexibility and comprehension monitoring. One way to encourage readers to entertain alternate interpretations and multiple perspectives is to present two reasonable hypotheses and ask which is the best given all the information in the text. Questioning may also help; for example, asking questions such as "Does this fit with other ideas in the story?" "Are there other ways to make sense of this?" "Where in the story does it say what you just told me?" Writing down reasonable hypotheses and testing them against the text should help, especially with problems of schema mainte-

nance. Again, automaticity in word recognition may need to be developed so that readers draw on context and background knowledge to facilitate decoding.

There are some common elements in all comprehension instruction. One is to begin with materials that are appropriate in terms of interest, content, and difficulty. Another is to provide instructional support through modeling and direct explanation that helps make the invisible processes involved in reading visible (Pearson, Dole, Duffy, & Roehler, in press). Finally, the think aloud approach to comprehension strategy assessment I have presented here should be considered as only one part of a comprehensive assessment program. To understand the causes of comprehension problems and make informed decisions about subsequent instruction, the teacher should know if readers (a) have adequate background knowledge, both general knowledge of the world and specific knowledge of the topic being read; (b) have an understanding of what is involved in meaning construction and comprehension monitoring; (c) are adept and confident in applying this knowledge to particular reading tasks; and (d) have prerequisite skills such as rapid, automatic word recognition.

Limitations

As with any assessment technique, this procedure has certain limitations. One limitation involves an awareness that the strategies a reader will use with one type of passage may not be the same as those used with other types of reading materials (Wixson & Lipson, 1984). Because reading is an interaction between the reader, the text, the task, and the context of the reading situation (Anderson & Armbruster, 1984; Jenkins, 1979), assessment of comprehension strategies should be varied to include texts that differ in length, content, difficulty, and genre; likewise, the purpose for reading should also be varied (Wixson & Lipson, 1984). Particularly important in comprehension assessment are observations of how readers deal with texts for which they have a great deal of background knowledge compared to texts for which they have little. Background knowledge, as we have seen, plays an enormous role in comprehension. Therefore, recognize that the results one obtains in any think aloud assessment will be specific to the unique combination of text, task, context, and reader background knowledge.

Other limitations involve the procedure itself and the materials that are used. First, asking children to think aloud following the reading of individual segments of a text may change their strategies and the meaning they derive from the text. Second, unlike the passages presented in this article, many well written texts, especially expository ones, state main ideas explicitly and at the beginning rather than requiring readers to infer them as they go along. Third, verbal reports are only measures of the reader's conscious, stated knowledge of cognitive processes, not those that may be tacit. Thus, for students who are less capable of thinking about their own thinking and reporting on it, the think aloud may underestimate their knowledge and abilities (Garner, 1987).

However, think alouds have several advantages over other types of verbal reporting: They involve highly specified tasks that produce more reliable results than hypothetical ones, and they lessen the problem of memory failure since the reporting is nearly concurrent with the processes being described (Ericsson & Simon, 1980). Therefore, think alouds do produce valuable initial hypotheses about readers' processing styles, which can then be tested in more natural reading situations.

Future Directions

The results of our field testing of think aloud as an assessment tool suggest as many new questions as they answer. For example, comprehension problems resulting from over reliance on bottom-up or top-down processing should be investigated developmentally. Would we find these types of problems in young children who are progressing normally for their age? Are some types of comprehension problems more common than others in younger children? Do the same readers exhibit different characteristics with different passages? Are there other categories of comprehenders that might be found? Future research and development of this promising assessment tool are required to address these questions.

In summary, the think aloud procedure for assessing comprehension can help teachers evaluate students' comprehension strategies such as the ability to generate appropriate hypotheses, integrate new information from the text with the hypotheses, and revise or abandon hypotheses if new information conflicts with them. Also, the teacher can learn how the reader goes about integrating information, such as visualization or elaboration techniques, and how confident the reader is in figuring out what the text is about. This provides information not readily available from more traditional product-oriented tests. As a result, teachers will acquire valuable information about students' strengths and weaknesses, both of which can be used to guide instruction.

References

Afflerbach, P.P., & Johnston, P.H. (1984). Research methodology on the use of verbal reports in reading research. *Journal of Reading Behavior, 16,* 307-322.

Alvermann, D.E. (1984). Second graders strategic preferences while reading basal stories. *Journal of Educational Research, 77,* 184-189.

Anderson, R.C., & Pearson, P.D. (1984). A schematheoretic view of basic processes in reading. In P.D. Pearson (Ed.), *Handbook of reading research* (pp. 255-292). New York: Longman.

Anderson, R.C., Reynolds, R.E., Schallert, D.L. & Goetz, E.T. (1977). Frameworks for comprehending discourse. *American Educational Research Journal, 14,* 367-381.

Anderson, T.H., & Armbruster, B.B. (1984). Studying. In P.D.Pearson (Ed.), *Handbook of reading research* (pp. 319-352), New York: Longman.

Brown, A.L. (1980). Metacognitive development and reading. In R.J. Spiro, B.B. Bruce, & W.F. Brewer (Eds.), *Theoretical issues in reading comprehension* (pp. 453-481). Hillsdale, NJ: Erlbaum.

Brown, A.L. (1987). Metacognition, executive control, self-regulation, and other more mysterious mechanisms. In F.E. Weinert & R.H. Kluwe (Eds.), *Metacognition, motivation, and understanding* (pp. 65-116). Hillsdale, NJ: Erlbaum.

Canney, G., & Winograd, P. (1979). *Schemata for reading and reading comprehension performance* (Tech. Rep. No. 120). Urbana, IL: University of Illinois, Center for the Study of Reading.

Ericsson, K.A., & Simon, H.A. (1980). Verbal reports as data. *Psychological Review, 87,* 215-251.

Garner, R. (1987). *Metacognition and reading comprehensian.* Norwood, NJ: Ablex.

Garner, R., & Alexander, P. (1982). Strategic processing of text: An investigation of the effects on adults' question-answering performance. *Journal of Educational Research, 75,* 144-148.

Genest, M., & Turk, D.C. (1981). Think-aloud approaches to cognitive assessment. In T.V. Merluzzi, C.R. Glass, & M. Genest (Eds.), *Cognitive assessment.* New York: Gullford Press.

Hare, V.C., & Smith, D.C. (1982). Reading to remember: Studies of metacognitive reading skills in elementary school-aged children. *Journal of Educational Research, 75,* 157-164.

Jenkins, J.J. (1979). Four points to remember: A tetrahedral model and memory experiments. In L.S. Cermak & F.I.M. Craik (Eds.), *Levels and processing in human memory* (pp. 429-461). Hillsdale, NJ: Erlbaum

Markman, E.M. (1981). Comprehension monitoring. In W.P. Dickson (Ed.), *Children's oral communication skills* (pp. 61-84). New York: Academic Press.

Marshall, N., & Glock, M.D. (1978-79). Comprehension of connected discourse: A study into the relationships between the structure of text and information recalled. *Reading Research Quarterly, 14,* 10-56.

Olshavsky, J.E. (1976-77). Reading as problem solving: An investigation of strategies. *Reading Research Quarterly, 12,* 654-675.

Paris, S.G., Lipson, M.Y., & Wixson, K.K. (1983). Becoming a strategic reader. *Contemporary Educational Psychology, 8,* 293-316.

Pearson, P.D., & Spiro, R.J. (1980). Toward a theory of reading comprehension instruction. *Topics in Language Disorders, 1,* 71-88.

Pearson, P.D., Dole, J., Duffy, G., & Roehler, L. (in press). Developing expertise in reading comprehension: What should be taught? How should it be taught? In S.J. Samuels

& A.E. Farstrup (Eds.), *What research says to the teacher* (2nd ed.). Newark, DE: International Reading Association.

Phillips, L.M., & Norris, S.P. (1986). Reading well is thinking well. In N.C. Burbules (Ed.), *Proceedings of the 42nd Annual Meeting of the Philosophy of Education Society* (pp. 187-197). Normal, IL: Philosophy of Education Society.

Rumelhart, D.E. (1980). Schemata: The building blocks of cognition. In R.J. Spiro, B.B. Bruce, & W.F. Brewer (Eds.), *Theoretical issues in reading comprehension* (pp. 33-58). Hillsdale, NJ: Erlbaum.

Spiro, R.J. (1980). Constructive processes in prose comprehension and recall. In R.J. Spiro, B.C. Bruce, & W.F. Brewer (Eds.), *Theoretical issues in reading comprehension* (pp. 245-278). Hillsdale, NJ: Erlbaum.

Spiro, R.J., & Myers, A. (1984). Individual differences and underlying cognitive processes in reading. In P.D. Pearson (Ed.), *Handbook of reading research* (pp. 471-501). New York: Longman.

Squire, J.R. (Ed.), (1987). The state of reading assessment [Special issue]. *The Reading Teacher, 40,* 8.

Valencia, S., & Pearson, P.D. (1987). Reading assessment: Time for a change. *The Reading Teacher, 40,* 726-732.

Wittrock, M.C. (1987). Process oriented measures of comprehension. *Reading Teacher, 40,* 734-737.

Wixson, K.K., & Lipson, M.Y. (1984). Reading (dis)ability: An interactionist perspective. In T.E. Raphael (Ed.), *The contexts of school-based literacy* (pp. 131-148). New York: Random House.

Developing Alternative Assessments: Six Problems Worth Solving

Reprinted from *The Reading Teacher* (1994), *47*, 420-423

Peter Winograd

Change, when it finally comes, often happens more rapidly than anyone could imagine or predict. This is certainly the case with assessment, particularly the assessment of literacy. Across the U.S., teachers are exploring and creating alternative methods of evaluating and assisting their children's growth as readers and writers. Traditional tests still exist, of course, but teachers interested in change can now turn to a rich body of literature dealing with portfolios, performance assessments, developmental checklists, conference guides, and other methods of alternative assessment.

The enthusiasm and optimism surrounding alternative assessments are certainly justified. But change involves challenge, and the changes in assessment are no exception. In this column I examine six challenges that face teachers interested in developing alternative assessments. These are "problems worth solving" because addressing them successfully will help us realize the full promise of alternative assessments.

Problem #1: Clarifying the goals of assessment. When we first think about developing alternative assessments we must ask, "What do we want to measure?" The identification of what is to be measured is no easy task.

One way to conceptualize the issue is by thinking of a continuum that ranges from goals that are very broad and general to goals that are extremely specific and narrow. One of the 1992 National Education Goals, for example, states that students will demonstrate "competency in challenging subject matter, including English, mathematics, science, history, and geography; and every school in America will ensure that all students learn to use their minds well, so they may be prepared for responsible citizenship, further learning, and productive employment in our modern economy" (National Education Goals Panel, 1992). This is obviously an important goal, but it is too broad to measure in any manageable way. At the other end of the continuum are very low-level goals that focus on isolated skills like "Students should identify the sound the letter *a* represents in the word *man.*" Such specific goals are often easy to measure but are rarely worth the effort.

Developing goals at just the right level on the continuum requires thinking about meaningful, authentic outcomes that are observable and useful. For example, "Students will become more self-reflective about their reading and writing" might be useful for teachers interested in helping students become more independent learners. "Students will be able to understand a wide variety of authentic reading materials" may be useful for teachers who want to focus on comprehension. "Students will develop an interest in reading" may be a useful goal for those interested in helping their students become lifelong readers.

After meaningful goals are identified, we must still ensure that they actually drive assessment and instruction. If meaningful goals are included in curriculum documents but the district or school still relies heavily on traditional multiple-choice tests, the testmakers' scope and sequence become the de facto goals of assessment and instruction. Thus, even though the curriculum may identify helping students develop a lifelong love of reading as an important goal, students are evaluated only on their ability to read short paragraphs and select the right answer from a multiple-choice format.

Problem #2: Clarifying the audiences to be addressed. Assessment can and should serve different audiences (Winograd, Paris, & Bridge, 1991). For example, assessment can help

- students become more self-reflective and in control of their own learning
- teachers focus their instruction more effectively
- educators determine which students are eligible for Chapter I [federally supported] programs, programs for the gifted, or special education
- parents understand more about their children's progress as learners
- administrators understand how groups of students in their schools are progressing as learners
- legislators and officials gauge the level of achievement of various cohorts of students across the state, the region, or the nation.

Traditional assessments are usually administered with an eye on accountability: Students are tested so that teachers can provide parents, administrators, or legislators with some proof of progress. To be sure, parents, administrators, and legislators are important audiences, and indeed, there is a healthy movement towards using alternative assessments for the purposes of accountability (Au, Scheu, Kawakami, & Herman, 1990; U.S. Congress, Office of Technology Assessment, 1992; Wiggins, 1989).

But the movement to alternative assessments is based upon the understanding that students and teachers are the most critical audiences and that assessments should be administered with an eye on learning. In other words, students and teachers engage in evaluation so that students can take control of their own learning and teachers can improve their instruction.

The important point here is that alternative assessments should first focus on serving students and teachers. The more we improve assessment for learning, the more satisfied we will be when we assess for accountability, especially as the assessments for accountability become more authentic.

Problem #3: Selecting and developing assessment techniques and tasks. The third problem worth solving is deciding how to gather assessment information. If traditional multiple-choice tests are no longer used, what techniques and tasks should replace them?

One way to address this challenge is first to focus on the goals to be evaluated and the audiences to be addressed. We can then gather samples of portfolios, anecdotal checklists, developmental checklists, rating scales, guides for student-teacher conferences, parent-teacher conferences, narrative report cards, and other forms of alternative assessments from other teachers, other schools, state departments of education (e.g., Kentucky, Maryland, Vermont), reading conferences. and some of the resources listed at the end of this column. These samples can be adopted, adapted, or used as models.

Problem #4: Setting standards of student performance. Information on students' performance is readily available in the classroom and may be gathered using alternative assessment. Interpreting all of this information has proven to be a considerable challenge.

The challenge is to move from traditional standards and measures to new forms of conceptualizing student performance. In the past, constructs like grade equivalents, age equivalents, percentile scores, or standard scores were used to measure students' growth. It did not matter that such scores were rarely understood by students or their parents or that they provided little useful information to teachers and administrators (Neill & Medina, 1989; Shepard, 1989). The perception that these kinds of scores are meaningful is difficult to change, especially when one is faced with the complexity of trying to interpret portfolios full of students' work samples, observations of students' behavior in real classrooms, or other kinds of evidence.

The issue of standards can be addressed through the use of rubrics. Rubrics are guidelines that describe student work in reading, writing, mathematics, and other content areas. Rubrics often have 3-, 4-, or 5-point scales that range from the highest quality of work to work of minimal quality. The rubrics contain words and phrases that describe the characteristics of each point on the scale. The scorer compares the work being evaluated to the descriptions or examples in the rubric.

Rubrics are useful because they help students, teachers, parents, and others understand what is expected for high-quality work. For example, students who have seen (or better yet, helped develop) the writing rubric will know how to define good writing. Rubrics make expectations explicit.

A group of outstanding primary teachers in Lawrenceburg, Kentucky (USA) wanted to help parents interpret the information the teachers gathered from observations. Some of the rubrics the teachers included on their report cards to the parents appear in the Figure.

Teachers circled the point on the rubric that most closely described each student's behavior during silent reading, group reading, and the writing workshop. The teachers also included narrative reports, but these rubrics helped parents see the developmental trend that occurs as children progress. *Independent* students get involved with what they are reading, can discuss what they have read, and can apply the writing process on their own. *Developing* students are somewhat involved in their reading, can answer questions about what they have read, and produce some writing; but teachers still must provide some modeling and support. *Beginning* students still need lots of guidance during free reading, group reading, and while writing.

Problem #5: Establishing methods of management. Developing alternative assessments and then gathering and interpreting various kinds of information takes time, and time is what teachers need most. Indeed, the most serious concern about the future of alternative assessments is that they are so potentially time consuming (Maeroff, 1991; Worthen, 1993).

Alternative assessments become more manageable when they replace traditional assessments rather than simply adding to the burden of testing. Unfortunately, too many teachers and students find themselves dealing with both traditional standardized tests and new forms of assessments. This is particularly true of schools and districts in transition, where one group of educators is willing to make changes, while another group is still adhering to more traditional approaches. In such instances, it is important that both groups spend time discussing which audiences are being served to see if a compromise can be negotiated between those interested in using evaluation to enhance student learning and teacher effectiveness and those who view assessment as a method of fulfilling the demands of accountability. Again, it is worth noting that there is a healthy movement to make the methods of assessment for accountability more authentic and aligned with the kinds of evaluation that enhance student learning and teacher effectiveness.

Another way to make alternative assessments more manageable is by providing teachers with adequate training (Maeroff, 1991; Winograd & Jones, 1992). For ex-

Rubrics Teachers Included on Report Cards to Parents

During super silent reading		
Involves self intensely with print	Maintains interest in print with additional support	Has difficulty being involved with print
During group reading		
Carries on a meaningful conversation about reading	Willing to answer questions about reading material with guidance	Unable to express thoughts or feelings about reading material
During writing workshop		
Shows independence using the writing process	Shows some independence; needs individual guidance to progress	Needs individual guidance to participate

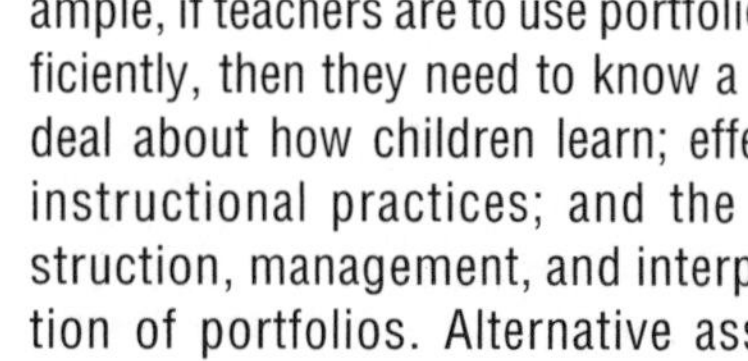

ample, if teachers are to use portfolios efficiently, then they need to know a great deal about how children learn; effective instructional practices; and the construction, management, and interpretation of portfolios. Alternative assessment, like most things, becomes easier with practice.

Teachers also need adequate time and support for collaborating with their colleagues. Expecting isolated teachers in lonely classrooms to carry the burden of assessment is simply unrealistic. In my experience, the most successful examples of teachers developing and using alternative assessments have taken place when small groups of teachers work together.

A fourth way to make alternative assessment manageable is by integrating assessment and instruction—embedding assessment in instruction—so that both happen at the same time. The advantage of integrating assessment with instruction is that time need not be taken away from teaching and spent on testing. This is a complex issue, and we shall examine It in more detail next.

Problem #6: Integrating assessment and instruction. A key criticism of traditional methods of assessment is that they fail to test what is taught during instruction. Indeed, increasing the alignment between meaningful instruction and meaningful assessment is one of the most important goals of reforming assessment. Achieving this goal clearly a problem worth solving.

Embedding assessment in instruction first requires an understanding of what is entailed in good instruction. This does not necessarily mean that we must solve debates between competing philosophies, but we must think about the most powerful and effective instructional activities used in our classrooms. For some, these instructional activities will include shared reading, book conferences, free reading time, cooperative learning groups, writing workshops, author's chair, and so forth. Other teachers may find other instructional activities more useful.

After we have identified effective instructional practices, we must think about the products, processes, behaviors, or other kinds of evidence that could be gathered during instruction to form the basis for assessment. Fortunately, there is a fair amount of information about how to complete this step. Developmental checklists, rating scales, guidelines for portfolios, and scoring rubrics provide some guidance about the kinds of evidence worth gathering during instruction.

But another step in the process of integrating instruction and assessment has yet to be addressed in any systematic fashion. After we have provided the richest instruction and gathered assessment evidence, we still need to interpret that evidence and use it to guide the next round of good instruction. The concept is not new, of course, but it is still a problem waiting to be solved, particularly now that we have moved beyond the teaching and testing of low-level skills to more complex and more meaningful student outcomes.

In summary, these six problems—clarifying the goals of assessment, clarifying the audiences to be addressed, selecting and developing the assessment techniques, setting standards of student performance, establishing methods of management and integrating instruction and assessment—face educators interested in developing alternative assessments. Solving these problems successfully will determine whether the move to alternative assessments is permanent or simply another educational fad.

References

Au, K., Scheu, J., Kawakami, A., Herman, P. (1990). Assessment and accountability in a whole literacy curriculum. *The Reading Teacher, 43,* 574-578.

Maeroff, G. (1991). Assessing alternative assessment. *Phi Delta Kappan, 73,* 272-282.

National Education Goals Panel, (1992). *The National Educational Goals Report, Executive summary.* Washington, DC, Author.

Neill, D., & Medina, N. (1989). Standardized testing: Harmful to educational health. *Phi Delta Kappan, 70,* 688-697.

Shepard, L. (1989). Why we need better assessment. *Educational Leadership, 46,* 4-9.

U.S. Congress, Office of Technology Assessment. (1992). *Testing in American schools: Asking the right questions*(OTA-SET-519), Washington, DC: U. S. Government Printing Office

Wiggins, G. (1989). A true test: Towards more authentic and equitable assessment. *Phi Delta Kappan, 70,* 703-713.

Winograd, P., & Jones, D. (1992). The use of portfolios in performance assessment. *New Directions in Education Reform, 1,* 37-50.

Winograd, P., Paris, S., & Bridge, C. (1991). Improving the assessment of literacy. *The Reading Teacher, 45,* 108-116.

Worthen, B. R. (1993). Critical issues that will determine the future of alternative assessment. *Phi Delta Kappan, 74,* 444-454.

Resources

Clay, M. (1985). *The early detection of reading difficulties* (3rd ed.). Portsmouth, NH: Heinemann.

De Fina, A. (1992). *Portfolio assessment: Getting started.* New York: Scholastic.

Fredericks, A., & Rasinski, T. (1990). Working with parents: Involving parents in the assessment process. *The Reading Teacher, 44,* 346-350.

Goodman, K. S., Goodman, Y. M., & Hood, W.J. (1989). *The whole language evaluation book.* Portsmouth, NH: Heinemann.

Graves, D. H. (1983). *Writing: Teachers and children at work.* Portsmouth, NH: Heinemann.

Harp, B. (1991). *Assessment and evaluation in whole language programs.* Norwood, MA: Christopher-Gordon.

Johnston, P. (1992). *Constructive evaluation of literate activity.* New York: Longman.

Kemp, M. (1989). *Watching children read and write: Observational records for children with special needs.* Portsmouth, NH: Heinemann.

Paulson, F., Paulson, P., & Meyer, C. (1991). What makes a portfolio a portfolio. *Educational Leadership, 48,* 60-64.

Routman, R. (1988). *Transitions: From literature to literacy.* Portsmouth, NH: Heinemann.

Sharp, Q. (1989). *Evaluation: Whole language checklists for evaluating your children.* New York: Scholastic.

Spandel, V. & Stiggins, R. (1990). *Creating writers: Linking assessment and writing instruction.* New York: Longman.

Tierney, R. J., Carter, M.A., & Desai, L. E. (1991). *Portfolio assessment in the reading-writing classroom.* Norwood, MA: Christopher-Gordon.

Valencia, S. (1990). A portfolio approach to classroom reading assessment: The whys, whats, and hows. *The Reading Teacher, 43,* 338-340.

Improving the Assessment of Literacy

Reprinted from *The Reading Teacher* (1993), *45,* 108-116

Peter Winograd
Scott Paris
Connie Bridge

Improving assessment is arguably the most difficult task facing those interested in educational reform. This is particularly true in the area of literacy, where insights in theory and improvements in practice have conflicted with traditional approaches to assessment (Valencia & Pearson, 1987). Our purpose is to examine recent thinking in the assessment of literacy and offer specific suggestions to educators interested in making assessment more congruent with instruction. We begin by briefly reviewing why changes in assessment are necessary. Then, we discuss four important guidelines for improving the assessment of literacy. Finally, we provide some illustrations of how to improve assessment.

Why Changes in Assessment Are Necessary

Literacy reflects both processes of learning and products of knowledge, so assessments must provide measures of both. But traditional assessments of literacy have been limited to tests of decoding, sight vocabulary, and comprehension of isolated sentences or short paragraphs. Many of these tests are administered to large groups of students who fill in bubbles on multiple-choice answer sheets. An increasing number of writers have expressed dissatisfaction with these methods of assessments (e.g., Haney, Madaus, 1989; Johnston, 1984; Miller-Jones, 1989; Nickerson, 1989; Resnick & Resnick, 1990; Shepard, 1989; Suhor, 1985) Thus, it is argued, assessments of reading need to change—traditional standardized achievement tests, many state-designed criterion-referenced tests, unit tests in commercial series, and perhaps even teacher designed objective tests. There are four reasons we believe reading assessments must change.

Traditional assessments are based upon an outdated model of literacy

Traditional assessments of literacy have been based upon an outdated and inappropriate model of literacy. Literacy research in the past two decades has changed the way we view reading and writing. For example, reading comprehension is now conceptualized as an interactive process in which readers use their prior knowledge along with text information to construct meaning (e.g., Anderson, Hiebert, Scott, & Wilkinson, 1985).

Moreover, we have come to appreciate that literacy is functional; it capitalizes on the development of speaking and listening skills and it is best learned in authentic settings with the help of adults. Traditional assessments that remove literacy from real purposes and uses, test artificial skills in isolation, and ignore the prior knowledge and motivation of the student violate these principles (e.g., Teale, 1988; Wixson & Peters, 1987).

These are not just theoretical issues. If new commercial reading programs, whole lan-

guage emphases, and literature-based programs are based upon different models of reading, then traditional tests cannot adequately measure children's literacy accomplishments. Misaligned tests force teachers to abandon their curricular goals to prepare students for skill-based tests. Teachers may feel obligated to spend time drilling their students on isolated skills and facsimiles of achievement tests in order to prepare them for misaligned tests. Lost instructional time, confused students, and frustrated teachers are all part of the price paid for assessments that do not conform to curricular reforms.

Traditional assessments prohibit the use of learning strategies

Many traditional assessments prohibit the use of learning strategies. During the past 20 years, educators have provided teachers with tactics to help students learn to manage their time, study, control anxiety, and increase or sustain motivation (e.g., Weinstein, Ridley, Dahl, & Weber, 1988; Winograd & Paris, 1988). In reading, teachers can help students learn to skim and scan text, form hypotheses, seek help from others, reread, use context, make inferences, and relate the text information to personal experiences.

But reading tests are usually solitary and timed exercises that penalize students who attempt to use these kinds of strategies. Multiple-choice tests may also cultivate the development of artificial test-taking strategies that are counterproductive in actual reading situations. For example, children may learn to read questions first and then search the paragraph for similar words in the stem and alternatives. Indeed, some of the questions may be answerable without reading the passage at all. Thus, some students learn to avoid reading the text to answer the questions expeditiously.And for others, the test can lead to confusion, cheating, or haphazard guessing. In sum, traditional tests can counteract the development of students' appropriate learning strategies and frustrate teachers and students alike.

Traditional assessments redefine educational goals

Traditional approaches to assessment may redefine the goals of education in ways that are counterproductive to students' motivation (e.g., Johnston & Winograd, 1985; Nicholls, 1989). When success in school is reduced to the knowledge demonstrated on traditional tests, the goals of school become defined in terms of comparative success on tests. This fosters competition among students for scarce resources (i.e., high grades, privileges, future opportunities), but not all students obtain these rewards. For lower achievers, "the losers" in this competition, there is increased anxiety, depressed self-esteem, cynicism about teachers and school, and devaluation of education (Paris, Lawton, & Turner, in press).

Traditional assessments are easily misinterpreted and misused

Information gleaned from traditional assessments is of limited use and is subject to misuse and misinterpretation (e.g., Neill & Medina, 1989). Traditional assessments that provide normative data on students' achievement are routinely reported in newspapers as if they were complete and accurate indices of a district's success or students' learning. But these tests are not valid measures of teachers or curricula; instead, they are measures of students' accumulated knowledge, test-taking skills, and socioeconomic status (e.g., Guskey & Keifer, 1989).

Moreover, the data are rarely understood by students or their parents and fail to provide useful information to teachers. Too many assessments measure only the number of questions answered correctly without assessing students' problem-solving skills and learning processes. A percentile rank or stanine provides little diagnostic information to teachers. Further, many traditional assessments were not designed to inform or benefit teachers, students, or parents; instead, they provide administrative means of accountability that are used in the allocation of funds. Money, in part,

makes testing a "high stakes" game which invites abuse.

Traditional assessments focus educational efforts on the wrong targets. Students learn isolated skills, teachers prepare students to take tests, students base their self-concepts partly on comparative success on tests, parents evaluate their children and their school districts with the wrong measures, and administrators spend excessive amounts of time and money giving and interpreting measures they believe demonstrate accountability. In the next section, we outline four guidelines that can improve educational assessment.

Guidelines for Improving Assessment

No single solution exists for problems that vary enormously from district to district. There are, however, some helpful guidelines, developed by recent research and exemplary practice, that educators interested in improving assessment should consider. It is important to note that two key assumptions underlie our guidelines. First, reforms and innovations in one aspect of schooling must be connected in coherent ways to other aspects of schooling. In this case, improvements in literacy instruction must be matched by congruent improvements in literacy assessment. Second, solutions will vary depending upon local needs. Thus, our guidelines are presented as flexible heuristics intended to initiate discussion.

Guideline 1: Clarify the goals of instruction

Establishing a theoretical framework and clarifying the goals for instruction provide the crucial foundation for a coherent curriculum. Then assessments can be selected which match the theoretical orientation. For example, if a process-writing curriculum is implemented, then one-time unassisted assessments of students' writing skills are unwarranted; instead, ongoing assessments of students' writing at various stages in the writing process are required, perhaps through a writing portfolio. If a literature-based language arts curriculum is implemented, then reading proficiency should not be measured by tests that assess vocabulary knowledge and comprehension of contrived passages; instead, students' reading growth should be assessed by examining how they read, comprehend, and respond to trade books, perhaps through reading conferences. A coherent curriculum depends upon the alignment of instruction and assessment.

Instruction should direct assessment; therefore, we should not feel required to assess what we do not teach. This is an important point for those who select to use commercially-prepared assessments, which often attempt to include all the skills that might be included on anybody's shopping list. Not every skill included in a test must be tested when, where, and in the manner dictated by that test. We must pick, choose, adapt, and adopt the measures that provide us with the information that fits our vision of reading and writing.

Guideline 2: Clarify the purposes of assessment

Clarify the purpose of an assessment and then select the tools most appropriate for that purpose (Cross & Paris, 1987: Johnston, 1983). Consider for a moment some of the diverse ways that assessment data are used in school districts: (a) to diagnose the instructional needs of a student or group of students; (b) to place students in appropriate materials; (c) to report educational progress to parents; (d) to rank students or determine standards for placement within advanced or compensatory programs; (e) to determine which students are promoted or retained; (f) to decide whether students are ready to graduate; (g) to demonstrate compliance with district, state, or federal mandates and guidelines; or (h) to satisfy the political need to show that schools are spending tax monies wisely. Educators must clarify the purpose of an assessment, and then select assessments that are compatible with that purpose.

Thinking about potential audiences is also a helpful way to clarify the purposes of assessment. For example, *students* find some kinds of assessments particularly useful for increasing their awareness of themselves as learners. *Teachers* find some kinds of assessments more helpful than others as they make day-to-day instructional decisions. *Parents* need certain kinds of information to understand how their children are progressing. *Administrators* need certain kinds of assessments to help them evaluate teachers, summarize a district's performance, or make the other kinds of decisions required of individuals in their positions. Finally, individuals in the *political community* (e.g., legislators, newspaper columnists, etc.) often use assessments to fulfill their own agendas. Different audiences need different kinds of information, but these assessments should support and enhance one another.

When selecting assessments, it is important to recognize three things: No single assessment can serve a district's multiple needs with equal effectiveness; assessment data can be used in a variety of ways; and no assessment instrument is appropriate for all purposes.

Guideline 3: Select multiple measures

No single instrument or technique can adequately measure achievement in reading (Johnston, l987b, 1989; Lipson & Wixson, 1986; Valencia & Pearson, 1987) since the reading process involves complex interactions among reader, text, task, and contextual variables. To account for this complexity, researchers and educators are exploring the effectiveness of literacy portfolios that contain a variety of measures (e.g., Lytle & Botel, 1988; Valencia, 1990). Most of the attention has focused on portfolios for classroom teachers. Assessments frequently included in portfolios are daily classroom observations; informal records of voluntary reading; interviews and checklists designed to assess motivations and attitudes; interviews that focus on a child's ability to engage in self-evaluation; and compositions written in response to what has been read. The important point is that a variety of measures that assess a broad range of performances and behaviors must be employed to understand children's reading and writing.

A caveat is in order here. Collecting, organizing, and interpreting the results of multiple measures can be time-consuming work for teachers. Some teachers are rightly skeptical about the new emphasis on portfolio assessment because it requires considerable time and effort. Any kind of assessment that simply adds to already full workloads is unlikely to be well received by either teachers or students. Thus, a crucial aspect of improving assessment is ensuring that teachers and students view the activities as *helpful* rather than disruptive or time-consuming.

We believe that teachers and students will endorse new forms of assessment if such assessments are manageable. Administrators need to provide teachers the time and support required to implement new forms of assessment. Then it is likely that teachers will come to view assessment as part of instruction, and students will begin to engage in assessment cooperatively and openly so that it can promote individual learning.

Guideline 4: Interpret results in ways that enhance instruction

The final guideline is the logical extension of the first one: clarify the instructional goals. The importance of interpreting assessment results in terms of what is valued cannot be emphasized enough. As Wiggins (1989a, p. 705) argues, "Do we judge our students to be deficient in writing, speaking, listening, artistic creation, finding and citing evidence, and problem solving? Then let the tests ask them to write, speak, listen, create, do original research, and solve problems." If it is believed that fragmenting language and language learning should be avoided during reading instruction, then students' ability to respond to whole texts that contain coherent, authentic language should be assessed. If teachers spend time teaching

students to be critical thinkers, then students should be judged on how well they answer open-ended questions, take risks, explore diverse interpretations, or analyze challenging texts (Lytle & Botel, 1988; Resnick, 1987).

Assessment data must be interpreted within the same framework that underlies instruction. We possess a rich repertoire of instructional techniques aimed at improving reading comprehension, facilitating writing, or nurturing a love of books, yet teachers often find themselves trying to explain percentile scores derived from a test of atomistic, isolated skills. Students, teachers, parents, and administrators need a clear understanding of what is valued in instruction, so they can have an equally clear idea of what assessment results mean.

In short, districts have a responsibility to educate their administrators, teachers, and constituents about the assessment measures they use and what the information does and doesn't mean. In addition, districts have a responsibility to create assessments that neither decrease teachers' time for instruction nor the students' motivation for learning. This can be best accomplished by ensuring that the assessment tasks used are meaningful and congruent with the tasks used for instruction.

A Model for Improving Literacy Assessment

In this section, we present a model that aligns instruction and assessment. The theoretical framework that underlies the model is our belief that children must become strategic readers (e.g., Paris, Lipson, & Wixson, 1983; Winograd & Paris, 1988). In order to achieve this overall objective, we focus on three overlapping and interrelated goals.

First, strategic readers are skilled (e.g., Anderson et al., 1985). They understand that reading should make sense, and hence they focus on meaning. Strategic readers discuss, interpret, and respond to what they have read, and they are fluent in that they recognize most words effortlessly and automatically. It is important to note that strategic readers are skilled at dealing with authentic, coherent texts; we do not support instruction (or assessment) that focuses on fragmented comprehension or decoding skills in isolation.

Second, strategic readers are motivated. They have the self-assurance it takes to be active learners, and they are willing to put forth effort, take risks, and question authors and teachers when the things they read fail to make sense. Strategic readers also regard reading as enjoyable and useful, searching out interesting books, choosing to spent time reading, and responding with enthusiasm to certain authors or topics.

Third, strategic readers are independent. They are able to transfer the skills and strategies they have learned in one situation to other situations when it is appropriate to do so (e.g., Palincsar & Brown, 1986; Resnick, 1987). These readers are able to handle a variety of authentic texts for a variety of different purposes (e.g., Paris & Winograd, 1990), and they are adept at planning their approach to reading depending upon their purpose, their familiarity with the topic, the type of text, and so forth. These students actively monitor their comprehension and engage in fixup strategies like rereading, paraphrasing, or reading ahead.

Given this framework, let us consider how different kinds of assessment information can be selectively used and interpreted in order to fulfill some of the needs of five major audiences: students, teachers, parents, administrators, and members of the political community. Note that while specific assessment techniques may vary, there is an underlying congruence among the curriculum, instruction, and assessment.

Helping students gain ownership of their learning

In a very real sense, students themselves are the most important audience for assessment data. Unfortunately, traditional methods and uses of assessment often leave students confused, cynical, and disillusioned about their educational experiences (Paris, Lawton, & Turner, in press). Consider, however, ways in which assessment data could be used to enhance students' involvement in their own learning.

One of the most important objectives in developing strategic readers is to help students become adept at monitoring their comprehension. Sharing the results of running records (Clay, 1985) with students can help them become more aware of the importance of self-corrections when meaning is disrupted. Audiotapes of oral reading that are recorded over the course of several rereadings of the same text can also help children keep track of their developing fluency (Dowhower, 1989; Samuels, 1979).

Interviews are particularly useful for helping students become more aware of their own progress (e.g., Graves, 1983; McKenna & Kear, 1990; Wixson, Bosky, Yochum, & Alvermann, 1984). Questions like "How have you improved in reading over the past month?" or "How have you improved as a writer?" can provide important insights for both teacher and student. "What reading goal will you set for yourself over the next two weeks?" or "What writing goal will you set for yourself?" can do much to engage students in their own learning. Indeed, such questions can be fairly general, like these examples, or they can be much more specific, like "How could you edit this piece of writing so that readers would be sure to understand what you are trying to say?" or "What strategies could you use to figure out the difficult words or parts of this chapter in your science book?"

Lists of books read and topics and authors enjoyed are extremely useful sources of information. Discussions based on these lists can help students become more aware of their reading interests and preferences. In addition, if students keep informal track of which books were easy to read and which were more challenging, they acquire a more sophisticated and accurate view of their own development as readers (Hansen, 1987).

Helping teachers make instructional decisions

Assessments for teachers are successful only to the extent that they improve instruction for individual students (Johnston, 1987a), and teachers' informal observations and intuitions about children's needs are far more useful than are scores from formal tests (Shavelson & Stern, 1981). Most beneficial are observations of students' behaviors and responses while engaged in meaningful reading and writing tasks in the classroom (Goodman, Goodman, & Hood, 1989; Morrow & Smith, 1990).

Classroom discussions, enthusiasm for or avoidance of certain authors or topics, spontaneous self-corrections of miscues that disrupt meaning, puzzled looks or questions asked in class, informal interviews, the quality of daily work, and anecdotal records all provide teachers with continual feedback and guidance on students' literacy development. Periodic use of running records, teacher-student conferences, interviews, and tests or examinations can augment and systematize the collection of information useful in making instructional decisions. Because teachers and students are the final recipients of this assessment data, they can determine which information is most important and how that information is best put to use.

Helping parents understand their children's progress

Parents want to know two things: Is my child progressing? and Is that progress consistent with the school's expectations for a child of her or his age? We concur with Lytle & Botel (1988, p. 151) that "parent conferences are the preferred mode of reporting to parents." Conferences enable

teachers to describe goals and share samples of the child's writing, tapes and charts of the child's oral reading fluency, lists of books read and topics and authors the child enjoys, and samples of the tests and examinations (e.g, Fredericks & Rasinski, 1990).

In many instances, however, teachers must rely on grades and communicate with parents through the use of report cards. In such instances, educators can take a number of useful steps. First, they can ensure that the format of the report card is congruent with the theoretical framework that underlies instruction. For example, if reading is treated holistically or if extensive voluntary reading is an important part of the school's curriculum, then the report card should reflect these views.

Second, when teachers must assign grades to students, then teachers and administrators should give systematic thought to which specific tasks and what "grade level benchmarks" (Au, Scheu, Kawakami, & Herman, 1990) will be used as the basis for evaluation. For example, a group of intermediate teachers may decide to assign grades on the basis of selected samples of the children's writing, total scores (not subscores) from the basal reader end-of-level tests, scores from teacher-made or commercially available tests and examinations, and information gleaned from the children's reading logs. The important point, again, is to select evidence that reflects fully the goals of the literacy curriculum.

Third, grades on report cards should be accompanied by narrative accounts (Afflerbach & Johnston, 1991; Johnston, 1989; Lytle & Botel, 1988). Such written formats communicate richer information than summary grades can convey. Teachers can talk about instructional goals, explain procedures for evaluation, or provide insight into the child's individual strengths and weaknesses.

Helping administrators and members of the political community make policy decisions

We have combined our discussion pertaining to administrators and to members of the political community because these two audiences share some common needs in terms of assessment and because both groups often focus on high-stakes, large-scale testing. We are not implying that administrators and the political community are the same audience with the same needs or the same agenda; clearly, they are not.

One of the needs that administrators have is for assessment information that will provide them with an overall view of student progress. In addition, administrators want assessment information that will drive instruction in positive ways and promote student achievement. Obtaining an overall view of student achievement and promoting instruction are often the stated goals of legislators and other members of the political community. Thus, the success of assessments for administrators and the political community is measured by how well they inform the public and by the incentives they provide for better instruction.

Unfortunately, traditional tests have rarely been successful for achieving these goals. Instead, they have provided the public with simplistic and misleading information (e.g., Kortez, 1988), and they have resulted in fragmenting the curriculum and disempowering teachers. The situation is exacerbated by the fact that teachers and administrators often have little say about what kinds of assessments will be used for the purpose of accountability.

Fortunately, a number of positive trends are occurring in large-scale assessment that could enhance the alignment between instruction and assessment. One of the most positive trends is the use of performance or authentic assessments (Wiggins, 1989a, 1989b). Authentic assessments are contextualized and complex, and they represent tasks faced by people in the real world. Such assessments often involve observing students engaged in important educational processes (e.g., discussing books they have read) or evaluating the products and outcomes of those processes (e.g., writing in response to reading).

Performance assessment tasks also can be derived from our framework for strategic reading. Skilled reading might involve asking students to write in response to something that they have read (e.g, Farr et al., 1990). For example, students might read two different editorials dealing with the same issue (e.g., crime control, pollution legislation). Then they would write a response that analyzes and evaluates the two different reading selections. Potential questions could include "Which author presents a more convincing argument and why?" or "How is your view of the topic different from or similar to the views presented by these two authors?" Students' responses could be judged in terms of whether they expressed the gist of the selections, compared and contrasted the selections in terms of the quality of the arguments, and articulated their own viewpoints.

Attitudes toward reading could be assessed by asking students to discuss books selected from their lists of books and magazines read for pleasure (e.g., during free reading at school). Possible discussion questions include "Why did you pick this book to read?" and "Tell me about this book." Students could be judged by criteria that include enthusiasm or other evidence that they view reading as relevant to their personal lives; evidence that they understood the gist of the book or experienced a strong personal response to something they read; or evidence that they engage in reading for pleasure on a regular basis.

Finally, independence in reading could be assessed by performance-based assessment tasks in content areas like science or social studies (Wiggins, 1989b). For example, students might complete science projects in which they identify a question, spend several days engaged in background research, prepare a written report, and present that report using graphs, charts, overheads, or other visual aids. Students could be judged in terms of the questions identified, research strategies, and ability to present what was learned visually, orally, and in writing.

The current educational reform movement in Kentucky offers an excellent case in point. The Task Force on Assessment (Council on School Performance Standards, 1989, Appendix E) argues cogently for authentic assessments using a double sampling approach: a sampling of students and a sampling of assessment tasks. The Task Force identified a number of advantages of such an approach including the fact that reliable indications of education progress can be obtained without consuming inordinate amounts of instructional time; that authentic assessment tasks can continue to be developed and included in the system; and that sampling of authentic tasks can drive instruction in positive ways by encouraging teachers to teach to a general goal (e.g., reading with understanding) while discouraging teaching to the particulars of the assessment task itself. The purpose of the Kentucky approach to authentic assessment *is* to determine the degree to which schools or districts are achieving designated learning outcomes. The purpose *is not* to provide diagnostic or normative information about individual students, nor is it to compare or evaluate individual teachers. Limiting the use of the statewide testing in this manner is important because it attempts to untangle separate and conflicting purposes that often plague statewide assessment programs. A sampling of authentic assessments combined with other measures like drop-out rates, measures of school attendance, and percentages of students succeeding in college, the military, or business can provide a more accurate picture of how a school or district is performing.

Summary

Our examples of how different audiences need different kinds of assessment information illustrate ways in which the assessment of literacy can be improved. Clearly, there are additional audiences to be addressed and assessment needs to be ful-

filled. Our examples were intended to illustrate, rather than exhaust, the possibilities for change. In each case, however, the guidelines are the same. We clarified our view of what is important in literacy instruction; we specified the purpose of the assessments; we used manageable multiple measures; and we ensured our assessments fit the needs of the audience while preserving the richness of our instructional curriculum.

References

Afflerbach, P., & Johnston, P. (1991). *Making sense of report cards: Conflicts in knowing and communicating.* Unpublished manuscript, University of Maryland.

Anderson, R.C., Hiebert, E., Scott, J.A., & Wilkinson, I.A. (1985). *Becoming a nation of readers.* Washington, DC: The National Institute of Education.

Au, K., Scheu, J., Kawakami, A., & Herman, P. (1990). Assessment and accountability in a whole literacy curriculum. *The Reading Teacher, 43,* 574-578.

Clay, M.M., (1985). *The early detection of reading difficulties* (3rd ed.). Portsmouth, NH: Heinemann.

Council on School Performance Standards, (1989). *Preparing Kentucky youth for the next century: What students should know and be able to do and how learning should be addressed.* Paducah, KY: Western Kentucky University.

Cross, D., & Paris, S. (1987). Assessment of reading comprehension: Matching test purposes and test properties. *Educational Psychologist, 22,* 313-332.

Dowhower, S. (1989). Repeated reading: Research into practice. *The Reading Teacher, 42,* 502-507.

Farr, R., Lewis, M., Faszholz, J., Pinsky, E., Towle, S., Lipschutz, J., & Faulds, B. (1990). Writing in response to reading. *Educational Leadership, 47*(6), 66-69.

Fredericks, A., & Rasinski, T. (1990). Working with parents: involving parents in the assessment process. *The Reading Teacher, 44,* 346-350.

Goodman, K.S., Goodman, Y.M., & Hood, W.J. (1989). *The whole language evaluation book.* Portsmouth, NH: Heinemann.

Graves, D. (1983). *Writing: Teachers and children at work.* Exeter, NH: Heinemann.

Guskey, T., & Keifer, E. (1989). *Ranking school districts on the basis of statewide test results: Is it meaningful or misleading?* Paper presented at the annual meeting of the American Educational Research Association, San Francisco, CA.

Haney, W., & Madaus, G. (1989). Searching for alternatives to standardized tests: Whys, whats, and whithers. *Phi Delta Kappen, 70,* 683-687.

Hansen, J. (1987). *When writers read.* Portsmouth, NH: Heinemann.

Johnston, P. (1983). *Reading comprehension assessment: A cognitive basis.* Newark, DE: International Reading Association.

Johnston, P., (1984). Assessment in reading: The emperor has no clothes. In P.D. Pearson (Ed.), *Handbook of reading research* (pp. 147-182). New York: Longman.

Johnston, P. (1987a). Teachers as evaluation experts. *The Reading Teacher, 40,* 744-748.

Johnston, P. (1987b). Assessing the process and the process of assessment in the language arts. In J. Squire (Ed.), *The dynamics of language learning: Research in the language arts* (pp. 335-357). Urbana, IL: National Council of Teachers of English.

Johnston, P. (1989). Constructive evaluation and the improvement of teaching and learning. *Teachers College Record, 90,* 509-528.

Johnston, P., & Winograd, P. (1985). Passive failure in reading. *Journal of Reading Behavior, 17,* 279-301.

Kortez, D. (1988, Summer). Arriving in Lake Wobegon: Are standardized tests exaggerating achievement and distorting instruction? *American Educator,* 8-15, 46-52.

Linn, R. (1985). Standards and expectations: The role of testing. *Proceedings of a National Forum on Educational Reform* (pp. 88-95). New York: The College Board.

Linn, R. (1990). Dimensions of thinking: Implications for testing. In B. Jones & L. Idol (Eds.), *Dimensions of thinking and cognitive instruction.* Hillsdale, NJ: Erlbaum.

Lipson, M.Y., & Wixson, K.K. (1986). Reading disability research: An interactionist perspective. *Review of Educational Research, 56,* 111-136.

Lytle, S., & Botel, M. (1988). *PCRP II: Reading, writing, and talking across the curriculum.* Harrisburg, PA: Pennsylvania Department of Education.

McKenna, M., & Kear, D. (1990). Measuring attitude toward reading: A new tool for teachers. *The Reading Teacher, 43,* 626-639.

Miller-Jones, D. (1989). Culture and testing. *American Psychologist, 44,* 360-366.

Morrow, L., & Smith, J. (Eds.). (1990). *Assessment for instruction in early literacy.* Englewood Cliffs, NJ: Prentice-Hall.

Neill, D., & Medina, N. (1989). Standardized testing: Harmful to educational health. *Phi Delta Kappen, 70,* 688-697.

Nicholls, J.G. (1989). *The competitive ethos and democratic education.* Cambridge, MA: Harvard University Press.

Nickerson, R. (1989). New directions in educational assessment. *Educational Researcher, 18,* 3-7.

Palincsar, A.S., & Brown, A. (1986). Interactive teaching to promote independent learning from text. *The Reading Teacher, 39,* 771-777.

Paris, S.G., Lawton, T.A., & Turner, J.C. (in press). Reforming achievement testing to promote students' learning. In C. Collins & J. Mangieri (Eds.), *Learning in and out of school.* Hillsdale, NJ: Erlbaum.

Paris, S.G., Lipson, M.Y., & Wixson, K.K. (1983). Becoming a strategic reader. *Contemporary Educational Psychology, 8,* 293-316.

Paris, S.G., & Winograd, P. (1990). How metacognition can promote academic learning and instruction. In B. Jones & L. Idol (Eds.), *Dimensions of thinking and cognitive instruction* (pp. 15-51). Hillsdale, NJ: Erlbaum.

Resnick, L. (1987). *Education and learning to think.* Washington, DC: National Academy Press.

Resnick, L., & Resnick, D. (1990). Tests as standards of achievement in school. *The uses of standardized tests in American education* (pp. 63-80). Princeton, NJ: Educational Testing Service.

Samuels, J. (1979). The method of repeated readings. *The Reading Teacher, 32,* 403-408.

Shavelson, R., & Stern, P. (1981). Research on teachers' pedagogical thoughts, judgments, decisions, and behavior. *Review of Educational Research, 41,* 455-498.

Shepard, L. (1989). Why we need better assessments. *Educational Leadership, 46*(7), 4-9.

Suhor, C. (1985). Objective tests and writing samples: How do they affect instruction in composition? *Phi Delta Kappan, 66,* 635-639.

Teale, W. (1988). Developmentally appropriate assessment of reading and writing in the early childhood classroom. *The Elementary School Journal, 89,* 173-183.

Valencia, S. (1990). A portfolio approach to classroom reading assessment. *The Reading Teacher, 43,* 338-340.

Valencia, S., & Pearson, P. (1987). Reading assessment: Time for a change. *The Reading Teacher, 40,* 726-733.

Weinstein, C., Ridley, D., Dahl, T., & Weber, E. (1988). Helping students develop strategies for effective learning. *Educational Leadership, 46*(7), 17-19.

Wiggins, G. (1989a). A true test: Toward authentic and equitable forms of assessment. *Phi Delta Kappan, 70,* 703-713.

Wiggins, G. (1989b). Teaching to the (authentic) test. *Educational Leadership, 46,* 41-47,

Winograd, P., & Paris, S. (1988). A cognitive and motivational agenda for reading instruction. *Educational Leadership, 46*(4), 30-36.

Wixson, K., Bosky, A., Yochum, M., & Alvermann, D. (1984). An interview for assessing students' perceptions of classroom reading tasks. *The Reading Teacher, 37,* 346-353.

Wixson, K., & Peters, C. (1987). Comprehension assessment: Implementing an interactive view of reading. *Educational Psychologist, 22,* 333-356.

From Informal to Informed Assessment: Recognizing the Role of the Classroom Teacher

Reprinted from *The Journal of Reading* (1993), *36*, 518-523

Kenneth P. Wolf

Imagine two scenarios:

(a) Ms. Knight walked slowly about her classroom, reading from the folded booklet in her hand. Her voice was clear and measured. Her students waited for the question at the end of each passage and then bent their heads towards their papers, filling in the small circles on their answer sheets with their newly sharpened number 2 pencils. Ms. Knight noticed that Tod, one of her students, was drawing small pictures on his scratch sheet. She sighed, and reminded him to concentrate. At the end of the test, she collected the students' papers and turned them in to the office. Although she would wait months for the official results, she held out little hope for Tod.

(b) Ms. Knight knew that Tod's writing lacked organization and his oral reading was halting. His standardized tests scores were abysmal. Yet, as she studied the art work in Tod's portfolio, she saw that he was able to convey a deep understanding of complex ideas and themes through his drawings. In one particular drawing, Tod captured the theme of "cycles" by illustrating the "life cycle" of an Anasazi clay pot from the hands of the ancient craftsman who shaped it, to the hands of the child who dropped it, to the hands of the archaeologist who reconstructed the pot hundreds of years later. Ms. Knight decided to build more instruction around Tod's art, encouraging him to use his artistic talents as a bridge to develop his oral and written language skills.

The two classroom scenes captured above present a contrasting view of assessment. The first depicts a formal assessment, a term commonly used to describe assessments such as standardized tests that are designed and scored by those outside the classroom. The second portrays an informal assessment, a label that generally refers to assessments developed and conducted by classroom teachers, and includes such activities as deskside conferences, observations, and reviews of student products.

The use of the term "informal" to describe the assessments that teachers carry out in their classrooms suggests that these assessments are subjective, capricious, casual, and possibly even misleading. In contrast, labeling the assessments conducted by those outside the classroom as "formal" implies that these assessments are objective, reliable, scientific, and, without question, accurate. The end result is that teachers' assessments of their students are dismissed by those outside of the classroom (and even by many teachers themselves) as untrustworthy, while

externally imposed assessments are embraced as the "true" tests of what students know and can do.

There is growing recognition, however, of the limitations of using formal assessments to measure student achievement (Archbald & Newmann, 1988; Report of the National Commission on Testing and Public Policy, 1990). Moreover, evidence is mounting that such tests undermine student motivation (Paris, Lawton, Turner, & Roth, 1991), deprofessionalize teachers (Smith, 1991), trivialize curriculum goals (McNeil, 1988), distort instruction practices (Haertel, 1990), and misrepresent student achievement (Cannell, 1987).

At the same time, respect for informal assessments is on the upswing, both for improving teaching and learning in the classroom (Calfee & Hiebert, 1989; Goodman, 1991) and for large-scale reporting (Brewer, 1990). Many have come to believe that the most valuable and valid information about student learning comes not from an isolated and decontextualized "snapshot" of student performance, but from those who work closely with students on a daily basis.

With these issues in mind, I would like to propose an alternative label for teacher-based assessment of students—a label that conveys respect for the kinds of every day assessments knowledgeable teachers carry out in their classrooms and that recognizes that teachers' assessments provide the most accurate and useful information about student achievement. When teachers have meaningful goals for instruction and clear purposes for assessment, and when they use a variety of strategies to observe and document their students' performances across diverse contexts and over time, these teachers are practicing not informal but *informed* assessment.

In the following sections, I will define informed assessment and describe its features, then discuss conditions that must occur if teacher-based assessment is to realize its full potential.

Informed Assessment in the Classroom

Informed assessment refers to the process that knowledgeable teachers engage in when they systematically observe and selectively document their students' performance through multiple methods, across diverse contexts, and over time as students participate in meaningful learning activities (see Figure).

A *knowledgeable teacher* is the foundation of informed assessment. The further we move away from commercially published, "teacher-proof" assessments and turn toward teacher-based assessment of students, the greater the need for teacher knowledge—about curriculum and instruction, about children and their development, and about the roles that language, culture, and social context play in learning. For assessment to be informed, teachers must apply this knowledge to set clear, sound goals for instruction along with carefully articulated performance standards and benchmarks for measuring student progress towards those goals.

Systematic observation of students at work—as they choose books, plan projects, write stories, solve problems, and discuss ideas—gives teachers a wealth of information about students' strengths, interests, and needs. As Yogi Berra is reported to have said, "You can observe a lot just by watching." "Kidwatching" (Goodman, 1985), however, must be guided by knowledge, for it is difficult to see if you don't know what you are looking for.

Observation is essential, but without some form of *documentation*, much of what has been seen will be either forgotten, or, more likely, remembered in a form that scarcely resembles the original artifact or event. Decades of research have illustrated the frailties of human memory (Bartlett, 1932; Miller, 1956), but documentation in the form of student work and teacher records can help to compensate for these limitations.

Documentation in many classrooms takes the form of student portfolios (Wolf, 1989). These collections of student work and reflections provide a visible record of student accomplishments, enabling both students and teachers to extend and evaluate student learning. In addition, some teachers keep classroom portfolios (Valencia & Calfee, in press), in which they record their observations of individual students and the class as a whole through written notes, checklists, and class profiles.

A caution is in order, however. While some documentation of products and processes is necessary, collecting student artifacts and recording observations can be a time-consuming task for teachers, and too much of an emphasis on documentation can interfere with teaching and learning. By carefully considering the goals for instruction and the purposes for assessment, however, teachers and students can be *selective* in the information that they gather so that it is both meaningful and manageable.

Multiple methods of assessment offer an array of windows on student learning. A paper written during a 45-minute session in response to a standardized prompt may provide a very different view of a student's writing ability than does a piece on a self-selected topic that has been through several drafts. No single assessment approach is sufficient for understanding all that is important to know about each student, but a blend of assessment strategies can help teachers build a more complete picture. Interviews with students, collections of student work, performance assessments, and pencil-and-paper tests are all potentially valuable sources of information.

Assessment should take place in *diverse contexts* because a student may vary greatly in his or her performance across texts, tasks, and settings (Lipson & Wixson, 1986). The same student who can comprehend and insightfully discuss *Beloved* by Toni Morrison (Knopf, 1987) may have difficulty understanding and commenting on an elementary textbook on electronics, even though s/he can decode all of the words (*e.g., circuit, voltage, ampere).* Similarly, the student who can write a trenchant rap song about racial injustice may appear to be a sophisticated writer, but when given the task of writing an expository piece on the same topic may be seen as much less competent.

Recognizing that a student who is a high performer in one context may be a poor one in another, even when the content being assessed is similar, suggests that for teachers to be able to determine the conditions that best support their students' development, they need to assess their students across a number of different settings and contexts. This particularly holds true for students whose backgrounds and cultures may be at variance with that of the mainstream school culture (Heath, 1983).

Assessment *over time* is important because learning is a continuous, dynamic process (Valencia, McGinley, & Pearson, 1990). Ongoing assessment provides teachers and students with regular feedback on their performance and enables them to adjust their actions accordingly. In addition, some features of students' performances are not apparent unless they are viewed on multiple occasions. The student who enthusiastically reads with his partner during buddy reading may not merit special attention unless the teacher notices that the student's partner does all of the reading day after day, or the student who is deeply engaged in writing a story each day during writer's workshop may not appear to be in need of assistance until the teacher determines that the student is continually revising the same draft over and over. It is sometimes only by examining a student or class's performance across a number of occasions that a pattern becomes visible.

Observing students as they are actively engaged in *meaningful learning activities* and examining the work that they produce not only present the most authentic and complete view of what students know and can do, but the most informative one as well. In many traditional classrooms, however, students are quite

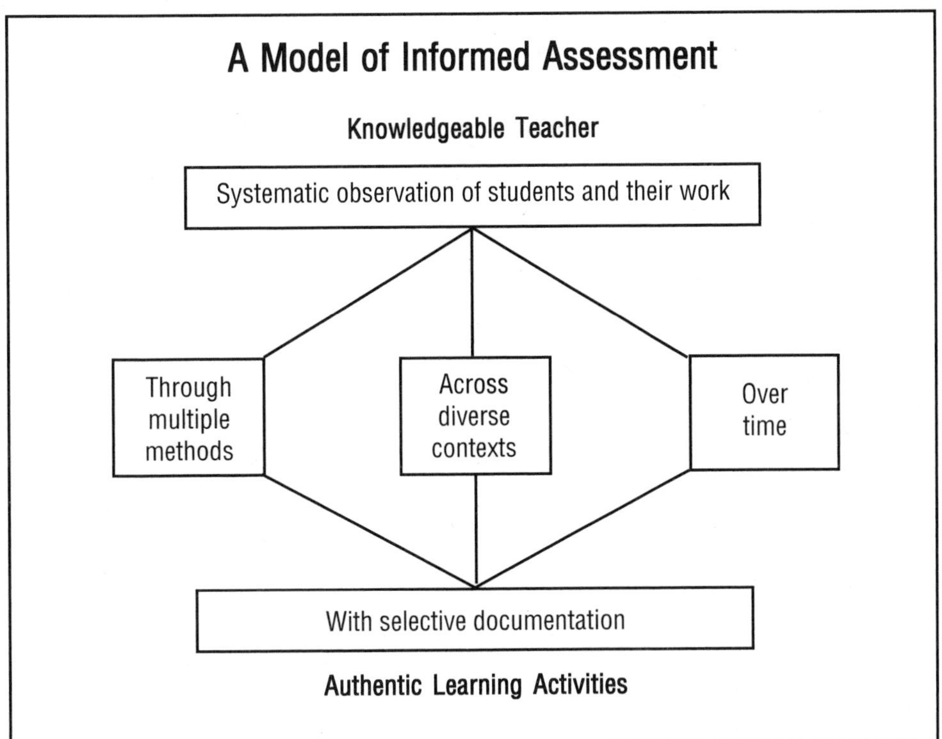

limited in the kinds of literacy activities that they engage in.

If students are confined to a narrow range of activities, the assessments that are carried out will be equally narrow in their portrayal of students—and teachers will have few insights into the range of talents and interests possessed by their students. If students work in isolation and complete fill-in-the-blank work sheets all day, there will be little information available to the teacher, for example, about students' success at collaborating with others or about their literary preferences. As Shulman, (1991, personal communication) has observed, it is difficult to fashion a silk purse assessment out of a sow's ear curriculum.

However, if the curriculum emphasizes process as well as products (Atwell, 1987), promotes high-level comprehension and composition (Graves, 1983; Pearson, 1984), values motivational goals as well as cognitive ones (Winograd & Paris, 1989), and allows students to pursue individual paths to literacy (Taylor, 1989), then the assessments that teachers conduct in their classrooms can be rich and valuable sources of information for guiding and reporting on student learning.

Support for Teacher-Based Assessment Outside the Classroom

While teacher-based assessment holds the promise of improving student learning and providing more authentic indicators of student achievement, it will have a limited impact unless two conditions are addressed. First, expanding the number of teachers who are practicing informed assessment will require greater preservice and inservice preparation in classroom assessment. Teachers receive little, if any, guidance in developing and interpreting classroom-based assessments (Stiggins, 1985; 1991). Curiously, however, while informed teacher-based assessment requires knowledgeable professionals in the classroom, involving teachers in assessment contributes to the process of teacher professionalization by allowing teachers to

move out of the role of technicians who administer assessments designed by others and into the role of decision-makers who act on assessments that they have created and conducted.

Second, extending the work of teachers who are practicing informed assessment will require greater respect and commitment from those outside the classroom. The individual teacher, no matter how knowledgeable and talented, will be limited in what he or she can achieve alone. Support for teacher-based assessment must occur at the school site and beyond. Effective assessment requires a setting in which teachers can work together to establish a sound and shared vision of the curriculum, to set clear goals for instruction and purposes for assessment, and to develop a coherent schoolwide system for evaluating and reporting on student performance.

In addition, a broader recognition, both within the educational community and society at large, of the critical role that teachers can play in the assessment process must take place as well. This recognition can best be achieved by educating the public about the limitations of standardized testing and by ensuring that teacher judgment is an integral part of any student assessment program.

In sum, assessment is informed, rather than informal, when it is carried out by knowledgeable teachers who draw on a variety of strategies to carefully observe and document their students' performances across diverse contexts and over time as students are engaged in authentic learning tasks. Informed assessment requires knowledgeable professionals in the classroom, but the individual teacher is restricted in what he or she can accomplish alone.

For teacher-based assessment to achieve its potential, it also requires a schoolwide commitment to alternative forms of student assessment, coupled with broader recognition of the importance of teacher judgment in the assessment process, both within the educational community and society at large. With these conditions in place, informed assessment by teachers can be a powerful lever for improving teaching and learning in our schools.

References

Archbald, D.A., & Newmann, F.M. (1988). *Beyond standardized testing.* Reston, VA: NASSP.

Atwell, N. (1987). *In the middle: Writing, reading, and learning with adolescents.* Upper Montclair, NJ: Boynton/Cook.

Bartlett, F.C. (1932). *Remembering: A study in experimental and social psychology.* Cambridge, England: Cambridge University Press.

Brewer, R. (1990). *The development of portfolios in writing and mathematics for state-wide assessment in Vermont.* Paper presented at the Institute on New Modes of Assessment, Cambridge, MA.

Calfee, R.C., & Hiebert, E.H. (1989). Advancing academic literacy through teachers' assessments. *Educational Leadership, 46*, 50-54.

Cannell, J.J. (1987). *National norm-referenced elementary achievement testing in America's public schools: How all fifty states are above the national average.* Charleston, WV: Friends of Education.

Goodman, Y. (1985). Kidwatching: Observing children in the classroom. In A. Jaggar & M.T. Smith-Burke (Eds.), *Observing the language learner* (pp. 9-18). Urbana, IL & Newark, DE: National Council of Teachers of English and International Reading Association.

Goodman, Y. (1991). Informal methods of evaluation. In J. Flood, J. Jensen, D. Lapp, & J. Squire (Eds.), *Handbook of research on teaching the English language arts*, (pp. 502-509). New York: Macmillan.

Graves, D.H. (1983). *Writing: Teachers and children at work.* Exeter, NH: Heinemann.

Haertel, E. (1990). Student achievement tests as tools of educational policy: Practices and consequences. In B.R. Gifford (Ed.), *Test policy and test performance: Education, language, and culture* (pp. 13-14). Boston, MA: Kluwer.

Heath, S.B. (1983). *Ways with words.* Cambridge, England: Cambridge University Press.

Lipson, M., & Wixson, K. (1986). Reading disability research: An interactionist perspective. *Review of Educational Research, 56*, 111-136.

McNeil, L. (1988). Contradictions of control, Part 2: Teachers, students, and curriculum. *Phi Delta Kappan, 69*, 433-438.

Miller, G.A. (1956). The magical number seven, plus or minus two: Some limits on our capacity for processing information. *Psychological Review, 63,* 81-97.

Paris, S.G., Lawton, T.A., Turner, J.C., & Roth, J.L. (1991). A developmental perspective on standardized achievement testing. *Educational Researcher, 20*, 12-20.

Pearson, P.D. (1984). Direct explicit teaching of reading comprehension. In G. Duffy, L. Roehler, & J. Mason (Eds.), *Comprehension instruction: Perspectives and suggestions,* (pp. 222-233). New York: Longman.

Report of the National Commission on Testing and Public Policy, (1990). *From gatekeeper to gateway: Transforming testing in America.* Chestnut Hill, MA: Boston College.

Smith, M.L. (1991). Put to the test: The effects of external testing on teachers. *Educational Researcher, 20,* 8-11.

Stiggins, R.J. (1985). Improving assessment where it means the most: In the classroom. *Educational Leadership, 43*, 69-74.

Stiggins, R.J. (1991). Assessment literacy. *Phi Delta Kappan, 72*, 534-539.

Taylor, D. (1989). Toward a unified theory of literacy learning and instructional practices. *Phi Delta Kappan, 71*, 184-193.

Valencia, S., & Calfee, R. (1991). The development and use of literacy portfolios for students, classes, and teachers. *Applied Measurement in Education, 4*, 333-345.

Valencia, S., McGinley, W., & Pearson, P.D. (1990). Assessing literacy in the middle school. In G. Duffy (Ed.), *Reading in the middle school* (2nd ed.). Newark, DE: International Reading Association.

Winograd, P., & Paris, S.G. (1989). A cognitive and motivational agenda for reading instruction. *Educational Leadership, 46*(4), 30-36.

Wolf, D.P. (1989). Portfolio assessment: Sampling student work. *Educational Leadership, 46,* 35-39.